S0-BJL-729

THE FOUR GOSPELS ON SUNDAY

**More from Fortress Press
by Gordon W. Lathrop**

The Pastor: A Spirituality

Christian Assembly: Marks of the Church in a Pluralistic Age
(with Timothy J. Wengert)

Holy Ground: A Liturgical Cosmology

Holy People: A Liturgical Ecclesiology

Holy Things: A Liturgical Theology

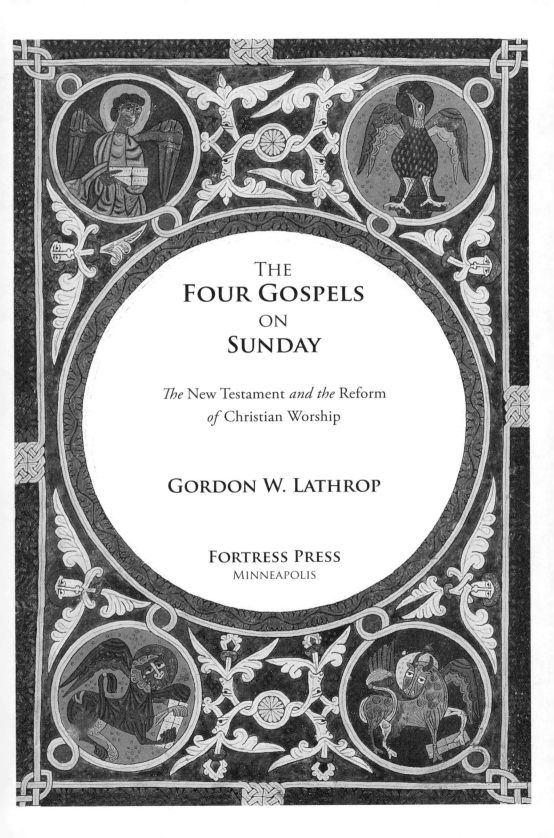

The
Four Gospels
on
Sunday

The New Testament *and the* Reform *of* Christian Worship

Gordon W. Lathrop

Fortress Press
Minneapolis

THE FOUR GOSPELS ON SUNDAY
The New Testament and the Reform of Christian Worship

Copyright © 2012 Fortress Press. All rights reserved. Except for brief quotations in critical articles or reviews, no part of this book may be reproduced in any manner without prior written permission from the publisher. Visit http://www.augsburgfortress.org/copyrights/contact.asp or write to Permissions, Augsburg Fortress, Box 1209, Minneapolis, MN 55440.

Unless otherwise noted, scripture quotations are the author's own translation or from the New Revised Standard Version Bible, copyright © 1989 by the Division of Christian Education of the National Council of Churches of Christ in the USA, and are used with permission.

Cover image: *Christ Enthroned and the Symbols of the Evangelists*, from the Beatus Apocalypse from Santo Domingo de Silos, 1109 (vellum), Spanish School, (twelfth century), British Library, London, UK / Topham Picturepoint / The Bridgeman Art Library International
Cover design: Laurie Ingram
Book design: Josh Messner

Library of Congress Cataloging-in-Publication Data
Lathrop, Gordon.
The four gospels on Sunday : the New Testament and the reform of
Christian worship / Gordon W. Lathrop.
          p. cm.
Includes bibliographical references and indexes.
ISBN 978-0-8006-9852-2 (alk. paper)
1. Public worship—Biblical teaching. 2. Bible. N.T. Gospels—Criticism, interpretation, etc.
I. Title.
BS2417.W65L38 2012
264—dc23   2011034371

The paper used in this publication meets the minimum requirements of American National Standard for Information Sciences—Permanence of Paper for Printed Library Materials, ANSI Z329.48-1984.

Manufactured in the U.S.A.
16 15 14 13 12   2 3 4 5 6 7 8 9 10

In grateful remembrance of

†
Willem Grossouw (1906–1990),
Bastiaan van Iersel (1924–1999),
and
Edward Schillebeeckx (1914–2009)
†

And in gratitude to
the Theology Faculty
of the University of Helsinki

Contents

PART TWO
The Beasts on Our Sundays: Assembly according to the Gospel

Preface

The four canonical Gospels, beginning with Mark, can be understood as lively critical proposals, documents of reform, addressed to ancient Christian assemblies. The books, of course, were most directly about Jesus. Written in the last thirty or so years of the first century of our era or the first decade of the second century, they clearly intended to invite their readers to reconsider who this Jesus was, that figure who had lived, taught, and been cruelly killed in the first third of the first century. The author of Mark initially, then the authors of Matthew and Luke, and finally the author of John each constructed a life and death account of Jesus, perhaps on the model of Hellenistic-era biographies, saying what the authors and their communities considered currently significant about the Jesus who had died some forty to eighty years before. The books were tools for remembering Jesus, as the Christian movement continued to spread throughout the Mediterranean area.

But the books were much more. They were accounts of the meaning of Jesus that belonged in a communal meeting, themselves symbols of the one of whom they spoke. They were books meant to convey what Paul called "the gospel," the oral proclamation of Jesus Christ that gives birth to faith. Indeed, the Gospel books seem to have been intended to be means for an actual communal encounter with this same Jesus, tools for "seeing the Lord."[1] They were texts that, in differing ways, carried the presence of the crucified and risen one into the assemblies where they were read or recited, by means of this presence inviting the people of these assemblies to rethink who it was they were encountering.

The Gospels were also texts that proposed some of the communal consequences that followed upon that presence. At least in part, the books invited

---

1. Cf. Marianne Sawicki, *Seeing the Lord: Resurrection and Early Christian Practice* (Minneapolis: Fortress Press, 1994).

those first readers to reconsider what the gathering of Christians—the Sunday meeting, the assembly—might itself be and in what ways those gatherings were fiercely at odds with the surrounding imperial culture of the times. They were as much calls for continuing reform in those meetings as were the early letters of the apostle Paul that preceded them by some years and influenced their origin. They were—and are—fascinating, in some cases even revolutionary, books.

For Christians now, they are still the most important books we know. They remain the primary source of what we can say responsibly about Jesus. More: as they functioned symbolically in the first- and second-century churches, bearing the presence of the crucified and risen one into the communities that read them, so that communal presence and those symbols still are life-giving to us. For all of the differences between those early Christians and ourselves, the reforms the books meant to propose come as proposals also to us today. As the books meant to say something important about the meanings and practice of ancient Christian meetings, they also can be seen to say something equally important about what we today call Christian worship.

This book is about those four Gospels. It approaches them especially as they spoke about the meaning of Jesus and, at the same time, about early Christian gatherings in various places throughout the ancient Mediterranean world. Furthermore, it approaches them as they continue to have a privileged place in Christian gatherings today, in the current liturgies of the ecumenical churches. With this book, I have wanted to think again about what the Gospel books actually are and how they work. I have sought to explore their critical proposals, proposals for the reform both of Christian faith and of communal ritual and ethical practice. I have thought about what might happen if the books were taken seriously and read honestly in Christian gatherings today. In this quite concrete way, I have hoped that this book is simultaneously about both Bible and liturgy, believing that they belong together.

The outline of the book is simple. Part 1 considers what the Gospels were originally and what connection they had to early Christian gatherings. It begins with an inquiry into the relationship between "gospel" and Gospel books and between the books and what we call "worship." Then it turns to examine how all four books may be related to the origins of the Eucharist, the beginnings of that centrally significant meal practice of Christians. It goes on to examine each of the four Gospels in turn, reflecting on each one's major and unique characteristics and the ways those characteristics might have been intended specifically to affect an assembly in its meetings. Part 2 then asks whether that effect may continue today. With the Gospels in hand, I consider several matters of current ecumenical liturgical importance, matters that in one way or another concern all Christians: assembly itself; the regular service of word and table in such an assembly; baptism as the practice of entering into this assembly; and leadership as it is carried out in the assembly. Finally, the last chapter summarizes the proposal of the book by arguing that the contemporary movement for liturgical reform in the churches has also been, at its best, a biblical movement, a recovery of biblical meaning, and that this movement may still be continued today. Thus, the order of questions is this: What are the Gospels? What did they say about ancient Christian worship? What do they say to Christian liturgical assemblies today? And how may we still engage in a biblical-liturgical movement for renewal?

At the outset of the book, I think a little about one ancient and continuing image for the Gospels: the four living creatures—"the Beasts"—of the Revelation to John. That image, which says a great deal about the relationship of the books and Christian assemblies for worship, occurs on the cover of this volume and recurs as an organizing idea throughout its text.

That there are four Gospels remains a fascinating challenge. Justin Martyr already spoke of them as plural when, in mid-second century, he said that they were read in assembly. They were, for him, the "memoirs of the apostles." Graham Stanton argues that "the decision to accept four gospels . . . was one of the most momentous ones taken within early Christianity, a decision which cries out for continuing theological reflection."[2] It is out of the desire to provide one part of such reflection that the present book has been written. The four come to their common, though tension-laden, purpose in assembly. The Gospels, of course, have been approached and read from many different perspectives, with many different tools. The form-critical research into early oral patterns of the Jesus tradition; the redaction-critical interest in the setting and intentions of the compilers of these traditions who were increasingly seen to be creative authors; the rhetorical-critical discussion of the ways in which the hearers of these books would have experienced their narratives and their arguments; and the social-critical inquiry into the cultural and political settings in which the books appeared—these all are legitimate readings. But here, in this present book, the mutual coherence between the four Gospels and the assemblies of Christians is the focus of interest. A Gospel

---

2. Graham N. Stanton, *Jesus and Gospel* (Cambridge: Cambridge University Press, 2004), 64.

book can be read with the meeting around it in mind, a meeting with which the book itself is at least partly concerned. And the Gospels can be read side by side, in concert and in tension with each other, all four together mattering to the meeting, even if three of the four are silent on any given day. We might call that method "liturgical criticism."

So this book is called *The Four Gospels on Sunday*. That "on" has both senses. The book discusses what the four Gospels of the New Testament have to say about the meetings of Christian assemblies, held principally on Sunday, and it discusses the actual use of those Gospels in current Sunday meetings: thus, the four as they speak *about* the Sunday meeting; the four as they are *used on* our Sundays.

I want to invite you, the reader, into the reflections of this book. The subject matter is immensely important. It arises out of a desire to hold together matters that have recently been too often put asunder: critical biblical studies and faithful liturgical studies, history and theology, diversity of Christian practice and unity in Christian life and meaning, orthodoxy and social criticism. Too often scholars of Christian worship have not paid attention to what biblical studies are doing nor to what may be accurately said about the Gospels. Too often preachers have communicated a kind of literalism about the text that has missed the excitement of its original location and intention and the present symbolic force of its message. Too often, the Gospels have been used by Christians in ways very much like the various strands of religious literalism that today threaten the very fabric of human life and of the earth. But, similarly, too often those who study the Gospel books—the very books that have been preserved because they mattered so much to Christian assemblies—have had nothing much to say about their assembly context, either ancient or modern, writing about them instead as if they were books only for the individual and for the scholar's desk. Furthermore, in matters I find intimately related to the reading of the Gospels—as I will try to make clear in this book—liturgical theologians have sometimes acted as if careful history did not matter, while biblical and liturgical historians have sometimes written as if they did not need to speak about their own theological presuppositions and their own historical and communal locations. Proponents of diversity have let unity go, and proponents of unity have acted as if unity means monolithic uniformity. And all of us have sometimes forgotten that orthodoxy, like the Living Creatures of the Revelation, is not tame. If it is genuine orthodoxy, it carries within itself a criticism of all empires and their imperial values, of all religion and its temptations to power and to self-assurance.

Honesty about the Gospels can knit these things—biblical studies and liturgical studies, diversity and unity, orthodoxy and social criticism, even history and theology—into a common web.

I have tried to do such knitting here, but the task is larger, more important, than this book can accomplish. Furthermore, I know that in making the arguments of this book, I also have a location. I am a confessional Lutheran pastor and liturgical theologian of the late twentieth and early twenty-first century, trained in critical biblical studies and formed in the theology of the cross, who has tried to work for the clarity and centrality of assembly, word, table, and baptismal bath in contemporary ecumenical Christian worship, who believes that this clarity and centrality will always carry important ethical implications, and who thinks that we are often tempted now to make only ourselves the center of our celebrations. I know that, at least in part, there emerges from this location things that will also show up in this book: my interest in avoiding fundamentalism and naïve biblical readings; my accent on meaning arising from the juxtaposition of the word of the cross to the meals of the church; my proposal that a reforming word can be the source of unity in the churches; my confession that by the power of the Spirit the risen crucified one acts in the meeting and in his meal; and my urging that baptism and Eucharist should always lead to remembering the poor. I trust that this location has not finally skewed my research and my conclusions. I hope, rather, that this location allows something true to be seen which might not otherwise have been seen, something true about both the ancient church and our current theologies. I hope that the historical part of this "something" can be tested in other research and that the theological part might be tested in faith, while both are tested in public discussion. I hope that this location may be responsibly in dialogue with what is actually in the Christian sources, especially in Paul and the Gospels, perhaps in the process casting some light on the sources themselves. And I hope that you will join in thinking about these things.

More than forty years ago now, I concluded my doctoral studies in the Netherlands. I had studied New Testament there with Bastiaan van Iersel, who was at the time working on the project that would become, among other things, his excellent *Reading Mark*, and with Willem Grossouw, who was working on a Galatians commentary and was still famous for his bridge-building *Bijbelse Vroomheid*, and I had studied hermeneutics with Edward Schillebeeckx, who was at the time giving the lectures that became his widely read "Jesus books." I was the sole Lutheran among these Vatican II Roman Catholic scholars. In 1969, I finished a dissertation on the symbolism in Mark 6:1-6 and defended it before these three. With this work done, I went on to become a pastor and to turn my attention further to the communal practice of the biblical symbols I had there begun to explore. I remember these three professors, however, with great affection and deep respect. I remember their remarkable and careful methods, their critical care for the church, their trouble from unimaginative and reactionary authorities, their love of life, and their honesty and wit. They are now, all three, dead. But I write this work giving thanks for them. Having now passed my own seventieth year, it is time for me to return to the place where I began with them, to explicit biblical studies.

But the intervening years do not disappear. Behind this present book there also stands my *Holy Things: A Liturgical Theology* (Fortress Press, 1993), the books that followed it, and the method of biblical juxtaposition those books sought to exercise. Juxtaposition will reoccur in what follows here. So will other central things from those books: Sunday, ordo, assembly, broken symbols, and cosmology. But now the focus will be on the Gospels, the Beasts. I believe that there, in the Gospels, read critically and in community, read as a primary source of the Christian liturgy and of the gospel which should animate that liturgy, we may still find public symbols "to hold and reorient, in material and social realities, our experience and our lives" (*Holy Things*, 3).

Much of this book was developed in papers, public lectures, and discussions held in a great variety of contexts.[3] In all of these places and events I met a warm

---

3. Especially, the Liturgical Theology Seminar of the North American Academy of Liturgy (NAAL), the Lutheran study group that meets at that Academy, and the Philadelphia NAAL chapter; the Spring 2009 and the Fall 2010 courses on Liturgical Theology at Yale Divinity School; the Ecumenical Liturgical Institute of Seattle University; the Sixth International Convegno Liturgico sponsored by the Community of Bose in Italy; the Sprunt Lectures at what is now Union Presbyterian Seminary in Richmond, Virginia; the Seminar Week lectures at United Theological College in North Parramatta, New South Wales, Australia; lectures at the University of Iceland in Reykjavik and at a course held at the cathedral school of Skálholt; study events for the pastors and other leaders of the Dioceses of Uppsala and Lund in the Church of Sweden; a meeting of the Nordic Research Council at Løgumkloster, Denmark; the Graduate Seminar on *kyrkovetenskap* at the University of Uppsala, Sweden; the Roman Catholic parish church of St. Peter in Cleveland, Ohio; the Chi Rho Lectures at Central Lutheran Church in Eugene, Oregon; retreats and continuing education events for the priests of the Diocese of New Jersey of the Episcopal Church and the pastors and other lead-

welcome and a lively conversation, for both of which I am deeply grateful. I especially thank those who invited and hosted me in giving the lectures or papers that have built toward the contents of this book, as well as those dear friends who have spoken with me about what became these same contents. Developed from these lectures and papers, some passages of chapters 2, 3, 4, and 7 have been published in a different form in several articles.[4] I also wish to express my gratitude to David Lott and Josh Messner, who have so carefully shepherded this manuscript into book form with Fortress Press, and to the Theology Faculty of the University of Helsinki, Finland, for the degree *Theologiae Doctor Honoris Causa*, presented in their Conferment Ceremony of May 27, 2011, and in my own seventy-second year, a presentation that was both movingly surprising and deeply encouraging to me.

The Gospel according to Luke tells the story of a man—Simeon—who had been looking for the consolation of his people by the coming of the promised Messiah. The story seems to propose him as an old man, since it tells that he had been promised that he would not die until he had seen this very Messiah and since it pairs him with the remarkable figure of Anna, a prophet of "great age" (Luke 2:36). Then, in the very Temple itself, the ancient place at the heart of the worship of Israel, the place of assembly before the face of God, Simeon takes the Child Jesus into his arms, and sings and speaks of God's mercy, the world's great hope, the sword of suffering, his own death, and the very Light of God, as beside him Anna speaks to all who will hear of the meaning of the Child. Luke's Simeon witnesses to the content of the gospel and of the Gospel book, but he also proclaims what that gospel means for his own existence. I take it as great wisdom that several traditions of Christian worship have regarded this text as an appropriate metaphor for the moment of receiving communion at the Eucharist, using Simeon's song as a song for the people of the assembly to sing in their own new temples when the holy bread and wine have been in their hands and they are about to be dismissed to witness and service and even possible death. But

ers of both the Eastern Washington/Idaho Synod and the Pacifica Synod of the Evangelical Lutheran Church of America; and lectures at Wartburg Theological Seminary in Dubuque, Iowa, and the Lutheran School of Theology at Chicago.

    4. *Ritröð Gudfræðistofunar—Studia Theologica Islandica* 27/2 (2008): 25–40; *Dopet i vår tid* (Uppsala: 2008) 107–17; *Worship* 83/3 (May 2009): 194–212; *Assemblea Santa: forme, presenze, presidenza* (Communità di Bose: 2009), 99–115; *Uniting Church Studies* 15/2 (December 2009): 1–10; *Kritisk Forum for Praktisk Teologi* 121 (September 2010): 5–22; and *Worship* 85/1 (January 2011): 68–53.

now, on this day, when I myself am a man of more than seven decades, I have meant to take the Gospel books into my hands as if they were the presence of the Child. I have meant to sing as well as I can of the Light of God, its promise to the whole world, its concomitant story of resistance and the cross, and the ways that Light and its story play out in the places where the assembly gathers before the face of God. I have meant also to tell what this revelation means to me. And, with greater thanks than I can express, I have meant to do this again side by side with the truth-speaking woman who has been as the prophet Anna for me and for many others.

Introduction

The Four Beasts of Revelation and the Gospels

He is the Way.

Follow Him through the Land of Unlikeness;

You will see rare beasts, and have unique adventures.

——W. H. Auden, "For the Time Being: A Christmas Oratorio"

The Beasts hold this book together. Or they do so, particularly, as they bring their fierce witness to the Lamb in the center. Around the Lamb, in one important image of classic Christian iconography, amidst all the worshiping elders and saints, there is a Lion, an Ox, a Human Being, and an Eagle, each holding or representing its own book. These Beasts are there all together on the cover of this book, which reproduces one early-twelfth-century version of this image.[1] They also recur in this book's subtitles and chapters, being especially discussed in chapters 1 and 8. The point is, of course, that the verbal image of the "four living creatures around the throne," drawn from Ezekiel 1 and especially from Revelation 4 and 5, was taken, in the second century C.E., as symbolic of the Gospel books. These "living creatures," these ζῷα, were already used in such a symbolic, metaphoric way perhaps a half-century or so after the Revelation

---

1. "Majesty," folio 7, verso of the *Silos Beatus*, Add. Manuscript 11695, in the British Library, London, completed at the Santo Domingo de Silos Monastery, Spain, in 1109. See also John Williams, *The Illustrated Beatus* I (London: Harry Miller, 1994), 11. Note that in this image Christ enthroned is in the midst of the Beasts, the object of their witness. The Enthroned One is, of course, as much of a metaphoric image as is the slain-yet-standing Lamb, and exactly of the same sort. Jesus never sat on a throne, certainly not in his death. Faith sees him there. The presence of this image behind the title of this book represents the hope that the present inquiry into the Gospel books—the Beasts—may serve to illumine the hidden yet manifest presence in the assemblies of the living one, the one who was dead but is now giving life from the throne.

itself was written and only shortly after the time when the four-Gospel collection was coming to be widely recognized in the churches. It was not many centuries until the originally verbal image began to be drawn and painted, as it still is today, with the intention of setting out a visual icon of the Gospels and their function. If Jesus Christ, crucified and risen, is the "Lamb," the one who mediates God to us and the one who has the key to the book of God's will, then, by this image-use, the Gospels themselves are as the "Living Creatures." Or, they are the "Beasts," to use the slightly archaic word of older English translations in order to emphasize that they are dangerous, not conventional, not tamed. The Living Creature that is "like a lion," the first one (Rev. 4:7), is usually taken to stand for the book we call Mark, the one "like an ox" to stand for Luke, the one "with a face like a human face" to stand for Matthew, and the one "like a flying eagle" to stand for John.[2] The attribution of those names of the supposed authors of the books, of course, is not much earlier than the attribution of each of the symbolic creatures to one of them, both developments having occurred more or less in mid-to-late second century.

Say it this way: the Gospels, freshly read in the context of an assembly, are among the "rare beasts" that W. H. Auden rightly says one encounters when one begins again to follow Jesus Christ as the Way.[3] Indeed, the Gospels also point to "unique adventures" in a needy yet beautiful world. And the paradoxes with which the Gospels are filled, their very inverting of words to mean new things and thereby bring us to see both God and the world anew, themselves make up a large part of Auden's "Land of Unlikeness."

While I think that the writer of the Revelation did not originally intend the Beasts to stand for the Gospels, there are four useful things about that writer's version of this apocalyptic image when it is taken as a metaphor for the Gospels: the Beasts themselves are *not the Lamb*; they do their work *in the midst of an assembly*; there are *four of them*; and they call for *the riders of judgment to ride throughout the earth*. Thus, they are witnesses to and worshipers of the "one seated on the throne" and the "Lamb standing as if it had been slaughtered" (Rev. 5:1, 6). They lead the assembly in its "Holy, Holy, Holy" (4:8) and its

---

2. Though the seventh-century Gospel book called the Book of Durrow, found in the Trinity College Library in Dublin, as well as some old Syrian traditions, has Mark as the Eagle and John as the Lion.

3. W. H. Auden, "For the Time Being: A Christmas Oratorio," in *The Collected Poetry of W. H. Auden* (New York: Random, 1945), 466.

"You are worthy to take the scroll" (5:9-10) and its "Amen" (5:14; 7:12; 19:4; cf. 14:3). They are diverse and yet united in their witness. And they call "Come!" (6:1-8) to the riders of "the four horses of the Apocalypse," just as they also pass out the bowls "full of the wrath of God" (15:7). Much of this book will explore these metaphors: how the Gospels bear witness and give truthful praise to God and to Lamb; how the Gospels belong in the assembly; how they work differently and yet together; and how the assembly around the Gospels is called by them to address the social structures of the world.

Also: they are not tame. They still have surprising things to say.

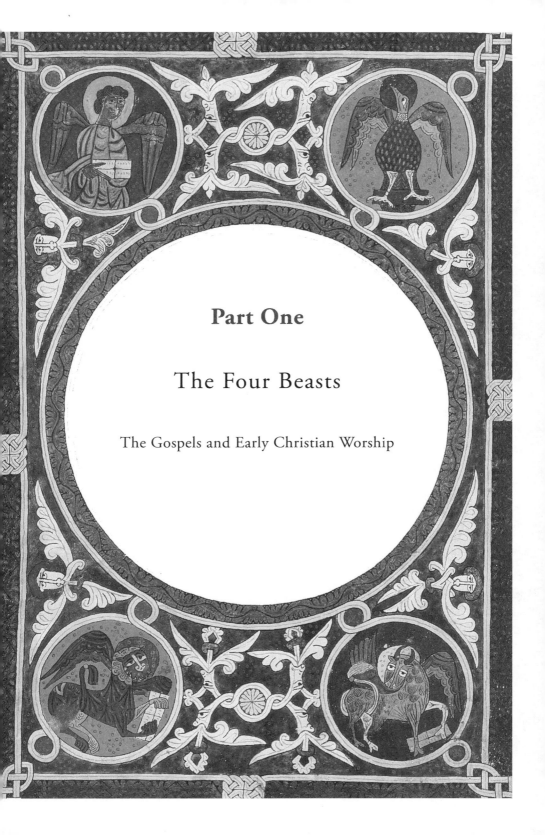

Part One

The Four Beasts

The Gospels and Early Christian Worship

1

Beginnings

Assemblies, "Gospel," Gospels

In most of the Christian assemblies meeting around the world today, a reading from one of the four Gospels—from Matthew or Mark or Luke or John—occupies a central moment in the worship service of every Sunday. This reading is a kind of pillar of the meeting, a reliably recurring ritual, a principal locus for meaning. In many assemblies, certain intensifying ceremonies accompany the Gospel reading and mark this moment as central. The assembly stands for the reading, facing the reader and the book. Or the reading is greeted with song. Or the Bible or Gospel book or lectionary is carried into the midst of the room, the assembly turns toward it and, perhaps, this movement is accompanied with candles and incense. Or, in the East, the book is brought out through the Holy Doors, which themselves carry images of the Gospel writers. Or all of these things occur. The preaching in the service usually follows the reading, often bearing special responsibility to articulate current meanings of the Gospel text that has been read alongside all the other texts. In a well-planned service, images from the Gospel text not infrequently fill the hymnody sung on that Sunday. If the congregation follows a lectionary—say, the Revised Common Lectionary—this very system of reading the Bible in community finds its coherence and its organization, in the first place, around the unfolding reading of Gospel texts. Indeed, the content of the feasts and seasons of the so-called "church year" is primarily brought to expression by whatever Gospel text is read. And, in some communities, the vigil of a feast or the Saturday evening vespers culminates in the reading of the Gospel text appointed for the feast or the Sunday immediately following.

Much of this practice has been going on for a long time. All of the Christian Sunday and festival lectionaries used throughout the centuries have been centered in the Gospel. The Western and Eastern liturgical ceremonies of its reading are very old, reflecting Roman and Byzantine court rituals. Already in the mid-second century, Justin Martyr said that "the memoirs of the apostles" were read in the Sunday meetings of the Christians with whom he was associated in Rome,[1] these "memoirs" having been already explicitly identified by Justin himself as "the Gospels."[2] Alongside "the writings of the prophets," these Gospels were then read, according to Justin, not necessarily in their entirety, but for "as long as there is time." The very Christian preference for using the codex, the bound book, rather than the widely used but unwieldy scroll, may well have been encouraged by having the Gospels in the meeting of the church, perhaps having all of them there, even if only one was being read. We know that the codex was invented in the first and second centuries, and that thereby books began to look like what we call "books" today, with pages sewn together and with the whole easily held in the hand. This primary Christian book form enabled the written Gospels to be bound in a single book and carried into the Christian house meetings or "shop-churches" to be read aloud.[3] Indeed, all four Gospels, copied out by hand on papyrus, could fit in a single ancient codex and thus be available to a community's reader.

Why this intense communal use? Was such a use envisioned by the books themselves, at their origin? And do the Gospels themselves have anything to say about the Christian meetings of the time of their origin or about the idea of a Christian meeting generally?

Mutual Coherence, Not Panliturgism

We need to be careful here. Such an attempt at biblical-liturgical thought—biblical studies aware of Christian worship, worship studies caring about the Bible—could be skating on thin ice. Good scholars have been here before, and they have quite frequently crashed though to the ruin—or, at least, to the scholarly rejection—of their project. There was a time not long ago when "it was fashionable

---

1. *1 Apology* 67.

2. *1 Apology* 66.

3. Cf. Graham N. Stanton, *Jesus and Gospel* (Cambridge: Cambridge University Press, 2004), 84–85, 165–91. Stanton interestingly proposes that the Christian preference for the *codex* may well have been due not only to its portability but to its countercultural sense of newness. These were new books, with a countercultural message. On "shop-churches," see Marcus J. Borg and John Dominic Crossan, *The First Paul: Reclaiming the Radical Visionary Behind the Church's Conservative Icon* (New York: HarperOne, 2009), 91. See further below.

to find liturgy everywhere"[4] in the Bible, a tendency that has come to be called, disparagingly, "panliturgism." I do not want to argue again that the organization of all four of the Gospels corresponded to the ancient synagogue calendar and its lectionary as these were reworked in primitive Christian practice[5] or that the Fourth Gospel was thoroughly and positively sacramental.[6] As much as I myself was at one time drawn by these proposals, I have come to see that there is very little evidence for them.[7] Nonetheless, I do think that these proposals and others like them were reaching toward something of importance, longing to bring to expression in some way the mutual coherence of New Testament Gospels and Christian assembly.

That assertion is the first thing to say. There was a kind of mutual coherence between the four Gospels and the ancient Christian Sunday meetings. It is not that the Gospels and the meeting practice of Christians were co-extensive. The Gospels were not direct scripts for the meeting. And, of course, they could be read elsewhere. But the Gospels presume the Christian assembly and include it within their reference. They seem to have been intended for communities, for reading or orally reciting the story of Jesus in those communities. These meetings existed before the Gospels did. So did the stories and sayings of Jesus. But the Gospels gathered those stories and those sayings together into an intentional form and made that form available to those meetings. Of course, they provided only one kind of book read or recited in the meeting. At least some gatherings of early Christians, perhaps influenced by synagogue practice, seem to have especially gathered around the "scriptures," the books of what we call the "Old Testament."[8] Or, since these small communities may not have owned or had access to an extensive collection of scrolls of the Torah or the Prophets, in

---

4. C. F. D. Moule, *Worship in the New Testament* (London: Lutterworth, 1961), 7. See also Paul F. Bradshaw, *The Search for the Origins of Christian Worship*, 2d ed. (New York: Oxford University Press, 2002), 47–52; and A. E. Harvey, "A Word from the New Testament?" in Martin Dudley, ed., *Like a Two-Edged Sword: The Word of God in Liturgy and History* (Norwich: Canterbury, 1995), 1–2.

5. Aileen Guilding, *The Fourth Gospel and Jewish Worship* (London: Clarendon, 1960); Philip Carrington, *The Primitive Christian Calendar: A Study in the Making of the Marcan Gospel* (Cambridge: Cambridge University Press, 1952); M. D. Goulder, *The Evangelists' Calendar* (London: SPCK, 1978).

6. Oscar Cullmann, *Urchristentum und Gottesdienst*, Zweite Auflage (Zürich: Zwingli, 1950).

7. Bradshaw, *The Search for the Origins of Christian Worship*, 48.

8. Consider the implications of Luke 24:27, 32 for the practice of the communities that heard this story.

Hebrew or in Greek, they may have had someone in their gathering who could recite parts of the scriptures or could read from notebooks containing *testimonia*, passages from Greek translations of the Hebrew scriptures collected together as handbooks of interpretation, especially handbooks for using the scriptures in understanding who Jesus was and what he did.[9] Certainly, some communities also began to copy and communally read and reread the letters of Paul.[10] But because of the importance of the story of Jesus to the identity of Christian communities, the Gospels grew to a preeminence, providing words for the meaning of the meetings of these communities and counsel for the practice of these communities. They demonstrated their coherence with the meetings of Christians, at least partly, by their interest in interpreting the very scriptures and *testimonia* already read there and interpreting them specifically of Jesus and his death. Indeed, they sought to join the basic books, the scriptures of the assemblies. The earliest fragments we have found of Gospel codices already often evidence a care in their creation, an "elegant literary hand" used in the copying and a universal use of the shorthand symbols for the sacred names of Jesus and God, the *nomina sacra*, all of which suggests the authoritative role of the books and the purpose, at least for these early copies, that they be reverently used and heard in assembly.[11]

If the Gospels themselves were not meant exclusively for this communal purpose, the meetings where they were to be primarily heard were still surely in their purview. Even the two places in the Gospels where a singular "reader" is called to "understand" (Mark 13:14 and its parallel, Matt. 24:15) may well be formal, metaphoric speech, belonging to apocalyptic style, or may be a call for the actual communal reader or some other communal leader to make this mystery clear in the assembled church when the book is read. The last suggestion may be all the more likely if the "desolating sacrilege" mentioned in these passages was in fact a statue of the Roman emperor or some other imperial cult object. This imperial statue was then not named in the text—to do so would be an act of probable sedition that would imperil any community that owned such a book—but the sense of opposition between the imperial cult and the Christian community was to be interpreted when the community gathered in the "house," where other

---

9. See Stanton, *Jesus and Gospel*, 182–85; and Martin Albl, *"And Scripture Cannot Be Broken": The Form and Function of Early Christian Testimonia Collections* (Leiden: Brill, 1999).

10. See 1 Thess. 5:27; cf. Col. 4:16.

11. Stanton, *Jesus and Gospel*, 192–206.

such mysteries are also disclosed.[12] Furthermore, the singular name of the person to whom the double volume Luke-Acts is addressed (Luke 1:3; Acts 1:1) may intend an idealized figure, representative of all the assemblies and of any "most excellent" friend of God who participated in the assembly with interest.

In any case, in the great range of people who made up the Christian communities of the first and second centuries, there were indeed people who were literate, people who could read aloud to the community.[13] Indeed, in classical times, reading was often out loud, recited, perhaps even intoned, and it often at least imagined hearers.[14] The image in the second-century book *The Shepherd of Hermas* of an ancient lady who is Ecclesia, the church, reading aloud to Hermas and then giving him a book to copy and to send to leaders in the churches for it to be read there[15] ought probably be taken as a relatively reliable picture of the copying, sending, and reading that went on in late-first- and early-second-century communities with the production of the Gospel books.

However, even if the books, like the letters of Paul, were largely intended for communal reading, it has become common to argue in recent biblical studies that relatively little can be said about the worship of the communities that were addressed by these letters or that made use of the Gospel books.[16] The texts are simply not interested in any systematic report of communal worship, and the local situations were most likely quite diverse. According to this argument, the individual elements of Christian gatherings that can be found as referenced in the New Testament—hymns, for example, or prophecy, or "speaking in tongues"—can simply not be organized into a widely valid, coherent picture called "early Christian worship."

---

12. Cf. Mark 9:28; 9:33; 10:10. See further below.

13. See Rodney Stark, *The Rise of Christianity: How the Obscure, Marginal Jesus Movement Became the Dominant Religious Force in the Western World in a Few Centuries* (San Francisco: HarperSanFrancisco, 1997), 29–47.

14. Cf. Richard Horsley, *Jesus in Context: Power, People, and Performance* (Minneapolis: Fortress Press, 2008), 4: "Even where texts existed in writing, they were almost always performed orally, before a group." See also the discussion in Whitney Shiner, *Proclaiming the Gospel: First-Century Performance of Mark* (Harrisburg: Trinity International, 2003), 14–16.

15. *The Shepherd of Hermas*, *Vis.* I:2:2; I:3:3; II:1:3-4; II:4:3. Cf. Pheme Perkins, *Introduction to the Synoptic Gospels* (Grand Rapids: Eerdmans, 2007), 39–40.

16. E.g., Ferdinand Hahn, *The Worship of the Early Church* (Philadelphia: Fortress Press, 1973), 2–3.

But the arguments of a scholar such as John Dominic Crossan have also invited us to see that at least the Gospel books that he calls "biographical"—the very four later gathered into the New Testament—have a deep, basic interest in how the story of Jesus is told in actual current communities.

> In this set [the four canonical Gospels] Jesus is located back in the late 20's of his first-century Jewish homeland, but he is also updated to speak or act directly and immediately to new situations and communities in the 70's, 80's, and 90's. There is an absolute lamination of Jesus-then and Jesus-now without any distinction of Jesus-said-then but Jesus-means-now. In Mark, for example, Jesus confesses and is condemned while Peter denies and is forgiven, but those specific events—dated, say, to the year 30—speak directly and were created precisely for a persecuted community in the year 70. . . . This lamination explains why the four canonical gospels could turn out so different even though they were copying from one another.[17]

For Crossan, what became normative about these books in the Christian community was the very Gospel form as marked by a dialectic between Jesus-then and Jesus-now: the Jesus whose concrete story was told in the Gospel book being the very risen Jesus encountering the community now; the crucified Jesus of an old and horrifying execution being the risen one whose wounds are encountered now as the wounds of history itself, of human brutality and inspired resistance, the response of the current Christian community being implied.[18] Crossan finds in this normative form a justification for the work of the Gospel commentator and the Jesus researcher today. But we need to note that for this normative dialectic between Jesus-then and Jesus-now to function, one needs two things: the book and the community reading the book. While on first reading the book may seem to be only about Jesus-then, it soon becomes clear to us that it is also and especially about how the Jesus-then is also the Jesus-now and about the assembly where that is seen to be so.

A Gospel book of this sort, then, went together with the Christian meeting. While book and meeting were not co-extensive, they were mutually coherent. This is not to assert panliturgism again, nor to find some special access to ancient

---

17. John Dominic Crossan, *The Birth of Christianity* (San Francisco: HarperSanFrancisco, 1998), 32.

18. Ibid., 39–40.

Christian liturgical practices. It is simply to argue that the four Gospels all presume a community, an assembly, a meeting, as part of what they are, as part of their very genre. If Crossan's "biographical gospels," the books that became "the programmatic gospels of sarcophilic Christianity,"[19] include an interest in the flesh of Jesus, the actual economic circumstances of ordinary life, and narratives of life and death, they also include an interest in meetings. Indeed, three of the four books significantly conclude with accounts of gatherings of the community. In two cases (Luke and John), these are clearly Sunday meetings.

The idea of mutual coherence might be illustrated by thinking first of all and especially about the Gospel according to Mark, the very book that does not at first seem to contain an account of a postresurrection meeting. I join the scholarly consensus that regards Mark as the earliest of the Gospels and, therefore, as the actual creation of what became the genre "Gospel."[20] Already when one begins to read the book, one catches the sense of the presence of an understood community of readers. So, the very first verse announces who Jesus is to the present readers (1:1). Thus, when, in the book's first miracle narrative, the possessed man in the synagogue says, to the surprise of everyone in the story, "I know who you are!" (1:24), the present reading community is already in on the secret. In fact, "being in on the secret" is one of the continuing characteristics of the entire book.[21] In Mark, only Jesus sees the heavens torn open at his baptism and hears the voice speak ("he saw," 1:10)—that is, only Jesus and the readers and hearers of the book. Then, time and again, when the "messianic secret" is urged upon unclean spirits or beneficiaries of Jesus' healings or the disciples themselves at the

---

19. Ibid., 38. See also my *Holy Ground: A Liturgical Cosmology* (Minneapolis: Fortress Press, 2003), 129–31.

20. It will be clear, in what follows, that I subscribe to several of the most basic matters of consensus in contemporary critical biblical studies: e.g., some sayings of Jesus and some Jesus stories circulated orally in early Christian communities; some of these sayings may have been gathered together in a now lost written source that scholars call Q or *Quelle*; the earliest written Christian books we have are the genuine letters of Paul, the Thessalonian letters, Galatians, the Corinthian letters, Philemon, Philippians, and Romans; the first written Gospel was the one we call "According to Mark," and it was written at about the time of the fall of Jerusalem and the destruction of the Temple, 70 c.e.; "According to Matthew" and "According to Luke" were both composed by authors who knew "According to Mark" and, perhaps, also Q; these books were written between 80 and 100 c.e.; the author of Luke may also have known Matthew; the writer of the Fourth Gospel, composed around the turn of the century, knew "According to Mark," and very likely the other two Gospel books, as well.

21. See further below, chap. 3.

confession of Peter or at the transfiguration—when they are all urged to keep silent concerning him—the reading or hearing community knows the secret and begins to see that this secret pushes toward the cross, only to leak out in the passion predictions, to become paradoxically plain in the assembly of the anointing woman (Mark 14:3-9) and at the supper before Jesus' death (14:17-25), as also at his trial (14:62) and death itself (15:39), and then, finally, to be revealed and proclaimed here, wherever the book itself is being read, in the word about the crucified risen one in the present assembly.

But there is more: when Jesus goes to sea, "other boats were with him" (4:36), an open narrative device that allows room for the hearing community to go along on the trip. The private explanations of the enigmatic parables (4:33-34; 7:17), of a difficult healing (9:28-29), of the implications of the second "passion prediction" (9:33-37), and of the saying about marriage (10:10) all open toward—indeed, *require*—continuing explanations and discussion in the current house churches. And the recurrent image of the *house* itself—another powerful Markan theme—as the place where Jesus is, as the place of teaching and healing and forgiveness, as the place of shared meals,[22] would have inevitably evoked in the minds of the readers or hearers the current houses of the church or shop locations of the assembly in the late-first-century communities that would have been reading this book. The very title, "the *kyrios* of the house," used for the eschatologically returning figure at the end of Mark's little apocalypse (13:35), may have carried a similar recognition: the one who is returning, the one for whom we are to watch, is the one to whom we sing as *kyrios* in our house churches.

These examples can be multiplied in the other Gospels. "Where two or three are gathered in my name, I am there among them," promises the Jesus of Matthew's Gospel (18:20). The risen one is known "in the breaking of the bread," asserts Luke (24:35), explicitly echoing an important practice that marks the gatherings of the church, according to the second volume of this Third Gospel (Acts 2:42, 46; 20:7, 11). And the Fourth Gospel itself is written so that "you" *plural*—one imagines an assembly—"may come to believe" (John 20:31). The four Gospels of the New Testament assume and refer to the meetings of Christian communities. And, when these books became available, the late-first- and early-second-century meetings of Christians came increasingly to find the books themselves attractive, challenging, important, and, finally, indispensable. The

---

22. Cf. Mark 1:29; 1:32; 2:1-12; 2:15; 3:20; 5:19; 5:38; 6:10; 7:17; 7:24; 9:28; 9:33; 10:10; 14:3; 14:14.

four Gospels and the Christian assembly have a mutual coherence. We can learn from that mutuality both something about the Gospels and something about what the Gospels were proposing for the meetings of Christians.

But if this coherence is indeed written into the books, if the Christian meeting is in some way envisioned in the books, we are brought to the question of genre. What, then, is a Gospel?

What Is the Gospel?

To answer that question, we must first ask what is meant by the word *gospel* at all. In order to begin to respond, we need to think a little more about the state of Christianity in the mid-to-late first and very early second centuries c.e., the time just before and during which the Gospels were composed. We will find the Christian use of the word *gospel* to originate in this period, and we will find it useful to investigate the origin of the Gospel books against the background of that word use.

In a highly regarded work, the sociologist Rodney Stark has argued that there were probably slightly more than 2,500 Christians in the world in the year 70, the likely year of the composition of Mark. By the turn of the century, shortly after the time of the composition of Matthew and Luke and about the time of the writing of John, there may have been more like 7,500 Christians.[23] The Christian movement was quite small. And it largely consisted of small groups, increasingly spread throughout the Mediterranean world and especially found in cities, groups that gathered in houses or tenement apartments or workshops or other small places. The letter of Paul to the Romans, probably written in the mid-to-late 50s of the first century,[24] clearly implies that the Christians in Rome at that time were a quite diverse lot, gathered in at least five different meetings and perhaps many more.[25] In Paul's word use, these gatherings are "churches,"

---

23. Stark, *The Rise of Christianity*, 6–7. The numbers given in Acts 2:41, 4:4, and 21:20 should probably be viewed as evidence of Luke's intention to present an ideal picture of the growth and spread of Christianity, not as reliable historical information.

24. Stark proposes that, in the year 50, there were a total of about 1,400 Christians. Some scholars have considered Romans 16, discussed here, to be a later addition to the letter, perhaps originally addressed to another city. For a clear refutation of that position, see already W. G. Kümmel, ed., *Introduction to the New Testament* (Nashville: Abingdon, 1966), 225–26. In any case, the demonstration of diverse assemblies found in Romans 16 is important for us, regardless of the original location of those assemblies.

25. So, the "church" in the house of Prisca and Aquila (Rom. 16:5); those with (or

ἐκκλησίαι, assemblies, like the assemblies before the Lord in the Hebrew scriptures,[26] and they are frequently characterized by the familial language— "relatives," "brothers and sisters," "a mother to me"[27]—that had come to express the communal character of the Christian movement. Indeed, Paul takes it upon himself to greet these gatherings in the name of all the other such assemblies throughout the world (Rom. 16:16), inviting them to exchange with each other the Christian ritual version of an ancient familial greeting, the "holy kiss."[28]

For the rest of the argument of this book it is important to note here that such assemblies were not a new or specifically Christian invention. In gathering as associations or clubs, in regarding each other as a kind of family, in meeting in households, in sharing meals, Christians were making use of a widespread pattern in Greco-Roman society. Such household-based associations were one important way in which people of the time were religious, one important way in which they sought to participate in the benefits of the gods, one significant basis for social organization in Hellenistic cities. Before the Christian movement and as one model for it, Jewish "synagogues" in the greater Mediterranean world also were organized much like these widespread "Gentile" associations.[29]

"from") Aristobulus ("the family of Aristobulus," 16:10); those with Narcissus ("the family of Narcissus," 16:11); the "brothers and sisters" who were with Asyncritus, Phlegon, Hermes, Patrobas, and Hermas (16:14); and the "saints" who were with Philologus, Julia, Nereus, his sister, and Olympas (16:15). For a contrary view, that the Christians of Rome at the time of Paul's letter may have constituted a single gathering of a few dozen people, see Bernard Green, *Christianity in Ancient Rome: The First Three Centuries* (London: T&T Clark, 2010), 31–33.

26. See my *Holy People: A Liturgical Ecclesiology* (Minneapolis: Fortress Press, 1999), 26–43. It must be noted that there is some evidence for the term ἐκκλησία being used not simply for the ancient Greek civic voters assembly but also for clubs and associations besides Christian ones. See Philip A. Harland, *Associations, Synagogues, and Congregations: Claiming a Place in Ancient Mediterranean Society* (Minneapolis: Fortress Press, 2003), 182, 283n1; and Richard S. Ascough, "Voluntary Associations and the Formation of Pauline Christian Communities: Overcoming the Objections," in Andreas Gutsfeld and Dietrich-Alex Koch, *Vereine, Synagogen und Gemeinden in keizerlichen Kleinasien* (Tübingen: Mohr Siebeck, 2006), 159. However, I think that Paul has biblical eschatology in mind in his use of the term.

27. One ought to compare the saying of Jesus in Mark 10:30: you will receive a hundredfold "houses, brothers and sisters, mothers and children, and fields with persecutions." The community in Rome seems to have had such multiple houses and alternative families, as well as the persecutions.

28. L. Edward Phillips, *The Ritual Kiss in Early Christian Worship* (Cambridge: Grove, 1996).

29. See Harland, *Associations, Synagogues, and Congregations*. See also Carolyn Osiek and David L. Balch, *Families in the New Testament World: Households and Household Churches*

It may be that Paul would call all of the Christian assemblies in Rome, together, by the singular word *church*—"the assembly of God that is in Rome"— as he did in his address to the Corinthian Christians (1 Cor. 1:2; cf. 2 Cor. 1:2). He certainly regarded all the Christians of the world together as "the whole church" (Rom. 16:23; cf. 1 Cor. 15:9), as a kind of great assembly before God. In any case, in the letter to the Romans, he addressed these various people and assemblies, bidding them "greet one another with a holy kiss" and bidding them avoid "dissensions and offenses" (Rom. 16:16-17).

But that intention is the point. The letters of Paul are addressed to assemblies and are both unifying and reforming in intent. All of Paul's letters seem to have been sent to gatherings like these in Rome, small groups spread throughout the Roman Empire. So, for example, Phoebe, a deacon of an assembly in Greece, near Corinth, seems to have been charged to carry the letter from Paul to Rome and make it available to the diverse gatherings he names (16:1-2). The first letter to the Thessalonians proposes a similar scenario of communal reading and hearing, also conjoined with the holy kiss (1 Thess. 5:27).[30] Even Philemon, seemingly addressed to an individual, also is sent to Apphia, Archippus, "and to the church in your house" (Philemon 2), thus dealing with its content, about the equality and freedom of a slave, as a public and communal, though also personal, matter.[31] Furthermore, all of the letters were critically reforming in intent. They invited the communities that read them to remember or to hear afresh what Paul regarded as the basic grounds for these assemblies, the source of their trust in God and of their unity, and they encouraged the participants in these assemblies to live out the implications of those grounds. In Galatians and 1 Corinthians, this reforming purpose is quite directly stated (Gal. 1:6-9; 1 Cor. 1:10-11). In the case of the Roman Christians, Paul says that he feels rather confident about them—about their knowledge and their goodness and their ability to instruct each other (15:14)—but he also says he writes to them all together (to "you" as a plural, to all these Roman assemblies) "on some points . . . rather boldly by way of reminder" (15:15).

(Louisville: Westminster John Knox, 1997); and Luke Timothy Johnson, *Among the Gentiles: Greco-Roman Religion and Christianity* (New Haven: Yale University Press, 2009), 138.

30. The later pseudonymous, "deutero-Pauline" or Pauline-school letter, Colossians, shows assemblies exchanging these letters for communal reading (Col. 4:16).

31. That Philemon is concerned with the necessary *freedom* of a slave is strongly and convincingly argued by Borg and Crossan, *The First Paul*, 31–45.

For Paul, both the authority he has for this "reminder" and its very content are what he calls "the *gospel*" (15:16). In this passage at the end of the letter to the Romans (15:14-21), Paul uses an extended metaphor: he is like a sacred public minister, a λειτουργός, a "liturgist," commissioned by the grace of God, doing the priestly service—as if in a new, worldwide temple—of turning the offering brought by the nations into an acceptable offering, made holy by the Holy Spirit. The image is most likely drawn from a passage of the prophecy of Malachi that was beloved of many first- and second-century Christians:[32] "For from the rising of the sun to its setting my name is great among the nations, and in every place incense is offered to my name, and a pure offering; for my name is great among the nations, says the LORD of hosts" (Mal. 1:11).[33]

It is that purifying work, bringing about that "pure offering," Paul means to be doing with the Romans, with his letter as with his planned presence. It is that work he believes he has been doing in all of his travels (15:19). But what is the meaning of this metaphor? For Paul, the content of his "sacred public ministry," his λειτουργία, is "Christ Jesus for the nations," and the content of his "priestly service," his ἱερουργεῖν, is the "gospel of God." In his metaphor, these are words for the same thing: the lively announcement of Jesus Christ, of his death, his resurrection, and his presence in the Spirit, as the very grounds for faith in God and the source of love turning toward a needy world. Such is the "gospel." Paul addresses this lively announcement to the assemblies. Indeed, for Paul, the very identity of the assemblies depends upon the gospel. So does their continual, faithful reform.

It is important to remember that the culture surrounding the early Christian communities was a culture full of temple sacrifices of all kinds, to all sorts of gods and to the Roman emperor himself, used for the sake of social and political cohesion. Christians often rejected these sacrifices, but their cultural omnipresence and importance made them the ready material for metaphor. The very metaphor, when used as here for the noncultic, nonsacrificial practice of announcing the gospel as the free gift of God and discovering a faith and a life according to the

---

32. Cf. *Didache* 14:2; Justin Martyr, *Dialogue with Trypho* 116–117; Irenaeus, *Against Heresies* 4.17.5.

33. Perhaps, indeed, Paul also has in mind a later passage of Malachi: "for he is like a refiner's fire . . . and he will purify the descendants of Levi . . . until they present offerings to the LORD in righteousness" (3:2-3). Gentiles and Jews, both, need such "purifying."

gospel, became a kind of negation of sacrificial practice.[34] Thus, it is no surprise that for Paul, whenever this metaphor occurs throughout his letters, the "offering" that such an announcement of the gospel brings about is not a cultic interaction enacted in the killing of animals, not a tit-for-tat with the divine, but faith (see Phil. 2:17), trust in God, and then, flowing from faith, one's own bodily life, turned in humility and love and mutual giving toward the other (see Rom. 12:1-13; Phil. 4:18).[35]

Again and again, Paul uses the word *gospel*, εὐαγγέλιον, as the short name for the basic thing he is called to serve and the content of what he is saying in both oral proclamation and letters. It is this gospel that he believes will do the needed "purifying," reminding, and unifying of the assemblies at which all of his letters aim. His letter to the Romans thus begins with his own identification as "a servant of Jesus Christ, called to be an apostle, set apart for the gospel of God" (1:1) and with the characterization of that gospel as the good news promised in the scriptures, the good news concerning Jesus Christ, born, dead, and risen, who is the Son of God and our κύριος. For Paul, this gospel reveals the central matter to which the scriptures point, the very scriptures with which the Christians in Rome were familiar and which many of the Christian communities were reading. But more than mere words, this gospel is "the power of God for salvation, revealing the very righteousness of God" (1:16-17). It comes in word and deed and sign (15:18-19), like what later Christians will call "the visible word" of God.

"Gospel" also recurs in Paul's other writings. His letter to the Galatians is a defense of the gospel he has proclaimed and a resistance to any other gospel (Gal. 1:6-9; cf. 2 Cor. 11:4), an assertion that this gospel is from God, given him "in a revelation of Jesus Christ" (Gal. 1:12). In his first letter to the Corinthians, he finds authority to address the Christian assembly in that city because he "became your father through the gospel" (1 Cor. 4:15; cf. 1:17). Indeed, it is obvious that he thinks of the gospel, the message about the cross of Jesus (1:18), as more than rhetoric (2:1) but as words that create, even give birth. This "word of the cross" is wisdom that looks like foolishness (1:23), strength that looks like weakness (2:3), yet the source of life and the presence of God's Spirit (1:17, 24; 2:1-4; cf. 1 Thess. 1:5). It causes people who trust it and live by it "to stand," in an age when

---

34. See my *Holy Things: A Liturgical Theology* (Minneapolis: Fortress Press, 1993), 143–49.

35. Paul uses the same metaphor in 1 Cor. 9:13-14, where "those who proclaim the gospel" are likened to "those who serve at the altar."

all is falling (1 Cor. 15:1; cf. Phil. 1:27; Rom. 16:25). Indeed, this "standing" or the "salvation" which the gospel brings about (Rom. 1:16), is a characteristic way that Paul speaks about his expectation that the world as we know it is ending and the gospel—the very revelation of the mystery of God which had been hidden until these last times—is the God-given means for life and survival. In this urgent time, this gospel brings or ought to bring Jew and Greek together, setting aside religious ways of distinguishing insiders and outsiders (Gal. 2:14). In this urgent time, it brings people to care for and give to the poor (2 Cor. 9:13).[36]

Perhaps the clearest delineation in all of Paul's writings of what he regards as the content of the gospel is given in the formal confession found in 1 Corinthians 15:3-8. There Paul, once again intent upon "reminding" the Corinthian assembly of the gospel in which they "stand" and are being saved, seems to pass on, in a traditional formula and in a catalog of witnesses, the central assertion: Jesus Christ died for us, was buried, was raised, and has appeared to the church and its leaders. This death and resurrection was "in accordance with the scriptures." Paul himself is among those to whom the risen one has appeared. Perhaps, indeed, given the numbers proposed by Stark, the assertion that the risen Christ "appeared to more than five hundred brothers and sisters at one time," an assertion otherwise unknown in ancient Christian testimony, may be an early way of saying that a few years after Jesus' death, the whole Jesus movement, in all of its meetings—and not only Peter and the Twelve and James—came to know that they were encountering Jesus Christ risen. In any case, the death and resurrection of Jesus are the content of Paul's gospel. What it means for faith and life that this death and resurrection are "in accordance with the scriptures," that they are "for our sins," and that they are good news is what then occupies much of Paul's writing and teaching.

Cultural Context for "the Gospel"

While the word *gospel* is found elsewhere and less centrally in other early Christian literature, its overwhelming use is in Paul.[37] So much is this so, that it has come to be widely regarded by scholars as likely that Paul himself was the originator of the Christian usage, at least of the word as a noun, in its singular,

---

36. See also the way 1 Corinthians 16, about the weekly collection for the poor, follows upon 1 Corinthians 15, about the content of the gospel.

37. See Stanton, *Jesus and Gospel*, 20.

absolute sense ("the gospel," without further modifier). But then the question of the background for Paul's use becomes fascinating. It certainly may be true that Isaiah 61:1-2 and other Old Testament passages about announcing "good news" had some effect on the idea in early Christianity that the preaching of Jesus Christ, his death and his resurrection, and the nearness of God's "kingdom" in him were "good news to the oppressed." But the evidence for this usage may not be as old as Paul (e.g., Luke 4:18 and Luke 7:22/Matt. 11:5, perhaps a Q text). Or, if the usage does recall a word of Jesus himself, it is important to note that the actual words used in Isaiah and in these Christian uses of Isaiah are verbs, not nouns. The source of Paul's unique use of "the gospel," a singular noun, remains a question.

But recently a startling answer to that question has been proposed. Linguists such as F. W. Danker and G. H. R. Horsley have carefully researched the Hellenistic use of the related word group. Of the noun in plural form, τὰ εὐαγγέλια, Horsley says, "The usage of the neuter plural noun is clear: it refers to good news (often emanating from a monarch), such as news of their victories or benefactions; and in particular, the word is employed of the sacrifices celebrated on such an occasion."[38] And now Graham Stanton demonstrates that in the time of the writings of Paul and the origins of the Gospels, the "monarch" concerned was overwhelmingly the Roman emperor.[39] Stanton has convincingly argued that the cultural home of this Greek word, the referential world which its use frequently called up, was the widespread and immensely important cult of the Roman emperor. So, Josephus (in the mid-70s) wrote of Vespasian becoming emperor in 69 C.E., that "every city kept festivals and celebrated sacrifices and oblations for such good news."[40] The cities, indeed, "celebrated gospels," ἑώρταζεν εὐαγγέλια, according to the literal Greek text. Here were those "sacrifices" called "gospels," of which Horsley spoke. The imperial "good-news announcements" were both invitations to festival and the festival sacrifices themselves.

Even more significantly, an inscription about the adoption of the Roman calendar (usually called the "Priene inscription" from its first discovery on the

---

38. G. H. R. Horsley, *New Documents Illustrating Early Christianity*, vol. 3 (Sydney: Macquarrie University, 1983), 13.

39. Stanton, *Jesus and Gospel*, 25–33. Cf. Helmut Koester, *From Jesus to the Gospels: Interpreting the New Testament in Its Context* (Minneapolis: Fortress Press, 2007), 3–4, 207, 217. *Pace* Rudolf Bultmann, *Theology of the New Testament*, I (New York: Scribner's, 1951), 87.

40. *Wars of the Jews* 4:10, in William Whiston, trans., *Josephus: Complete Works* (Grand Rapids: Kregel, 1972), 545. Cf. Perkins, *Introduction to the Synoptic Gospels*, 1–2.

west coast of Turkey in a ruined town not far from ancient Ephesus, but in fact found very widely in many Greek cities of Asia Minor) read in part:

> It is subject to question whether the birthday of our most divine Caesar spells more of joy or blessing, this being a date that we could probably without fear of contradiction equate with the beginning of all things [τῇ τῶν πάντων ἀρχῇ], if not in terms of nature, certainly in terms of utility, seeing that he restored stability, when everything was collapsing and falling into disarray, and gave a new look to the entire world that would have been most happy to accept its own ruin had not the good and common fortune of all been born: CAESAR. Therefore people might justly assume that his birthday spells the beginning of life and real living [ἀρχὴν τοῦ βίου καὶ τῆς ζωῆς] and marks the end and boundary of any regret that they had themselves been born. . . . and Caesar . . . transcended the expectations . . . not only by surpassing the benefits conferred by his predecessors but by leaving no expectation of surpassing him to those who would come after him, with the result that the birthday of our God signaled the beginning of good news for the world because of him [ἦρξεν δὲ τῷ κόσμῳ τῶν δι᾽ αὐτον εὐαγγελίων].[41]

The inscription, placed in temples erected to the emperor, then went on to establish the calendar as beginning with the birthday of Augustus and as observed by festivals and games, by sacrifices and the installation of local magistrates: the beginning of the year and the beginning of legal terms was, according to the decree of the provincial Greek council of Asia, to coincide with the birthday of Augustus and thus with the "beginning of all things" and the beginning of good news.

While this calendar inscription probably originated very early in the first century C.E., it was still standing in many places in Asia Minor and still playing a role in the determination of social, political, and religious life in the time of Paul's ministry. Indeed, we may take it as evidence of the values involved in the imperial cult as that cult was known throughout the Roman Empire. Although Asia Minor may have had its own religious culture in such matters,[42] the giving

---

41. F. W. Danker, *Benefactor: Epigraphic Study of a Graeco-Roman and New Testament Semantic Field* (St. Louis: Clayton, 1983), 216–17. Greek text from Robert K. Sherk, *Roman Documents from the Greek East* (Baltimore: Johns Hopkins University Press, 1969), 329–33.

42. S. R. F. Price, *Rituals and Power: The Roman Imperial Cult in Asia Minor* (Cambridge: Cambridge University Press, 1984).

of divine honors to the emperor and the accompanying games, processions, and sacrifices were a kind of social glue in the whole ancient world, one that was experienced as very attractive and as involving all classes, one with which it would have been very difficult to dissent.[43]

It appears that Paul did so dissent. Very likely Paul himself was the source of the singular use of τὸ εὐαγγέλιον for the announcement of the death and resurrection of Jesus. When seen next to the plural use of the word in imperial announcements, it seems that this singular use had a polemic intent. For Paul, there is only one reliable, life-giving, world-founding gospel as there is only one κύριος (1 Cor. 8:6). With this insight, we come to see the dangerous, existentially powerful implications of all that Paul says about "the gospel." He is resisting the religious ideology of the powerful and oppressive state that wishes everyone to praise the "stability" that state brings. And he is doing so by announcing the paradoxical good news of one who was killed by that very state. Far from participating in the sacrifices, festivals, and games that belonged to the imperial cult, those imperial public liturgies, Paul sees his nonsacrificial, noncultic announcement of the gospel of Jesus Christ as his "priestly service" and the responding faith in God, awakened throughout the world, as the only "pure offering" of the nations. Paul is constantly recalling the crisis of the death of Jesus as the very crisis and turning point of the world, the beginning of the radical healing of all things. He is proclaiming the resurrection of this Jesus and interpreting both his death and resurrection in continuity with and using images from the Hebrew scriptures. In so doing, he is engaging in a profoundly critical religion, one that inverts and reinterprets what the available religious gestures— sacrifice and festival, for example—and thus what life and the world, power and stability, freedom and hope all actually are.

It is to this dangerous gospel that Paul was calling the small assemblies of Christians to whom he writes. These communities probably had come to exist in ways that were quite socially recognized and acceptable: licit *collega*; supper clubs; gatherings for the like-minded. There were many such clubs in any Hellenistic city.[44] But Paul, because of the one Lord of the gospel, may have been calling the Galatians to avoid the religious observance of the imperial year and the imperial

---

43. Stanton, *Jesus and Gospel*, 26–28. On the world-stabilizing force of Greco-Roman religion, see also Johnson, *Among the Gentiles*, 93ff.

44. See Harland, *Associations, Synagogues, and Congregations*.

festivals (Gal. 4:8-10).[45] Because of the eschatology of the gospel, he may have been warning those who propagandize about and rely on the "peace and security," the stability, of the Roman emperor (1 Thess. 5:3).[46] Because of the content of the gospel, a content even made known to "the whole imperial guard," he may have been inviting the Philippians to a humility and mutual service like what they sing about in Jesus Christ and radically unlike that of the emperor (Phil. 1:12-13; 2:1-11).[47] But in all of his writings, he was calling those little assemblies—hardly noticeable assemblies, at first—to a faith and a way of life radically out of step with the social compact, the distribution of power and wealth, and the very description of the world supported by the worship of the emperor as "savior," "lord," "son of god," and source of the "beginning (or foundation) of all things," the "beginning of real living," and the "beginning of good news for the world." He was inviting them to a complex process of sorting, accepting, and rejecting elements of their own culture.[48] He was urging that they characterize their own versions of the Hellenistic local assemblies in a uniquely Christian way.

The words are made to crack, turn around, invert. The symbolic force of the words is broken. So, "assembly," ἐκκλησία, is an ordinary Greek word with a usual reference to a gathering of free citizens, perhaps in Paul's day to many a gathered "club." But in Paul it becomes a word transformed by its reforming, biblical content: the assembly called before God for the sake of the world, like the assembly found in the scriptures and expected at the end of time. For Paul, the gospel is making these gatherings into ἐκκλησία, church, God's assembly, and doing so in accord with the promises of the Hebrew scriptures. Furthermore, as we have seen, in Paul "offering" and "priestly service" are no cultic interactions at all, but the announcing of the new gospel and the awakening of faith. These "priestly services" can include the assemblies where the gospel is announced for the sake of awakening faith. But they can also include Paul's travels throughout the world, especially as he is gathering a collection for the needs of the poor. So also for him "gospel" itself is a word brought under new tension. It trails the

---

45. Stanton, *Jesus and Gospel*, 41–43; cf. Thomas Witulski, *Die Adressaten des Galaterbrief* (Göttingen: Vandenhoeck & Ruprecht, 2000), 158–68.

46. Stanton, *Jesus and Gospel*, 47–48; cf. J. R. Harrison, "Paul and the Imperial Gospel at Thessaloniki," *Journal for the Study of the New Testament* 25 (2002): 71–96.

47. Stanton, *Jesus and Gospel*, 48–49; cf. Borg and Crossan, *The First Paul*, 212; and Peter Oakes, *Philippians: From People to Letter* (Cambridge: Cambridge University Press, 2001), 147–74.

48. Harland, *Associations, Synagogues, and Congregations*, 198f.

smell of the imperial cult along with it, but then surprises and breaks those con-notations. Perhaps a memory of Isaiah 61 assisted in this linguistic change: in Jesus Christ good news is indeed announced to the wretched and the poor, not only, as in the imperial "gospels," to the collaborating rich and powerful. In any case, for Paul there is only one Son of God, only one Lord, only one "through whom are all things and through whom we exist" (1 Cor. 8:6). This is not Augus-tus nor any of his successors. It is Jesus Christ, the low and despised one, the crucified. The proclamation of this one, of his life and death, of his "accession" as Lord, and of the forgiveness that is through him—the proclamation of the gospel—is a word full of paradoxical power. It is both an invitation to festival and the festival observance itself, but not in triumphalism nor in the sacrificial manipulation of power. Rather, by its word of the crucified, the Christian gospel gives life, brings to birth, makes faith in God possible, and turns one toward the needs of the neighbor. For Paul, such a word can repeatedly turn a dinner club or a gathering of the like-minded into a church.

The Death of Paul and the Origin of a First Gospel

As far as we know, Paul was executed by the Roman imperial authorities. It is no wonder, given the nature of his gospel. But, for our purposes, there is more to say. An important argument can be made that this death had something to do with the appearance of the kind of book we call a Gospel.

We do not know precisely when Paul was killed. At first, he and the tiny groups to which he related would not have been particularly noticed publicly, except as a minor religious irritation. But then, apparently, he was noticed. Or he and many other Christians were noticed—and cruelly killed. The writer of Acts reports that Paul came to Rome but gives no further end to the story: com-ing to Rome fulfills the outline of the book (Acts 1:8), and any further account of an official Roman execution would be counterproductive to the book's irenic purposes, its desire to show that faith in Jesus Christ does not have to undermine a just government. The presentation of Paul in Acts as a Roman citizen (22:25-29; 23:27), a presentation that has no support in any of Paul's own writings, probably stems from the same intention and probably is not a historical fact. The late-second-century tradition that Paul was beheaded in Rome was probably created out of this earlier Lukan idea, beheading being the "humane" form of capital punishment given to citizens.

But the late-first-century letter from the Roman church to the church in Corinth, called the *First Letter of Clement*, does make it clear that Paul was killed in Rome. His death most likely took place at more or less the same time that Peter was killed there, and most likely with a great many other Christians: "To these men [Peter and Paul] with their holy lives was gathered a great multitude of the chosen, who were the victims of jealousy and offered among us the fairest example in their endurance under many indignities and tortures" (*1 Clem.* 6:1).[49] The great probability is that the event to which this letter refers, the deaths of Peter and Paul and a "great multitude" of others, is the Neronian persecution of Christians. In 64 c.e., the emperor Nero made the Christians of the city into scapegoats for the great Roman fire, and he proceeded to kill a large portion of them in horrible ways. Peter and Paul were probably among this number, not executed with singular dignity, but tortured and massacred in Nero's garden and at his "games," along with many other Christians.[50] It is not so much that the faith of these Christians was understood and fearfully rejected by those whose power it threatened. It is, rather, that their faith and their way of life, at least as Paul urged and interpreted it, made of them a people radically out of step with ordinary social norms and so made them vulnerable to a weak and monstrous emperor's need to blame a subgroup, redirect the public anger (which suspected him of the fire), and cruelly entertain the masses with public tortures and killings.

If this is so, then Paul died, to use the words that the Gospel according to Mark places in the mouth of Jesus at the "first passion prediction," among "those who lose their life for my sake, and for the sake of the gospel" (8:35). Indeed, he was among those who left family and house for the sake of Jesus and the gospel (10:29), and received manifold new family members and welcoming houses, but received them along with persecutions. He himself was among those who brought the gospel in proclamation to the nations (13:10), and so was betrayed and handed over and hated and put to death.

That these three occurrences of the singular noun "the gospel" in Mark, out of the total of seven such occurrences in the book, seem so close to Paul's own usage of the word and, furthermore, that these three occurrences could be used to recall and describe Paul's own death, raises the question as to whether the

---

49. Translation in Kirsopp Lake, *The Apostolic Fathers* I (Cambridge: Harvard University Press, 1959), 19.

50. See the convincing argument in Garry Wills, *What Paul Meant* (New York: Penguin, 2007), 157–70.

author of Mark knew the work of Paul. The question is intensified by the sense that the term "the gospel" is overwhelmingly a Pauline term and by the fact that the other four uses in Mark (1:1; 1:14-15; 14:9) are also strikingly like Paul. Mark uses the singular noun, never the verb, and uses it either absolutely or modified as the "gospel of Jesus Christ" (1:1) or the "gospel of God" (1:14), both reflecting Pauline usage. As in Paul, the gospel is juxtaposed with Jesus Christ, as essentially the same thing (the gospel is Jesus Christ, who is both its first preacher and its content for the world), in the manner of biblical parallel speech.[51] Furthermore, the question about the author of Mark knowing the work of Paul is intensified if both the proposal about Paul's death under Nero in 64 c.e. and the current consensus regarding the date of Mark at about 70 c.e. are correct. Then Mark's interest in "the gospel," the very interest with which the book begins, could in some sense be in succession to Paul, carrying on his work in a new way. Did the author of Mark know the writings of Paul?

I propose that the answer is yes. Perhaps, in the small company that made up mid-first-century Christianity, this author knew Paul himself and lamented his awful death. In any case, several scholars have pointed out the considerable correspondence that exists between the vocabulary of Mark's Gospel and Paul's word use,[52] a correspondence that is not limited to but certainly comes to expression in the immensely important word *gospel*. Even more decisively, Joel Marcus has demonstrated the series of overlapping themes and interests between the Gospel according to Mark and the letters of Paul:[53] the crucifixion of Jesus as the apocalyptic turning point of the world; Jesus' victory over demonic powers; the gospel as prophesied in the scriptures; Christ as a second Adam;[54] both a dualism in faith and a tendency to a certain universalism (Mark 10:45; Rom. 11:32); a negative sense about Peter and about Jesus' family; the gospel as good news for sinners; the gospel as for the Jews first but also for the Gentiles; a common attitude toward the

---

51. Mark 8:35; 10:29; cf. Rom. 1:1 and 15:16. "My sake" and "the sake of the gospel" are not two different things, but one thing spoken of in two juxtaposed and mutually reinterpreting ways. So also, "servant of Jesus Christ" and "set apart for the gospel of God" (Rom. 1:1) are not two different things. Neither are being a "minister of Christ Jesus" and doing "the priestly service of the gospel of God" (Rom. 15:16).

52. Stanton, *Jesus and Gospel*, 18–25; M.-J. LaGrange, *Évangile selon St. Marc* (Paris: Gabalda, 1929), clvii and 17–18; P. Rolland, "Marc. lecteur de Pierre et de Paul," in E. van Segbroek, et al., eds., *The Four Gospels*, 2 (Leuven: Leuven University Press, 1992), 775–78.

53. Joel Marcus, "Mark—Interpreter of Paul," *New Testament Studies* 46 (2000): 473–87.

54. Especially in Mark 1:13 and 9:2-8; cf. Rom. 5:12-21 and 1 Cor. 15:21-22.

food laws (Rom. 14:14; Mark 7:19); and, most especially, a Christology centered on the cross, a thoroughgoing *theologia crucis*. Both Paul and Mark use the perfect passive participle "the one who was crucified," ἐσταυωμένος, to describe the risen one whom their books proclaim (1 Cor. 1:23, 2:2; Gal. 3:1; Mark 16:6).[55] One might add yet more themes, especially the understanding of the followers of Jesus as an alternative "family," as brothers and sisters and mothers (Mark 3:33-35; 10:28-31; cf., e.g., Romans 16); the sense that the gospel calls for and creates faith (Mark 1:15; cf., e.g., Rom. 1:1-5); the idea that church leaders should be servants and stewards (Mark 9:35; cf. 1 Cor. 4:1); and the common interest in the "mystery" or the secret being revealed (Mark 4:11, 22; 1 Cor. 2:1, 7; 4:1).

The author of Mark knew and was at work interpreting Paul. But the author of Mark did not write letters to the churches as Paul did. He or she wrote a new kind of book. One might imagine something like this: with the deaths of Paul and Peter and the many other Christians who were killed under Nero, the Christian communities knew they were facing serious persecution. That persecution had also been breaking out in other places. One person, a person who understood what Paul was trying to do, also understood that these deaths meant a huge loss in the way the communities had access to the traditions and meanings of Jesus. Stories and saying of Jesus—and sayings of prophets who were speaking in the name of the risen Jesus[56]—circulated orally, perhaps even in notebooks, but these stories and sayings had to be brought together in a book, authoritatively. Paul himself had made use of and passed on a few sayings of Jesus or prophetic sayings in the name of the risen Jesus,[57] but Paul was now dead. The book to be written would include a few more sayings than Paul—though still relatively few—but it would report them with the same sense of power and authority they had held for Paul. The "gospel" might continue to be talked about in Christian communities, but that gospel needed to have a reliable content. The tradition quoted in 1 Corinthians 15:3-4 would need to become a narrative, since such a narrative could give cohesion to fragmented communities and carry the scriptural authority of a world-founding epic. The assemblies and clubs that consid-

---

55. Marcus, "Mark—Interpreter of Paul," 480.

56. It is important to realize that some of the sayings of Jesus had such a postresurrection origin.

57. See, for example, 1 Cor. 7:10, 40; 9:14; 11:23-25; 14:37; 1 Thess. 4:15. Especially 1 Cor. 7:40 and 14:37 makes clear that some of these sayings may well have come from Christian prophets or from Paul's own act of prophecy.

ered themselves part of the Jesus movement were under pressure to conform or simply to follow their own ways. They still needed to be addressed, as Paul had addressed them, "reminding" them, calling them again and again to the heart of this gospel, making the "houses" of their gatherings places of the mystery of God revealed.

Perhaps the author of Mark had one such community in mind. It might have been the remaining Christians of Rome, as the later tradition imagined the origin of the book,[58] or it might have been some group in Galilee or Syria, nearer to the destroyed Temple and the "desolating sacrilege" set up at Jerusalem (Mark 13:2, 14), as some modern scholars theorize.[59] Or perhaps the author really did imagine that the book was for all the communities of Christians,[60] to be spread among that small number throughout the world of the time, just as Paul's letters had begun to spread. We do not need to choose. In any case, the author knew that the communities saw themselves as under potentially murderous pressure, and meant to set out again the story of the death of the Lord as the most reliable help, a story that could gather into itself the current suffering and hold it under the resurrection promise. The book she or he wrote was a book for the persecuted.

Very likely, the many deaths in Rome and the growing number of deaths elsewhere had also brought about a subtle shift in the eschatological expectations of this successor of Paul. What he or she would write would still speak with apocalyptic language, but hidden in the text would be clear clues that with the death of Jesus the promised judgment of the nations had already begun, the promised day of God had dawned.[61] The nations are already being judged now, in those who suffer and die, just as in their crucified Lord. In this regard, the author would slightly differ with Paul. The book's word for the persecuted would

58. Eusebius, *Ecclesiastical History* 2:15:2; 6:14:6. Cf. Irenaeus, *Against Heresies* 3:1:1: after the "departure" of Peter and Paul, Mark wrote. For recent arguments for Rome as the location of the writer, see Adam Winn, *The Purpose of Mark's Gospel* (Tübingen: Mohr Siebeck, 2008).

59. For example, Willi Marxsen, *Der Evangelist Markus* (Göttingen: Vandenhoeck & Ruprecht, 1959).

60. See Richard A. Burridge, "Who Writes, Why, and for Whom?" in Marcus Bockmuehl and Donald A. Hagner, eds., *The Written Gospel* (Cambridge: Cambridge University Press, 2005), 110–11.

61. Note, for example, that the phrase "in the evening, or at midnight, or at cockcrow, or at dawn" (13:35)—the times for the coming of "the κύριος of the house"—is replicated in the times given throughout the following passion story. Note also that the drinking that is to take place "new in the kingdom of God" (14:25) does take place in the story, with sour wine on the cross (15:36). See further below, in chap. 3.

not simply be comfort. It would also lay down a way to go on, a way to be the community of Jesus in the way of the cross, even as the eschatology shifted away from the expectation of an immediate, open *parousia* of the Lord and an observable victory of the community. In the present moment was already the dawning dominion of God, in every encounter with the hidden but risen Lord. Indeed, the assemblies of Christians needed to know who was the risen one they were encountering in their meetings and at their meals and how he was still, precisely, the crucified, the ἐσταυωμένος. For all of these reasons, in succession to Paul and in nuanced change, the author would write a book that recounted the beginning and the root content—the ἀρχή—of the gospel.

Or perhaps it was not like this. Perhaps there were many authors of the work. Perhaps parts of it—say, the account of Jesus' death or the collection of parables that would make up the current chapter 4—were already largely composed and circulating. And of course, the resultant book, however composed, would have been influenced by available models or inevitably read as like them: it would be seen as a Christian version of a Hellenistic *bios*, a recognizable form for the biography of great figures.[62] In creating a narrative, it might have been influenced by the manner of ancient novels.[63] It might carry some of the traits of the great Greek epics, especially in its circular composition and its sense of the weight and importance of the story.[64] All these things are possible.

But, one way or another, the book was also something new, something else. So much is clear: in whatever way it came about, the Gospel according to Mark reflects the Pauline interest in "the gospel," the Pauline interest in the crucifixion of Jesus as the turning place of the world, the Pauline interest in the resurrection of Jesus, the Pauline sense that the gospel of the crucified comes with a life-giving and faith-creating power, and the Pauline interest in saying all this to an assembly or to assemblies—to the house churches that are echoed in the frequent Markan "house"—for the sake of their ongoing reform. However, if the apostle Paul himself was an ambassador of Christ (2 Cor. 5:20), a kind of stand-in for the presence of the risen one in the assemblies, and if Paul's letters were a kind of

---

62. See Richard A. Burridge, *What Are the Gospels? A Comparison with Graeco-Roman Biography* (Grand Rapids: Eerdmans, 2004).

63. Cf. Perkins, *Introduction to the Synoptic Gospels*, 23.

64. See Dennis R. MacDonald, *The Homeric Epics and the Gospel of Mark* (New Haven: Yale University Press, 2000); and Mary Douglas, *Thinking in Circles: An Essay on Ring Composition* (New Haven: Yale University Press, 2007), xii. See also chap. 3 below.

stand-in for his own presence, then this idea was even intensified in the Gospel according to Mark. The book, read in the assemblies, was intended as an encounter with, even a seeing of the Jesus Christ crucified and risen whom the book describes.[65] Jesus-then is indeed Jesus-now, in the assembly. The eschatological moment comes here. Such is the new intention of the book, more than the Hellenistic *bioi* intended to be, more even than Paul's letters. This was a newness needed by the times—by the eschatological shift, by the situation of persecution, by the ongoing and threatened meetings of the assemblies, by the communal fragmentation, by the need for the life-giving power of the gospel.

Still, the book shares with Paul the knowledge that this gospel is antiimperial. It is not only that the "desolating sacrilege" set up in the Temple (13:14), which seems to have been one of the occasions for the writing of the book, most likely referred to the statue of the *Sebastos*,[66] the emperor as the most "worship-worthy" one, as indeed god and son of god. It is not only that the death of the crucified is recounted in a way that makes clear the radical difference of this lowly one with all imperial pretension and power.[67] It is that the book itself is called "the beginning of the gospel of Jesus Christ, the Son of God" (1:1).[68] That is most likely its title, perhaps the one clear title we have in all of the original texts of the Gospel books:[69] *The ἀρχή of the gospel.* This title is almost exactly like the wording of the Priene calendar inscription,[70] only now in the Pauline singular, now about a very different "son of God," and now directly contrary

---

65. See Marianne Sawicki, *Seeing the Lord: Resurrection and Early Christian Practices* (Minneapolis: Fortress Press, 1994); my *Holy Ground*, 128–29; and chap. 3 below.

66. *Sebastos* is the Greek translation of the word "Augustus," but it carries more religious content: "the worshiped one."

67. See especially Marcus J. Borg and John Dominic Crossan, *The Last Week* (New York: HarperOne, 2006).

68. "Son of God," in the title, remains textually unsure, being supported especially by the Vaticanus, the Byzantine tradition, and the Vulgate. The parallel to the Priene inscription and the imperial cult seems to me to argue for its inclusion. So does the important Markan idea that the community of hearers is in on the "secret."

69. Of course, it can be argued that Mark 1:1 refers only to the immediately following account of John the Baptist, the baptism of Jesus, and especially the beginning of Jesus' preaching, *his* "evangelizing." It is then not a title of the work but a description of the opening section. Again, I think that the parallel to the Priene inscription and the use of the Pauline singular noun, rather than the verb, supports the idea that 1:1 is the ancient title of the book.

70. See M. Eugene Boring, et al., *Hellenistic Commentary to the New Testament* (Nashville: Abingdon, 1995), 169; and Winn, *The Purpose of Mark's Gospel*, 97, 179.

to the pretense of the emperor's cult. This title, rather, draws one into the book that follows and so points to the mercy and truth, the weakness and suffering of the Jesus-then—the beginning, the ground—who is the saving and healing, risen Jesus-now, as the assembly in the power of the Spirit stands before God around him. The book is revolutionary and calls upon the assemblies that read it to be countercultural, for the sake of a wider, deeper healing and stability of all things. In a certain sense, the book has from its outset a sacred character, like the announcements and proclamations that would be the basis for festivals and sacrifices in the imperial cult. But it is also a subversion of this kind of sacrality, a holy calling to another way.

What the book is comes to expression in the title: it is the beginning and grounds of the gospel, a gospel that is needed by the assemblies, proclaimed and celebrated in the "houses," and a gospel utterly at odds with the many, lying "gospels" of the imperium. That "beginning" points toward the assemblies where the gospel will occur on the grounds of this beginning. "Beginning" implies and coheres with assembly. And it witnesses against the imperial cult that found all beginnings of life and festival in the doings and person of the emperors.

The author of Mark, then, for the first time, creates a new genre—a kind of book that will later be called a "Gospel." It is not exactly made new, out of whole cloth. It depends upon the circulating stories and sayings of Jesus, upon the Pauline idea of "gospel," upon Hebrew scripture passages long used by Christians to interpret the meaning of Jesus, perhaps upon the methods of *bioi* and Homeric epics. But it is largely intended for assembly use, and it means to do a new thing, to be the grounds for proclaiming the gospel of God and thus a means for the encounter with the risen crucified one, his hidden death revealed for what it is and thus the hidden secret of all things revealed. In doing this, it is brilliant. I think that it is the astonishing creation of a fine, literate, Pauline-formed but independent theologian. It may not be the most elegant Greek. In that sense, like its subject, it is humble. But it is neither simple nor simple-minded. Its conceptions of the function of symbol, juxtaposed image and overlaid speech, its idea of word-event occurring in assembly, its balance of mystery and epiphany are complex and astonishing. Indeed, I join the Christian tradition in gladly confessing it to be the result of the inspiration of the Spirit of God, but exactly an inspiration that has a real human history, a flesh that goes with the spirit.

And Then, the Four

In the next three decades, the Gospel according to Mark seems to have been read at least some places among the Christians. In any case, it seems to have awakened the interest of a few people or a few communities to create other books like it, perhaps even in order to supersede it. It is right to argue that the authors of Matthew and Luke both made use of it. The shape of Mark became largely the shape of the other two. The three books, together, have been called "the Synoptics" for just this apparent common shape. Furthermore, the very wording of Mark often survived in the other two, albeit with an intentional editing and smoothing out of the Markan text and a leveling of some of the Markan paradoxes and complexities. What both of the other two Synoptics did, however, was seek to expand the collection of the sayings of Jesus, both of them perhaps relying upon the oral or notebook tradition of Q, while also each turning to unique material that we otherwise do not have.[71] For them, a faithful representation of Jesus in the assemblies needed to include more of his teaching. What they also both did was turn back slightly from the eschatological adjustment of Mark, reintroducing a somewhat stronger sense of a future event, a day of the Lord to come. They did this, apparently, in the years between 70 c.e. and the end of the century, Matthew probably between 80 and 90 c.e, Luke later, most likely between 90 and 100.[72] Perhaps they did it for specific communities, though we know from extensive quotation in second-century writers that these two books came to be widely read, probably more widely read than Mark. The greater number of second-century manuscript fragments of the Gospels are fragments of Matthew. And, while the two-volume work of Luke-Acts is addressed to a single, perhaps idealized reader named Theophilus, the work seems to present itself as a kind

---

71. A significant and compelling argument can be made, however, that Matthew used and expanded Mark, that Luke used both Matthew and Mark as its only written sources, that the author of John knew all three of the earlier books, and that alongside all of this an oral tradition about Jesus and his teaching still continued, evolved, and expanded. In such an argument, a strong accent is placed on the intentional creativity of each of the authors and the hypothesis of there being a "Q" at all is eliminated. This case was made cogently by Austin Farrer in his "On Dispensing with Q," in D. E. Nineham, *Studies in the Gospels* (Oxford: Blackwell, 1955), 55–88, esp. 85. See also Michael D. Goulder, *Luke: A New Paradigm* (Sheffield: Sheffield Academic, 1989/1994), 22–23; and Mark S. Goodacre, *Goulder and the Gospels* (Sheffield: Sheffield Academic, 1996).

72. See, recently, L. Michael White, *Scripting Jesus: The Gospels in Rewrite* (New York: HarperOne, 2010), 312 and 335.

of new epic of Christianity,[73] intended for widespread reading among Greco-Roman Christians. Indeed, perhaps the books were originally intended for all of the Christian assemblies then known in the world.

Then, at about 110 c.e. or so,[74] came the fourth book, the one we call "According to John." If one reads carefully, it, too, evidences a knowledge of Mark, following something like the same outline and fascinatingly expanding on Markan themes.[75] The author very likely also knew Luke and perhaps also Matthew,[76] but his (or her?) eschatology—sometimes called "realized"—is written as if this author understood and agreed with the hidden speech of Mark and brought the matter to yet more open expression. In any case, in John the whole outline is filled out with extensive theological discourses as well as with a series of "signs" that reveal who Jesus is.

None of these three was as Pauline as was the author of Mark. Still, they were certainly interested in the "gospel." While the singular noun "the gospel" occurs less frequently and less centrally in these other books, Luke does use the verbal form extensively. Indeed, the angels at the outset of "According to Luke" "proclaim good news" to Zechariah and to the shepherds (1:19; 2:10) about the preparation for and the birth of Jesus. And Jesus, at the outset of his ministry in Luke, quotes Isaiah 61:1-2 and inhabits its promise of "good news to the poor" (4:18). In "According to Matthew," the most extensive beginning of Jesus' preaching is the Sermon on the Mount, and there, at the outset, in the Beatitudes, beginning with "blessed are the poor in spirit" (5:3), Jesus may be being presented as doing exactly the announcement of good news to the poor that the text of Isaiah 61 envisions.[77] In Matthew, furthermore, the phrase "this gospel of the kingdom" (24:14) or simply "this gospel" (26:13) may very well refer to the book itself or, at least, to its content.[78]

While there is no such word use in "According to John," there in the first line of the book is that startling reuse of the Markan word ἀρχή, "beginning." In the Fourth Gospel, of course, what is there in the beginning is "the word." Already

---

73. Koester, *From Jesus to the Gospels*, 235.

74. White, *Scripting Jesus*, 358.

75. So, for example, in the Markan passion story, the "temple-builder" image and the "I am"—the divine name—both play a role (Mark 14:58, 62). In John, the former has become a story at the outset of Jesus' ministry (John 2:13-22) and the later an astonishing, revelatory event at Jesus' arrest in the garden (John 18:6).

76. Cf. White, *Scripting Jesus*, 354–55.

77. Cf. 4:23. See Stanton, *Jesus and Gospel*, 14–15.

78. Ibid., 57–58.

in Paul, "word" and "gospel" can be used synonymously (e.g., Phil. 1:12-14).[79]
The same is probably true for Mark (2:2; 4:14; 4:33). In any case, in both Paul
and Mark the content of the gospel is Jesus Christ himself. The same is true of
the Fourth Gospel's "word," as this idea is illumined by Hellenistic *logos* speculation and by a play on the opening words of Genesis. Moreover, in this prologue
to "According to John," the interest is in how this content of the word relates to
what the Priene inscription calls "the beginning of all things." It seems as if the
antiimperial character of "According to Mark" has spilled over into this further
Gospel book, this further reworking of the intention of Mark. All things have
come to be through Jesus Christ the Word, not through the emperor.

When one recalls that the calendar inscriptions and the imperial cult, generally, were also deeply interested in the birth of Augustus, then it is no surprise
that "According to Matthew" and "According to Luke" start with diverse versions
of the story of Jesus' birth. Indeed, Luke even dates the birth story with "a decree
. . . from Emperor Augustus" (2:1), demonstrating at once both the obedience of
Mary and Joseph to the imperial decree, their peacefulness, and the radical difference of this birth of another sort of "savior" or benefactor among the poor.[80]
It is also fascinating to note that the author of Luke also begins the book with
a reference to the beginning, the ἀρχή (Luke 1:2).[81] Perhaps this word is to be
expected at the outset of a book. But I think it more likely that both the power
of Mark's evocation and reversal of the imperial cult and the importance of this
first Gospel for the formation of the others have carried further reflection on "the
beginning" into both Luke and John. Luke thinks of the beginning of the gospel
(of Jesus Christ, not the emperor), that gospel now called "the word" (Luke 1:2).
John juxtaposes Genesis 1:1 and thus thinks of the beginning of all things in
that same word (and not in the advent of the emperor). In any case, besides the
general shape of the book, all three of the other Gospel books do seem to catch
some version of Mark's interest in "gospel" (or "word") and some breath of the
countercultural sense of that gospel.

They catch yet more. I am arguing here that the first example of the Gospel
book genre, created in about 70 C.E. and called by us "According to Mark," was

---

79. Ibid., 47–49.

80. Frederick Danker thinks that Luke intentionally sets the image of Jesus as "benefactor" against the kind of imperial "benefaction" praised in the Priene inscription. See his *Luke,
Proclamation Commentaries* (Philadelphia: Fortress Press, 1987), 29–30.

81. See also Acts 1:1, where a verbal form of "beginning" is used.

primarily addressed to assemblies. It was meant to be read at gatherings in the very "houses" that are reflected in its narratives and promised in its "you . . . will receive a hundredfold . . . houses" (10:30). It was to be read there as a means to see the risen one present in the assembly. While the other Gospels do not follow the same method that Mark does, revealing that presence as a kind of hidden epiphany breaking out of the layered and symbolic speech of the text, they have nonetheless gotten the point. All three of the other books conclude with accounts of assemblies, in each case presented as paradigmatic for all Christian assemblies. In Luke, it is Emmaus and then the gathering of all the disciples in Jerusalem (Luke 24). In Matthew, it is the baptismal sending of the community and the promise "I am with you always," a reprise of the earlier "where two or three are gathered in my name, I am there among them" (Matt. 28:16-20; 18:20). And in John, the meetings are recurring, every Sunday—as, by then, was the pattern of the churches—and are to be filled with the presence, word, forgiveness, sending, and Spirit of the risen Christ. The book is to be read there as enabling faith (John 20:19-31). These final images of the books are important indications of their most basic intentions, of the reasons for the books being written at all. The books have in common that interest in assembly, although they address the assemblies in differing ways.

Second-Century Reception of the Four

What shall we call these books? One of them calls itself "The beginning of the gospel of Jesus Christ" (Mark 1:1). Another may be proposing "This gospel of the kingdom" (Matt. 24:14). Otherwise, the earliest forms of the text were without title. But as the books came into the second century, they were increasingly called "The gospel according to _____." This use, of course, implied that there is a single gospel, a word alive in the assemblies and filled with the presence of the one Lord, but that there are a diversity of witnesses to that gospel. It is a splendid point, and one that ought not be taken for granted. The books themselves, for all that the latter three make use of the first one, seem to envision that each book is quite enough. After all, if the books purported to tell the truth about Jesus, then the inconsistencies among them might be seen as making the Christians vulnerable to a charge of lying or invention. Stanton argues that the very fact that Matthew incorporates most of Mark in his book is "an indication that he intended that his Gospel should replace Mark's, and that it should become *the*

Gospel for Christians in his day."[82] Similarly, Luke is aware of earlier attempts. He proposes to do the thing correctly that others have undertaken, finally writing an "orderly account for you" (1:3). And the Johannine community, in its probably later appendix to the Gospel, does not think they need all those other books that could fill the world. They most likely treasure only the book that they regard as the testimony of the beloved disciple (21:24-25). It is then amazing that the four Gospels survived and even thrived, seemingly against the intention of at least three of the authors. It is the more so, since at least one Christian, called Tatian, in the mid-second century actually attempted to weave all four into a single narrative: his resulting book was called the *Diatessaron*, "arising from four," and it was a book that was remarkably successful in Syriac-speaking Christianity in subsequent centuries. The temptation was to try to find a single reliable access to history, to Jesus-then.

But Tatian's text was not the deepest result of the use of the books in the churches. Some time in the second century, bound in a single codex, they began to be called by the names we still use today: "The Gospel according to Mark," "*kata Markon*"; "The Gospel according to John," "*kata Ioannen*"; and so on. By such titles, the point was made that the truth about Jesus will be best told in a juxtaposition of these witnesses, not by the absolutizing of one. In fact, as Irenaeus of Lyon would later warn,[83] to cling to just one would probably lead to distortions. But then the joint witness finally took place preeminently in the assembly. The gospel in the assembly could be both a transcending and a reconciliation of the original purposes of the individual books. Stanton argues that "by accepting the fourfold Gospel, the early church acknowledged that the gospels are not histories" but "theological witnesses to Jesus Christ in narrative form."[84] And the primary place of this witness, as envisioned by the books themselves, was the assembly. Here again, I gladly join the confession of the church that regards both each of the four and the very fact that there are four as gifts from the Spirit of God, but gifts that have a real human history, a flesh that goes with the spirit.

As the years continued, the books began to be called "Gospels," in the plural. I am following that custom in what follows in this present work, as I also make use of the standard shorthand "Matthew, Mark, Luke, and John." I do so hesitantly. Not only do we not really know, from the texts or from contemporary

---

82. Stanton, *Jesus and Gospel*, 87.
83. *Against Heresies* 3:11:7.
84. Ibid.

witnesses, the names of the authors of these books, but we also do not know the gender of these authors. At least "Mark," it seems to me, runs a good chance of having been written by a woman (the apostle Junia, perhaps, of Romans 16:7?),[85] because of the positive role of women in the text (e.g., 7:24-30; 14:3-9; 15:40-41) but also because of their final failure (16:8). It might be a faithful woman who could best set out that ambiguity. But I hesitate mostly because of our need to see again the remarkable difference of these books. In a sense, they are not themselves "the gospel" but its beginning, its witness, the materials for its proclamation. In a deep sense, they are not plural, like the imperial announcements, for they witness together to one person, one event, one presence. They are not ordinary biographies. They are not, finally, competing narratives. They are not tame. Nonetheless, "Gospels" it will be. And "Matthew, Mark, Luke, and John"—but with a constant suspicion that these are the wrong names. "The Gospel according to one like a Lion, one like a Human Being, one like an Ox, and one like an Eagle," rare beasts all, may be closer to the truth.

There are, astonishingly, four. And they are not the same. Garry Wills speaks of them as four "Reports": from the suffering body of Jesus (Mark), from the teaching body of Jesus (Matthew), from the reconciling body of Jesus (Luke), and from the mystical body of Jesus (John).[86] While one might want to be careful with the word *report*, Wills helpfully includes both witness to Jesus and witness to the life of the churches in his titles.

Others have recently argued that there are also more than four. In that regard, Helmut Koester has wisely said that the texts that continued to be central to the life of the churches were texts that carried centrally a witness to the death and resurrection of Jesus, the very death and resurrection that was also celebrated at the heart of the ongoing meal tradition of the church.[87] We will explore this connection between Gospels and meals further in what follows.[88] But Koester also points out that the "sayings tradition," the possible source of the "Gospel of Thomas" and others of the various second-century texts that were later treasured by Christian Gnostic groups, had little accent upon historic, communal continuity.

---

85. Were Junia the author, interestingly, "Mark" would indeed be the "memoirs" of an apostle, as Justin calls the Gospels (1 *Apology* 66 and 67), and not because it was attributed to a companion of Peter, as Papias and Irenaeus later did. See above, n.58.

86. Garry Wills, *What the Gospels Meant* (New York: Penguin, 2008), vii.

87. Koester, *From Jesus to the Gospels*, 38.

88. See chap. 2 below.

The "sayings," without narrative, without an interest in communal meals and meetings, and without the passion account, could indeed have religious meaning for individuals but not for communities.[89] They could express general religious ideas, even "wide truths of life," but not reform proposals for assemblies. What is more, Pheme Perkins argues that much of the second-century "apocryphal gospel" material "was created by the growing prominence of the four-Gospel canon in Christian life and worship. It does not contain much first-century Jesus tradition. Nor should the adoption of a Gospel canon for Christian worship and instruction be viewed as an example of ecclesiastical repression."[90] So, while the spread of the four may have evoked competition, there was not an "ecclesiastical structure" to be repressive. There was simply the mutuality between the late-first-century Gospel books and the assemblies. It is those earlier books, the four, the ones that arose out of a clear interest in and mutual coherence with the assemblies, that I am exploring here.

That this communal, reforming, reorienting intention for assemblies belonged to the early purpose of the Gospels seems to have been understood and read in the books themselves by at least some Christians in the second century. So, for example, already Ignatius of Antioch, in his letter to the church at Smyrna sometime in the first two decades of that century, calls for the church to pay attention to the prophets and "especially to the Gospel, in which the Passion has been revealed to us and the Resurrection has been accomplished" (Ign. *Smyrn.* 7:2b).[91] The "gospel" here, of course, could be the Pauline word meaning the oral proclamation of Jesus Christ, but when it is paired with "the prophets" it seems more likely that Ignatius is already envisioning the reading and preaching from a book. That book then shows forth the death of Jesus and the presence of his resurrection in the assembly. Ignatius appeals for attention to these things as a way to correct misconceptions of what God is doing and a way to ground the unity of the assembly: "flee from divisions" (7:2c). Then, the *Didache*, probably an early-second-century writing and compilation (that included some much earlier material), mentions "the gospel," perhaps meaning a book, and does so in connection to matters of assembly practice: the text of the Lord's Prayer, the reception of traveling prophets and apostles, and the

---

89. Koester, *From Jesus to the Gospels*, 234.
90. Perkins, *Introduction to the Synoptic Gospels*, xvi.
91. Translation in Lake, *The Apostolic Fathers* I, 57. Cf. also Ign. *Smyrn.* 5:1.

practice of mutual correction (8:2; 11:3; 15:34).[92] It is even more clear that Justin, writing in Rome in the mid-second century, has the books in mind. In describing the presence of Christ in the Eucharist, he first says, "For the apostles, in the memoirs composed by them, which are called Gospels, have thus delivered unto us what was enjoined upon them; that Jesus took bread . . ." (*1 Apol.* 66),[93] and then he continues with one version of the "institution narrative." It is these "memoirs of the apostles" which are reported as being read in the Sunday meeting of Justin's assembly (*1 Apol.* 67). Justin then asserts that this whole meeting and its content, the content being presented in the *Apology* and being summarized by the report of the baptismal and eucharistic practice of this assembly at the end of the *Apology*, is the result of the teaching of the risen crucified Christ, a teaching that may be especially known in the Gospels.

Then, toward the end of the second century, it was Irenaeus of Lyon who compared the four books to the four faces of the living creatures of Ezekiel 1 and the four Beasts of Revelation 4–7 and 14.[94] In the midst of the living creatures of Ezekiel is the fire of the presence of God. In the midst of those same Beasts, as the image was reused in the Revelation, are the throne of God and then the presence of the Lamb who was slain. Around them, in Revelation, is the assembly of the elders, surely a reflection of the assembly of the church. The first thing that the Lamb does is open the scroll in the hand of God. The Lamb is the key to the book. Perhaps it is not only that Irenaeus found the image of the beasts apt to what he regarded as the single aim of the diverse Gospel books, apt because there is a single presence in the midst of the four different creatures. He may also have found the image apt to the very use of the Gospels: their witness in the midst of the assembly, calling the assembly toward the throne and the Lamb and toward the Lamb as the key to the very book of God. The Gospels are not simply like the Beasts in their fourness and their difference. They are also like the Beasts in their common function: witness to the presence of the one crucified living one, the one who is the meaning of the book of the will of God; witness to that presence in the midst of a book-reading, meal-keeping (cf. Rev. 3:20; 22:14,17), singing-and-

---

92. Cf. Matt. 6:9-13; 10:5-10; 18:15-20. It seems as if the community of the *Didache* knew "according to Matthew."

93. Translation in *Ante-Nicene Fathers* I, 185.

94. *Against Heresies,* 3:11:8. Note that Irenaeus identifies John as the Lion and Mark as the Eagle, unlike the common and ongoing tradition of the West. Iconography in the East knows both traditions. See Leonid Ouspensky and Vladimir Lossky, *The Meaning of Icons* (Crestwood: St. Vladimir's Seminary Press, 1982), 113.

praying assembly of the church; and witness to that presence as witness against the murderous structures of the world. Irenaeus thus gives evidence for the fact that by the late second century the widespread practice of the churches included the four.

* * *

So what was a Gospel? If we are speaking of the four, of the books that belong to the genre first inaugurated by Mark, then it was a book intended to bear witness to the meaning of Jesus Christ and to do so, for the most part, in assembly. Such a book aimed at the ongoing reform of that assembly. It meant to be received as scripture, side by side with and interpreting any other scriptures read in the meeting. It meant to be word of God, witnessing to Jesus, in an assembly gathered in the Spirit. Or, rather, it meant to be the ground for and the beginning of the spoken and signed announcement of the gospel in that same assembly, an announcement that invited and gave birth to faith and that turned its hearers, in countercultural ways, in love toward their neighbors. More: this Gospel book functioned itself as a symbol of the presence of the crucified and risen one, and it spoke a symbolic language as it enacted that function. In its writing, it articulated the Jesus-then in order to enable speech about the Jesus-now. And it did all this with an explicit interest in resistance to destructive religious and cultural patterns of the time and an interest in the well-being of more than only the community that read the book.

The four did this common work in different ways. As time went on, the four also came to do this work side by side. We need to explore both those different ways and that side-by-side work, after we first look at the manner in which the Gospels, in one way or another, addressed the meals of the church. There are many ways to read these books, many questions that may be asked of them. We will be reading them here with primarily one question in view: As they speak of Jesus-then becoming Jesus-now, what are they saying about and to assemblies?

These Gospels are still read among us, in present-day Christian assemblies. The genre "Gospel," its coherence with assembly, and its ancient calls to reform still resonate in our time, in our liturgies. The very coherence between Gospels and assembly has an edge. As we have considered that edge in the first and second centuries, as we have looked at the origin of the Gospels and their early purpose, questions have also arisen for us.

37

Thus: Do we read the Gospels in our assemblies in order to hear the gospel there? What would that mean for our understanding and practice? Do we too easily turn the books into historical reports of Jesus-then, with no interest in Jesus-now? Or do we make the linkage between our times and those times only by our imagining "what it must have been like" or by our turning the teaching of Jesus into universal laws and "wide truths of life," even though the Gospel books themselves are interested in neither thing? Do our preachers deal with the texts as if they were literal reports? Does our general practice meld the four into one, single story, overlooking the striking differences? Does the ancient rejection of the imperial cult and its "gospels" have continuing relevance for us? What functions like that cult in our times? Do we help the people of our assemblies to know that these books arose in the late first and early second centuries, as witnesses to Jesus Christ crucified and risen, as calls to assembly, as countercultural moves—like the Beasts?

2

The Gospels and Meal Meetings

Then what do these Gospels say about worship?

First of all, we need to note that when we are discussing early Christianity, the words *liturgy* and *worship* may be anachronistic and misleading. The Christian community had meetings, and the evidence is that these meetings were frequently for the sake of a shared meal. The meal came to be of considerable significance, but "worship" might not be the first term one ought to apply to it. Christian communities certainly praised God. They worshiped. They gave thanks at table. They sang. Both the letters of Paul and the Gospels may reflect this singing by the hymns that are quoted and included in these texts. But "worship" is not all that paleo-Christians did when they gathered. It may be more accurate to say, simply, they held a meal at which, at least by Paul's advice, the gospel was proclaimed.

Furthermore, as we can tell from Paul's language in Romans 15:16, this announcing of the gospel ought be taken only metaphorically as a "liturgical service." If the gospel was a subverting form of the imperial announcements, with their calls to sacrifice and festival in honor of the divine emperor, then that gospel of Jesus Christ did indeed call to a new kind of "liturgy." But, reformed in the way that Paul envisioned, the gathering of the assembly, its hearing and interpretation of the scriptures, its prayers and its hymns, its meal proclaiming Jesus, and its care for the poor would then be a "liturgy" metaphorically, the public cultic event of the imperial temples inverted, humbled, saved. It would be the religious meeting criticized, made widely accessible, centered on the gospel and on the reorienting imagery and symbols of the Hebrew scriptures as these are reknown in Jesus, and turned to a new purpose.

But we might use the word *worship* more generally. We might thereby not so much be carefully describing what paleo-Christian assemblies did as expressing a trust in there being some continuity between what we call "Christian worship" today and what happened in those meetings in houses and tenements and shops in the first and second centuries. Expressed in this way, the question is an important one. The answer we have been pursuing is simply this: between assembly and the four Gospels there is a significant coherence. The Gospels are primarily addressed to communities in their meetings. They are addressed, like the letters of Paul, with "reminding" and reform in mind, for the sake of a new anchoring in the gospel so that the hearers might "stand" in a falling time, so that the hearers might believe and hope and turn in love to their neighbors, so that world itself might have a new beginning. These events in the gospel were certainly understood to take place in the presence of God, as God's gift, in God's mercy, and so, in that sense, could be called "worship." Along with Paul, these events in the gospel, enabled by the Gospels, could be called a new kind of "liturgy." We will discover, as we proceed, that the Gospels did imply one or the other specific thing about the practice of the assemblies as they read scripture, prayed, held meals, baptized, remembered the poor, and, especially, held meals. When the Gospels were read in assembly, they did cast a light on these things.

There might be one important objection to this proposal: Are not the books too long to be have been read in assembly very often? Perhaps. But when we think about the mid-second-century note of Justin in Rome, that the reader read "for as long as there is time,"[1] it is not clear that this is the case. Furthermore, I have been arguing that the Gospel texts already were understood as sacred texts, as soon as they were available to the churches. Then, to the extent that the churches were aware of synagogue practice, they would also have been aware of the reading of selected sections or pericopes (cf. Luke 4:17), and to the extent that they made use of notebooks or collections full of "testimonies" from the scriptures, they would already have known brief readings. While the whole book or all the books may have been known, the Gospels might also have been read or recited in part in any given meeting. The primary thing to note is not only that the Gospels were read aloud communally, but that they sought to reorient any Christian meeting around the presence of the crucified risen one.

Christianity as a Meal Fellowship

But those meetings were, for the most part, meal meetings. The early Christian movement seems to have come into existence and to have continued to spread as a meal fellowship. At least recent historical scholarship has strongly urged

---

1. *1 Apology* 67.

this idea, in a fairly wide consensus. Some scholars[2] have proposed that "commensality," or the open table, so marked the early movement gathered around Jesus that this commensality continued also after his execution.[3] Perhaps he had been at the center of free bread and fish distributed in intentional contrast to the food-distribution system of Roman-occupied Palestine, and this resistance in some way continued. Perhaps he was known for meals celebrated as a sign that the reign of God is made available also to the marginalized and the religiously impure, and this sense of an eschatological dawn continued. Perhaps both ways of understanding and prolonging Jesus' meals were true. In any case, by this conception, sharing food was then one of the authentic ways of remembering Jesus and continuing his eschatological proclamation.[4]

Other scholars[5] have argued that the only likely way for any association to gather and spread in the Hellenistic first and second centuries of our era was as a supper club. Such a "club" or *collegium* would inevitably have made at least some kind of use of the Greco-Roman meal pattern of *deipnon* and *symposion,* first the sharing of food and then the sharing of drink along with "entertainment" or conversation.[6] Such a supper club would also have been marked by the Greco-Roman banquet ideology, the ways shared eating was seen as providing social identity and cohesion. Such patterning and ideology were to be found in Hellenistic Jewish Palestine as well as throughout the first- and second-century Romano-Hellenistic world. By this conception, the meal pattern and ideology should be seen as having deeply influenced much material in the New Testament, including Paul's interest in meals and food[7] and, especially, the very way

---

2. For example, John Dominic Crossan, *The Birth of Christianity: Discovering What Happened in the Years Immediately after the Execution of Jesus* (San Francisco: HarperSan Francisco, 1998), 423–44; and Marianne Sawicki, *Crossing Galilee: Architectures of Contact in the Occupied Land of Jesus* (Harrisburg: Trinity International, 2000), 179, 182, 185–86.

3. Already Norman Perrin, *Rediscovering the Teaching of Jesus* (New York: Harper & Row, 1967), 104–5: "the most reasonable explanation of the fact of early Christian communal meals is that they are a continuation of a regular practice of the ministry of Jesus."

4. Cf. Sawicki, *Crossing Galilee,* 160.

5. Preeminently, Dennis E. Smith, *From Symposium to Eucharist: The Banquet in the Early Christian World* (Minneapolis: Fortress Press, 2003). Cf. Hal Taussig, *In the Beginning Was the Meal: Social Experimentation and Early Christian Identity* (Minneapolis: Fortress Press, 2009). See also my *Holy People: A Liturgical Ecclesiology* (Minneapolis: Fortress Press, 1999), 29–30, 187–90.

6. On the pattern of the Hellenistic meal, its *deipnon* and *symposion,* and on the use of this pattern in Hellenistic Judaism, see my *Holy People,* 186–88.

7. Cf. Gal. 2:11-14; 1 Corinthians 8 and 10–11; Romans 14.

that the story of Jesus was told. Indeed, as Dennis Smith says simply, "early Christians met at a meal because that is what groups in the ancient world did."[8] And the Christian groups were among many such groups in Hellenistic cities.[9]

Of course, these two assessments of the background for early Christian meal practice—the commensality of the Jesus movement and the patterns of Greco-Roman banquet practice—are not the same. But neither are they necessarily inconsistent with each other. Both can be true. On the one hand, the Gospel tradition, with its many references to meals found throughout the layers of that tradition, probably does recall something of the actual meal practice of the historical Jesus and something of the way he interacted with the regnant customs, boundaries, economies, and meanings of meals in his context. Even if one fundamental concern of the New Testament Gospel books involved the proclamation of the presence of the risen one in the then-current meal practice of the churches, the many stories of Jesus and meals were most likely not simply projections by the later meal-keeping church. If the historical Jesus was a preacher of the nearness of the dominion of God, then his meals probably were intended as prophetic signs that also spoke the content of his preaching, and his followers probably did grasp and continue something of his eschatology. The communal taking of food "with glad and generous hearts" (Acts 2:46), described by Luke, may rightly be seen as continuing in commensality, *Festfreude*,[10] and free distribution the theme of the "foretaste of the feast to come" that had been enacted by Jesus. Jewish eschatology included the expectation of the great feast for all peoples at the end (cf., e.g., Isa. 25:6-10), and thus meals welcoming sinners and occasions of open distribution could have been powerful prophetic "signs," conjoined with and part of the actual preaching of Jesus. Such a powerful eschatological sign would have been continued by the communities that remembered Jesus.

On the other hand, if the early Christian movement carried along within itself a religious reason for holding meals—a continuation of the idea of eating already the eschatological feast, for example—then the culturally available way of doing that would have been the *deipnon* and *symposion*, the meal and the

---

8. Smith, *From Symposium to Eucharist*, 279.

9. See Luke Timothy Johnson, *Among the Gentiles: Greco-Roman Religion and Christianity* (New Haven: Yale University Press, 2009), 138, and, especially, Philip A. Harland, *Associations, Synagogues, and Congregations: Claiming a Place in Ancient Mediterranean Society* (Minneapolis: Fortress Press, 2003).

10. See Bo Reicke, *Diakonie, Festfreude, und Zelos in Verbindung mit der altchristlichen Agapenfeier* (Uppsala: Lundequist, 1951).

shared cup and shared meanings, of the Hellenistic supper club. One might argue that the supper-club assessment, with its rigorous search for comparative cultural models and actual evidence, is primarily *historical* in method, while the kingdom-meal assessment, with its somewhat greater interest in meanings, is more methodologically *theological*.[11] In any case, both estimations of the evidence come to this bottom line: the early Christian movement came into existence in the first century and largely continued into the second century as a meal fellowship. The meetings we have been considering, the meetings addressed by Paul and then by the Gospels, were meal meetings. Such possibly second-century counterevidence as the *Gospel of Judas*, with its polemic against the meal-keeping disciples,[12] might then be taken as an exception that proves the rule. The author of that book wanted his or her readers to distinguish themselves from the ordinary practice of Christian communities, from their thanksgiving at a shared meal, perhaps indeed from what was already being called "the Eucharist."

If we want to ask about the relationship of the four Gospels to paleo-Christian meetings, we do well to inquire first about what those Gospels are saying about meals. The Gospels' concern for meal meetings can provide a central test case for our question and a way to shape our method.

Meals and Diversity of Practice

But current scholarship has come also to another widespread assertion—if not quite a *consensus*: those meals in primitive Christianity were quite diverse.[13]

---

11. The conception of history and theology operative here considers the two disciplines as distinct but interpenetrating. I regard liturgical theology as primarily concerned with the theological meanings of enacted symbols and rituals and with the pastoral practices and continuing reform necessary for those meanings to continue to shine forth. But such theology cannot ignore good history if it wishes to be concerned with what is and what has been, indeed if it wishes to be connected to a real tradition of Christian symbol making. History asks questions about what has been, about the actual state of that tradition, carefully evaluating the evidence that may help answer these questions. But these questions often arise from both theological need and the current situation. In any case, I do not want to dissolve history into the subjective projections of the historian, but I also do not want to ignore the historian's own interest in influence and meaning.

12. Rodolphe Kasser, et al., eds., *The Gospel of Judas* (Washington, D.C.: National Geographic, 2006), 20–21. Here is one of those later books called "Gospels" that does *not* evidence a mutual coherence with assembly.

13. See, especially, Paul F. Bradshaw, *Eucharistic Origins* (London: SPCK, 2004), and Andrew McGowan, *Ascetic Eucharists* (London: Oxford, 1999). See also Andrew McGowan,

According to the scholars who have especially made this assertion, the historical evidence will not allow us easily to sketch a single line of development in Christian eucharistic practice, with one central or normal model from which other practices were deviations. The evidence, from ancient Christian assemblies, of diverse patterns and diverse *agape* meals, of bread and water meals, bread-only meals, cup-first meals, Eucharist with full meals, Eucharist without full meals, and so forth, is simply too great. The unified Eucharist happens later, as a function parallel to the other codifications and centralizations of the conciliar and imperial church.[14]

The point should be granted. In many ways, it is a point that should be seen as a necessary implication of the consensus about widespread meal keeping in early Christianity. Meals are always local events, with local food, local meeting places, local participants, local customs. Of course they are diverse, especially so in a time when Christian communities had no particular instruments of extensive uniformity. Furthermore, the point should be granted especially by liturgical theologians who have too frequently joined the facile assertions of a perceived single early pattern—"the way it was done in the early church"—as a way to cajole current assemblies into a new practice, as if history implied necessity and as if history were simple.

But the point should not be exaggerated, nor should it go without critique. The historians who have helped us to see this ancient diversity also have a point of view. While the discipline of history rightly seeks for evidence, holds itself vulnerable to being proved wrong, and attempts to construct publicly testable models of the past, and while the results of this work are valuable to us all if we care to be talking about the actual conditions of our world, we must still remember that historians begin also in a certain personal and cultural place, with a source for their hypotheses and inquiries. So it is of considerable interest that the argument for ancient diversity arises in our late modern time, with its huge suspicion of any uniformities.[15] In this case, however, that location for the historians and

---

"Food, Ritual, and Power," in Virginia Burrus, ed., *Late Ancient Christianity*, vol. 2 of *A People's History of Christianity* (Minneapolis: Fortress Press, 2005), 145–64, and Harry O. Maier, "Heresy, Households, and the Disciplining of Diversity," in Burrus, *Late Ancient Christianity*, 213–33.

14. See Bradshaw, *Eucharistic Origins*, chaps. 6 and 8. See also the final chapter of Smith, *From Symposium to Eucharist*.

15. It also arises most especially from the work of Paul Bradshaw, a gifted Anglican scholar who has resisted one established tradition of his own Anglican community, the tradition of a

that way of asking the question seem to have allowed us all to see an important thing that had otherwise escaped our vision—the actual ancient diversities of Christian meal practice.

But this diversity-privileging point of view may also have obscured several things not so congruent with our late modern location. Within all that diversity in the earliest churches we can discover also the ancient operation of certain unifying tendencies. These may have included at least: (1) the Christian use of or reaction to or reinterpretation of more or less the same Hellenistic and Hellenistic-Jewish meal pattern;[16] (2) the emergence in different Christian communities of the theme of unity (for example, in Pauline, deutero-Pauline and Johannine sources)[17]—a theme that may indeed have been a Christian version of Hellenistic banquet ideology; and (3) the general Christian interest in the remembrance or continuation of the meal practice and meal meanings of Jesus.

It is especially the remembrance and use of the Jesus tradition that is of interest here. While we do not have direct access to the oral traditions about Jesus that circulated in the decades after his death, we can assume a number of things. The doublets in Mark and Matthew of the story of the feeding of the multitude, for example, indicate that story's wide circulation in differing communities. Many levels of the oral tradition seem to have contained sayings like "Look, a glutton and a drunkard, a friend of tax collectors and sinners!" (Luke 7:34; cf. Matt. 11:19), and such sayings seem to indicate that an exceptional meal practice was one of the important things remembered about Jesus. The Lord's Prayer, in both its Matthean and its Lukan forms (two slightly diverse forms again probably evidencing a wide oral circulation), contains a bread petition that might best be understood as a prayer for the "bread of the morrow," the very beginning taste of the eschatological banquet.[18] This prayer, which may indeed root to the historical Jesus, is a Christian parallel to the *Kaddish*, the important eschatological prayer of the Pharisees and then of the synagogue. The very parallels in language make the uniqueness and importance of the bread petition, which has no place in that

---

single, legally enforced liturgical rite, has sought to overturn the legacy of Gregory Dix when it was taken as an historical orthodoxy that established such a rite, and has gladly chosen to work as a "splitter." See the opening two paragraphs of Bradshaw's *Eucharistic Origins*, vi–vii, and see his *The Search for the Origins of Christian Worship*, 2d ed. (New York: Oxford University Press, 2002), ix–x.

16. So helpfully sketched by Dennis Smith.

17. See 1 Corinthians 12, Ephesians 4, and John 17.

18. Cf. Joachim Jeremias, *The Prayers of Jesus* (Philadelphia: Fortress Press, 1978), 100–102. See also my *Holy People*, 33–34, 76–78.

synagogue prayer, stand out the more. It may be that the presence of these oral fragments in early Christian communities would have mattered to and interacted with those communities' own understandings of what they were doing with their meals.[19]

But what early Christians were doing with their meals was neither universally excellent nor universally praised. Important, communally basic meals were taking place in Corinth, for example. But Paul, in 1 Corinthians 10–11, is enraged about the economic disparity accentuated by the practice in the Corinthian assembly: "one goes hungry and another becomes drunk" (1 Cor. 11:21), a drunkenness that may have been locally interpreted in Corinth as justified eschatological *Festfreude*, a rejoicing that the meal participants had already arrived among the saved but a disparity that Paul found presumptuous and appalling.[20] The same Paul, according to the account in Galatians (2:11-14), also objected to the ways in which Peter allowed issues of ritual purity to destroy commensality at Antioch. Probably much later, the letter of Jude (v. 12) complains about the morals of some participants in the "love feasts." And Acts reports a controversy over the fair distribution of food and the role of the leadership in serving tables (Acts 6). Even if the account of this controversy is largely a Lukan construct, narrated for the purposes of his view of church history, it probably does reflect the presence of such food controversies in ancient Christian communities. Thus, the diverse Christian use of the banquet tradition, even or especially as it may have remembered the eschatology of Jesus, was not entirely praiseworthy. If we are to listen to Paul or the author of Jude or of Luke-Acts, not all of these widely diverse ancient meals in Christian meetings were worth continuing or emulating. The first century, even in its diversity, is not a candidate for what is sometimes called the "golden age of liturgy." The idea that there is such an age, always to be emulated by later generations, is a historical-theological-liturgical will-o'-the-wisp, the search for which we ought finally to agree to renounce.[21]

---

19. Cf. Maier, "Heresy, Households, and the Disciplining of Diversity," 214: "Early Christian memory located Jesus in household settings to help believers elucidate and interpret their own household patterns of assembly and the rituals and teaching that went along with them."

20. Cf. 1 Cor. 10:12: "So if you think you are standing, watch out that you do not fall."

21. See John F. Baldovin, S.J., "The Usefulness of Liturgical History, *Worship* 82 (2008): 7.

Luke and Paul and the Meal Meetings

It may be all the more important, then, to see that when the Gospel books brought the oral traditions about Jesus into constructed whole compositions, part of the intention of each of the authors was likely to have been the reform of the meal practices of the churches, the reform of the most likely way in which the Christians met.[22] Certainly this could be so for the writer of Luke, for whom meals were of great importance. The story of the meal at Emmaus (24:13-35) seems to have been intended to help the churches that received the book to understand that their first-day meetings for reading the scriptures and holding a meal should be meetings for interpreting those scriptures as sources for the meaning of the death of Jesus (24:27) and holding the meal as an encounter with the crucified risen one (24:35). But then the other meals with which the Gospel book is full—the "ongoing feast" that has continued into the church, in the view of the author of Luke-Acts[23]—also carried a word to the practice of the then-current communities. The Christian assembly, in its practice of meal and baptismal bath, ought not forget the meal of the widow or the bath of the leper (4:14-30). The Christian meal is to be like the meal with Levi (5:27-38), with the sinful woman (7:36-50), with Mary and Martha (10:38-42), with the returned prodigal (15:1-2, 11-32), and with Zacchaeus (19:1-10), to name only a few Lukan stories.[24] Among the Synoptic Gospels, it is Luke alone that includes in the narrative of the Last Supper, in the long text,[25] the reforming phrase exactly

---

22. Taussig, *In the Beginning Was the Meal*, 36–43, provides a very helpful summary of the close relationship that can be seen between all early Christian literature, including the Gospels, and meals.

23. Arthur A. Just Jr., *The Ongoing Feast: Table Fellowship and Eschatology at Emmaus* (Collegeville: Pueblo, 1993).

24. On the Lukan meal stories, see further below, chap. 4.

25. *Pace* Bradshaw, *Eucharistic Origins*, 5, I regard the long text of Luke as the more original. It has by far the better manuscript tradition, being contradicted only by the idiosyncratic Codex Bezae and some Syriac and Old Latin versions. It contains the cup-bread-meal-cup sequence that corresponds to the Mishnaic version of the Hellenistic Jewish *deipnon/symposion* when the festal *kiddush* cup was used first; it thus corresponds to the Lukan tendency to reproduce accurately his reading of Jewish ritual practice (as in the synagogue meeting of Luke 4). And it makes use of the Pauline "do this" in a way that corresponds with the whole Lukan interest in reforming the meal practice of local Christian communities, if my argument about Luke is right. The later short text could have easily been created by a copyist who no longer knew of the Jewish cup-bread-meal-cup sequence, thought to present only one cup with the bread, sought to make the word about the bread parallel to that of Mark's Gospel, and—perhaps—himself or herself knew of a Christian cup-bread practice.

corresponding to and probably taken from Paul's version of this narrative: "Do this in remembrance of me" (22:19). The meal in the church, however it is celebrated, is to be done as the *anamnesis* of the Jesus who was killed and yet is still encountered at table. These central meal characteristics—the ones accentuated by the climactic Lukan narratives of the Last Supper and of Emmaus—are being urged by the Gospel exactly so that the meal keeping of the churches may be the meal with the widow, with Levi, and with Zacchaeus, and may thus become the breaking of the bread and distribution to the poor imaged in Acts 2:42-47. The writing of Luke-Acts had a purpose, and part of its purpose seems to have been the deepening of meal meaning and the extending of meal practice. Especially in meal meetings, this Gospel was urging that Jesus-then is to be seen as Jesus-now.

As we have seen, the four canonical Gospel books were not primarily "histories." They were intended by their authors to be books about and themselves symbols for the meaning of Jesus in the life of the churches. The canonical Gospels were words into the present of the church, including important words of criticism and reform. Of course, the Gospels give glimpses of the historical Jesus, but their own estimate of the importance of these fragments of remembrance is that such fragments animate that faithful current preaching, meal keeping, healing, and food distributing, which are the source and sign of trust in the authentic presence of Jesus Christ in the present time.

If this estimation of purpose may be true for Luke, it is fascinating to note that especially a story of the risen one encountered at a meal—the Emmaus story—serves to organize and focus the point of the various meal stories from the life of Jesus as these are set out in the first book, the Gospel. Then that story is the bridge between the stories of Jesus' meals and "the breaking of the bread" in Acts, between the Gospel narratives and the practice of the church. Luke's redaction, creation, and ordering are certainly at work with the Jesus stories, some of which may have come from the oral traditions. But it is a resurrection story that finally has the central, interpretive place as the Jesus tradition is placed in Luke's "orderly account" (1:3) for the sake of the life of the church. Luke builds upon and encourages the sense in the Christian community that the one who was executed is also the one encountered in the continuing meals of the church.

Such a use of the reinterpreted Jesus tradition to speak the meaning of Christian meals and to seek their reform, however, had an earlier history. Part of that tradition formed the ground to which Paul appealed as he sought to reform the meal practice of the assembly in Corinth. Paul wanted to urge the Corinthians to know that "as often as you eat of this bread and drink of the cup, you proclaim the Lord's death until he comes" (1 Cor. 11:26). He wanted them to know the communal and ethical consequences that follow from this proclamation. He wanted them to understand the necessary discernment of the body of Christ in the excluded and the poor. He wanted them to consider abolishing the full meal (11:22, 34; cf. 8:8), to be replaced instead both by the accented frame of the meal (the bread of the beginning of the *deipnon* and the cup of the concluding *symposion*, both seen to speak of Jesus' death) and, perhaps also, by the weekly collection for the poor (16:2). He wanted the "supper club" to be reformed. He draws the source of that reform from his understanding of the Jesus tradition.

The actual account of the meal of Jesus "on the night when he was betrayed" (11:23) Paul has "received from the Lord." It is possible, of course, that Paul here is quoting a small piece of the oral tradition—perhaps a part of the developing passion story—that he has learned from somewhere. The problem is that he does this kind of quoting nowhere else. It is perhaps more likely that Paul means it when he says he received this account "from the Lord." That is, he has the account himself directly in a vision or revelation from the risen one[26] or he has it from a prophet or prophets who have spoken in the name of the risen one (cf. 14:37). If some members of the assembly at Corinth in some sense regarded their meal as marked by the celebration of the resurrection already—the arrived eschaton—then Paul wants them to know that the risen one is the crucified one and that the heart of this meal is to bear witness to his death.[27] The "institution narrative" is taken by faith to be a word from the risen one for the reform of the assembly.

Perhaps this narrative first began to be heard in Pauline communities and so spread to later use in the Gospels. Or perhaps, given the significant variants in those later Gospel texts, it is older, having arisen from Christian prophets in the time since Jesus' death and having circulated in diverse ways. Or perhaps, again, it really is from Paul, and those variants can all be interpreted as rightly belonging to the redactional intentions of the evangelists. In any case, the very

---

26. See Smith, *From Symposium to Eucharist*, 226. That Paul ordinarily understands *kyrios*, when spoken of Jesus, to mean the crucified risen one, can be seen in such passages as Rom. 1:4; 4:24; 1 Cor. 1:7-8; and in the uniquely Pauline usage *en kyriō*, as in 1 Cor. 4:17 and 9:1-2.

27. Perhaps the supper bears witness like the Passover bore witness to the affliction of the Hebrews; "behold this is the bread of affliction" has become "this is my body that is for you."

source of the Pauline form of this word "from the Lord" makes it unlikely that the narrative gives us any substantial historical information about the meal of the historical Jesus in the days in which he was being arrested, tortured, and killed. For the Christian community, it might be asserted that access to the meaning of those days came most clearly not by eyewitnesses (they all ran away; they all were traumatized!), but from the church's encounter with the risen one.

The Pauline text "from the Lord" is the oldest account of the Last Supper that we have. The next oldest account, that in Mark's Gospel, is intertwined with the Markan purpose of predicting and interpreting the passion and resurrection beforehand (14:21-25; cf. 8:31; 9:31; 10:33-34), a purpose best seen as an insight that the church also believed it had from the risen one—that is, also, "from the Lord."[28] Indeed, the present or present passive tense of both texts[29] belongs in the mouth of the risen Lord speaking in the church, even if it is narratively located "on the night when he was betrayed" (1 Cor. 11:23; cf. Mark 14:12, 17-18). The much later Western ecclesial use of a more consequent and historically literal future tense ("will be given . . . will be shed . . ." is the phrasing of the Roman Mass) is significantly not present in this Pauline text "from the Lord" or this Markan text articulating the Gospel's sense of Jesus' presence in the life of the church.

In any case, Paul is aiming to speak a critical word with a goal quite similar to the one still alive in Luke's Gospel about thirty years later: to call the meal practice of a local community to remember the crucified risen one and to care about the poor. In Paul, the center of this word is a narrative "received from the Lord." In Luke, the whole Gospel structure is made to carry, among other things, the interest in reforming the church's meals. Paul makes an appeal to end the practice of full church suppers,[30] with their inevitable exclusions and inequities, in favor of a ritual meal that breaks into the usual practice of eating and changes the way of seeing food and the world, our neighbor and God. Paul wants Christians to see that if they may eat from the "table of the Lord," they can and should also end their participation in temple feasts for other "lords," perhaps especially

---

28. See Smith, *From Symposium to Eucharist*, 226.

29. In Paul, "this is my body that is for you" (1 Cor. 11:24); in Mark, the blood "is poured out for the many," that is, for all the great crowd of needy people (Mark 14:24).

30. The community reflected in Justin's writings in mid-second-century Rome (see *1 Apol.* 67) seems to have heard Paul. The meal has become the accented frame of the meal, with a single prayer over both bread and cup, and most food—or money to buy food—is being given away to the hungry rather than eaten in the meeting.

those imperial "lords" of the other "gospels" (1 Cor. 8:10; 10:21). Luke gathers all the meal stories of Jesus to reinforce such reforming proposals. If having supper together is "what groups in the ancient world did,"[31] then both Paul and Luke are seeking to reorient that expected behavior toward new meanings and unexpected boundary breaking. Though Paul sought reform, a reforming word was obviously still needed decades later, when Luke's Gospel was written.

Mark, John, and Matthew on Meals

While Mark's Gospel has no "do this" and no Emmaus story, it can be argued that the Gospel carries a similar purpose. As we have seen here, the book is interested in the meetings of the Christian assemblies, is coherent with those meetings, the current versions of the "houses" of its narrative. The book is interested in the "secret" of the identity of the crucified one being known and revealed in those meetings. The Gospel book functions as a comment on and a proposal to the assemblies of the churches. Indeed, one can say that the book itself, as a whole, is the missing resurrection appearance of the end: it is intended as an appearance of the risen one in the assembly.[32]

But then the Markan warning against the "yeast of the Pharisees and the yeast of Herod" (8:15) is a warning to the churches.[33] This "yeast," most likely here a synecdoche for meal practices in general, is reflected in the banquet for the powerful given by Herod in Mark 6 and the purity requirements of the Pharisees in Mark 7. These accounts of meal practice form important counterimages in this first half of Mark's Gospel. The former meal includes a horrible *symposion* at which women entertain the upper-class men, as was the widespread custom, and a prophet is cruelly killed, in a murder that itself foreshadows the death of Jesus (9:11-13). The latter purity rules mask real sin and would exclude the

---

31. See above, n.5.

32. See below, chap. 3, and see my *Holy Ground: A Liturgical Cosmology* (Minneapolis: Fortress Press, 2003), 128–35. Cf. Austin Farrer, *The Glass of Vision* (Westminster: Dacre, 1948), 145. See also my *Holy Things: A Liturgical Theology* (Minneapolis: Fortress Press, 1993), 29.

33. The passage Mark 8:14-21 may function as the important conclusion to the first full section of Mark's Gospel, the section that might be called "In Galilee." Or, differently figured, it may be the conclusion to a section about meals that stretches from 6:6b to 8:21. In any case, it is an important word. Cf. Bas van Iersel, *Reading Mark* (Edinburgh: T&T Clark, 1989), 20, and see below, chap. 3.

Syrophoenician woman, the Gentile "dog" of 7:24-30. The accounts become, then, negative images for the life of the churches, churches that are called away from a ruling elite that does not serve, from a devotion to purity rules, and, in both cases, from a misuse of women. But in direct contrast to the "yeast of the Pharisees," the meals of Jesus in Mark include the free distribution of food to the multitudes (6:30-44; 8:1-9), the eating with tax collectors and sinners (2:16), food for the once-dead daughter of Jairus (5:43), those metaphorical breadcrumbs for the Gentile woman with the unclean daughter (7:28-29), and even that eating with defiled hands (7:2). Indeed, the meals of Jesus include the continued distribution, at the hands of the disciples ("you give them something to eat!" 6:37) of those twelve baskets-full and seven baskets-full of leftovers.[34] Furthermore, as a transition to the passion, that cup of the death of Jesus that the disciples will drink (10:38-39) contrasts with the "yeast of Herod" and is part of the invitation to a way of service rather than a way of domination (10:42-45).

Then, in Mark, the passion story is interpreted with not one but two meals. The first of these (14:3-11) is a direct counterimage of the banquet of Herod.[35] In contrast to the "yeast of Herod," the woman who enters the banquet room does not cause the death of Jesus but speaks in gracious sign of this death, helping us to see both what the meal means and that we do still have the poor with us for us to remember at our continuing meals (cf. Deut. 15:11). This is no entertainment of powerful men combined with a murder. Here the *symposion* is replaced by a woman preaching in sign, showing forth the death of the Lord. Then at the Last Supper, the Markan Passover meal, the *symposion* is also replaced (14:17ff.). The bread and the cup that witness to Jesus' death take place in the midst of the *deipnon*, the meal—overshadow the meal, even *replace* the meal, it seems—while the cup after the meal, so characteristic of Hellenistic and Hellenistic Jewish meal practice, has here become first the cup in the garden (14:36) and then the drink of sour wine on the cross (15:36). Indeed, for Mark, in the characteristic hidden and paradoxical way of this Gospel, this cup in the garden and this drink on the cross are the very drinking of "the fruit of the vine . . . new in the kingdom" (14:25), the drink that indicates the actual arrival of the eschatological day.

The Gospel of Mark, then, presents a series of meal accounts that can be read as intending a reinterpretation and reorientation of the meal practices of the assemblies that read the book. If those meal practices of the churches included a

---

34. See below, chap. 3, n.32.
35. See the argument in my *Holy People*, 192.

sense of eschatological meaning, then that meaning is refocused—much as in 1 Corinthians 11—on the crucifixion of Jesus.[36] If those meals included a strong sense of boundaried community, then those boundaries are broken open by the woman who gives the sign of Jesus' death and who will always be remembered in the proclamation of the gospel, by the poor who remain with us, and by the *symposion* that opens out onto the garden and the cross. The risen one appears in the assembly by means of the book but also by means of the meal. And that risen one is the crucified one, acting in the church's meal to give himself away: "Take, this is my body," my encounterable self (14:22). This was a radically different celebration than those sacrifices, temple meals, and games that would have followed upon the announcement of the "gospels" of the imperial cult.[37] It was also a deepening and reversing of the values involved in simply belonging to a supper club.

A similar argument could be made for the late-first-century or early-second-century Gospel "according to John."[38] There the discourse about the Living Bread (6:25-71) and the insertion of the foot washing as the principal content of the final meal of Jesus (13:2b-5) are, just as in Mark, not ritual instructions but metaphoric commentary. For John, the *deipnon* becomes the foot washing and the *symposion* the "farewell discourse" (John 13–17), the speech about the "going away" and the "coming again" of Jesus in the assembly. These images are intended to call the community to understanding the depth of their meals as an encounter with the crucified risen one who gives himself away in love. In some ways, both the criticism of "the food that perishes" (6:27) and the very fact that the foot washing virtually replaces the "Last Supper" in the Johannine account could be taken as antieucharistic or antisacramental words in this Gospel. It may be wiser to consider that the churches known by this evangelist also had meetings at which there were meals, perhaps already becoming ritual meals. But

---

36. If Paul was arguing against a "realized eschatology" at Corinth, an idea that the participants in the meal were already risen and enjoying the Great Feast of God at the end as "kings" (1 Cor. 4:8; cf. 15:19), he was doing so by still holding out an eschatological promise to be realized. The resurrection of the crucified Jesus is the first taste of that promise. But the very proclamation of his death "until he comes" entails a changed communal ethic. Mark seems to accept but also slightly nuance this proposal. The cross *is* the arrival of the Day. The crucified one is the risen one. The communal meal is to insert its participants in this paradoxical and saving reality.

37. See especially Taussig, *In the Beginning Was the Meal*, 115–43.

38. See my *Holy People*, 193.

the evangelist means to call these communities to deepen their understanding of these meals, to find in them not their own excellence and fellowship, but the gift and the love and, indeed, the "flesh and blood" of Jesus. John, too, writes for reform.

As does Matthew. It is true that Matthew shifts the warning about the leaven of Herod and the leaven of the Pharisees away from its implications about meal practice, explicitly interpreting it rather as a warning against the teaching of the Pharisees and the Sadducees (and dropping Herod; Matt. 16:5-12). But the anointing woman still plays a role in Matthew's passion story (26:6-13). So does the bread and cup at the Last Supper, overshadowing the meal itself and set out "for the many." But it is Matthew's Gospel that adds the words "for the forgiveness of sin" to the gift of the cup (26:28), perhaps indicating a growing interest in a communal practice more intently focusing on a ritual meal. Indeed, it is Matthew that introduces a line that will play a role in the ongoing history of Eucharist: "Do not give what is holy to dogs" (7:6), and Matthew has the Wedding Banquet parable ("Invite everyone you find to the wedding banquet," 22:9), together with its paradoxical addition about discipline ("How did you get in here without a wedding robe?" 22:12). Then the forgiveness of sins in the cup and the gift poured out for "the many" are all the more striking, a gift that both heightens and trumps the discipline. Furthermore, Matthew—like Luke—includes in the book the Lord's Prayer (with its bread petition, 6:11), the word about Jesus as a "glutton and a drunkard, a friend of tax collectors and sinners" (11:19), and the astonishing parable of the kingdom as a woman leavening a huge batch of holy bread, enough for an epiphany of God (13:33).[39] Matthew uniquely has the Last Judgment parable, with its image of the giving of food to the hungry (25:35), and the Sermon on the Mount, with its counsel not to worry about food (6:25-34). The Matthean temptation account has the full quotation from Deuteronomy 8:3: "One does not live by bread alone, but by every word that comes from the mouth of God." One could imagine this word, next to the Pauline counsel against the centrality of food (Rom. 14:17; 1 Cor. 8:8; 11:22), as a cautionary word to the Christian supper clubs: they should be eager not simply for food, but food with the word about the crucified, food for the sinners, and food for the poor. In any case, Matthew seems to want to continue at least some of the Markan meal reform but also to deepen the meal's theological and soteriological significance and its discipline.

---

39. On the yeast parable, see my *Holy Things*, 24–27.

Eucharistic Origins

In reading this New Testament material, I propose that we have been observing the origins of the Eucharist. Those origins are not, therefore, hidden behind the texts we have, in some inaccessible period of history. Rather, the origins are being enacted before our eyes in these texts as we see that the diverse meal practices of first- and second-century Christianity were being brought under the apostolic and evangelical critique which called for these meals to show forth the death of Jesus until he comes. Later in the history of Christianity, in interpreting the Fourth Gospel, Augustine said that "the word comes to the element and so there is a sacrament."[40] I think that he read both that book and all the Gospels correctly. The *element*, in this case, is the meal practice of early Christianity, in all of its diversity, in its many ways of using and of understanding the Hellenistic *deipnon-symposion* tradition, and in its sense of the meal being already an eschatological feast. The *word* is then the call of Paul and of the evangelists—all of them, in this case, continuing this concern of Paul—speaking as in the name of the risen Lord, that this meal, in whatever form it took, must proclaim the death of Jesus Christ and thus be good news for the actually poor of the times. The *word* is the reforming gospel of Jesus Christ, the crucified and risen one: the way we know the new thing about God and the world, namely the way we know of God as triune, going out in love for the life of the world.

By this proposal, I do not mean to suggest that all the meals of the churches after the execution of Jesus and before this apostolic and evangelical reform were *not* Eucharist. Rather, the question of whether they were Eucharist or not is anachronistic. We might guess that they were diverse meals with diverse meanings, on the way to becoming Eucharist; they were sometimes continuations of the meal practice and meal meanings of the Jesus movement and sometimes distortions or betrayals of that practice and those meanings. In any case, with the possible exception of the *Didache* (on which, see below), the materials for an answer to the question, materials about meal practice before Paul, are inaccessible to us, capable of reconstruction only by conjecture.

A possible historical reconstruction of the early development of the Christian assembly meals, thus one such conjecture, could look something like this: in the face of the trauma experienced by the community around Jesus when he was violently arrested and killed—perhaps in refuge from that trauma, perhaps

---

40. *In Johannem* 80,3.

in spite of that trauma, perhaps both—this community did continue to gather. As Dennis Smith has argued, the primary mode of gathering available to them was the shared meal. As Christianity spread, meal communities spread. Perhaps, as Marianne Sawicki and others have argued, something of the meal values alive in the time of the movement around Jesus did continue to influence these early Christian meals: they were interpreted as eschatological signs or as the arrival of eschatological joy. They were already being interpreted with images from the Hebrew scriptures. They were, however, as is characteristic of meals and as has been argued by Paul Bradshaw and others, local and diverse. It is very likely that these meals became one of the most important locations of the growing conviction in these communities that the crucified Jesus was alive or—to use language borrowed from the Maccabean and apocalyptic traditions[41]—was already, as first fruits of the end time, "risen." Indeed, encounter with the risen one came to be a theme of some meals. One could say that the voice of the risen one was heard there, beyond the trauma of the community, transfiguring the trauma.[42] Into the midst of this diverse practice, Paul and then the evangelists urged the direct proclamation of the cross.[43] The eschatologically flavored meals, even the meals that now understood that the resurrection of Jesus was part of the down payment on the end time, could easily become meals focused only on "us," for "our" joy and satisfaction, forgetting the poor and running, in Mark's terms, the danger of the leaven of Herod and the leaven of the Pharisees.[44] Such meals could easily forget or tame the challenge of the gospel to the imperium. Instead, as Paul and the evangelists testified, the crucified risen one himself acts here in the meal. "Shared meal," especially shared meal as interpreted eschatologically, became a language one could use and re-form, a language for inverting and breaking,[45] in

---

41. Cf. 2 Macc. 7:14; 12:43; 2 Esd. 2:23.

42. See Dirk G. Lange, *Trauma Recalled: Liturgy, Disruption, and Theology* (Minneapolis: Fortress Press, 2010).

43. Cf. Helmut Koester, *From Jesus to the Gospels: Interpreting the New Testament in Its Context* (Minneapolis: Fortress Press, 2007), 289.

44. If there might be two strands of tradition behind the synoptic accounts of the Last Supper, as several scholars have proposed (see Bradshaw, *Eucharistic Origins*, 6–10), then the eschatological strand may indeed be the older one, with the words about the cross death of Jesus arising from the Pauline tradition or from those unnamed prophets and inserted first by Mark. Along with the cup in the garden and the drink on the cross, this insertion fits the redactional intention of the evangelist.

45. On the "breaking" of symbols, see my *Holy Things*, 27–31, and passim.

order to speak the meaning of Jesus and his death, to encounter Jesus himself so speaking, and to turn with him toward the needy world. Indeed, as Mark has it, the end time has dawned at his cross and reaches toward the world, toward "the many," in this cross meal.

The history of the Eucharist would thus see a variety of meal practices undergoing a steady revaluation, continuing on toward further revaluations as the church emerged from persecution. The growing similarities in eucharistic practice, then, would be due not only to the fourth-century imperial interest in a unifying church but also and more profoundly to the common orthodox Christian heritage of the reforming word of the apostle and the Gospels. A faithful theological evaluation of that history would confess that the Eucharist takes place in the church as the gift of the crucified risen one, acting in the life of the church, reinterpreting our meals to a larger meaning.

In following this history, it might be especially interesting to note the current scholarship that argues that the account of the Eucharist in the *Didache*[46] may well be quite early, perhaps even earlier than Paul. If this is so, the very absence of reference to the crucifixion of Jesus in the prayers of *Didache* 9–10 could be taken as evidence of the continuing sense of silenced trauma in the Christian community: How could one speak of such an unspeakable thing, even though it is hidden in the inaccessible experience of the community? But then the very

---

46. See Kurt Niederwimmer, *The Didache*, trans. Linda M. Maloney, Hermeneia (Minneapolis: Fortress Press, 1998), 44 and n.17. I take the Eucharist outlined in *Didache* 9–10 to follow fairly closely the Hellenistic-Jewish banquet pattern, echoed also in the Lukan long text: first a cup that corresponds to the *kiddush*-cup; then the broken bread that begins the meal, the *deipnon*. Brief prayers, using the often-favored Christian thanksgiving pattern rather than a *berakah* pattern, are spoken over both of these. Then, after the meal ("after you are satisfied with food," 10:1), there follows the lengthy thanksgiving, like the Jewish *birkat ha-mazon*, over the cup of the *symposion*. That a shared cup really is envisioned here is indicated both by the threefold form of the prayer in relationship to its antecedent prayer over a cup and by the invitation and warning at the end of the text: "if any one be holy, let that one come; if any be not, let that one repent" (10:6). One might also compare the structure of this last prayer over a cup to the structure of the prayer of Polycarp over the end of his life as over "the cup of Christ" (*Martyrdom of Polycarp* 14:1-3). On the structure of the Eucharist in the *Didache*, including the parallels in Mishnaic Judaism and in the *Martyrdom of Polycarp*, see already and especially, Thomas J. Talley, "From Berakah to Eucharistia: A Reopening Question," *Worship* 50 (1976): 115–37, reprinted in R. Kevin Seasoltz, ed., *Living Bread, Saving Cup* (Collegeville: Liturgical, 1982), 80–101. For a very different reading of the *Didache*, with which this construction disagrees, see Bradshaw, *Eucharistic Origins*, 24–42.

freedom of the prophets in giving thanks—"Let the prophets hold eucharist as they will" (10:7)—could also point to one possible locus (as we have considered above) for the voice of the risen one to say through the prophets, "This is my body, given for you; This is my blood shed for the many." Such a word from the prophets may not have changed the actual words of the prayers in the community of the *Didache*. Those prayers also might not have been changed had the community (or the redactor who compiled the *Didache* in the early second century) read 1 Corinthians or Mark. But such a word from a prophet or such reading of the Gospel, if it had been listened to, might have taught the community yet more profoundly what it meant to speak of the "life and knowledge that you made known to us through Jesus your Servant" (9:3), and it might have assisted in revising or at least criticizing the warning, "Do not give the holy to dogs" (9:5), as an example of the leaven of the Pharisees.[47] The crucified gives life and knowledge; indeed, the crucified shares the lot of the dogs. Further, reading a Gospel—say Mark or John—might have reinterpreted the interest of the *Didache* in the eschaton ("Let grace come and this world pass away," 10:6) and might have strengthened the connection between the community meal and concern for the poor. Still, whether it is from the mid-first century or the early second century, we can regard the text in the *Didache* as one important example of the Eucharist in formation and, as I think, one place in need of the reforming word of Paul and of the Gospels. Also, the *Didache* provides no example of the golden age. Rather, it is a moving contact with one ancient Christian practice, a practice in profound need of correction and breaking.

So, the Gospels speak critically about the assemblies of the ancient church by speaking especially about meals.

But then, might we look more directly at each one of these old Gospel books, hear more directly the witness of each of the Beasts in the assembly? While the books had a certain common and unifying tendency in the ways they continued to seek to reform and deepen the meal practice of the churches, they were not all the same book. Their differences are also important.

Again, from the original functions of the Gospels, questions arise for our practice, for current Christian assemblies: Do we continue to keep a meal at the center of our

---

47. In any case, it is fascinating that, at least by the late fourth or mid-fifth century, such ancient eucharistic warnings have evolved to have a communal answer: "Only one is holy, Jesus Christ!" See Cyril of Jerusalem, *Mystagogical Catecheses* 5:19.

meetings? Indeed, is it clear that the Eucharist among us is a meal, even though it is only the fragment of a meal? Is it celebrated with staple food and festive drink, with generous and beautiful vessels, with beautiful table prayers, with locally diverse practice, and yet with a sense of festive sharing? But, even more, is it clear that having a beautiful dinner is not enough, when its abundance and beauty are only for us? Does this feast proclaim the death of Jesus and the present gift of the risen one? Is it open for all to come and eat and drink, while sending both its participants and its necessary excess into a hungry world? Is collection for the poor connected to our Eucharist? Does the meal sign the mercy of God for the healing of the world? Are these references—to the crucified, to the "many," to the poor, and to a world in need of healing—what we mean by the "discipline" of the table?

3

Mark in Detail

"There You Will See Him"

But let us turn explicitly to Mark, to the book that is the First Gospel, at least as far as we know. We have already begun to reflect here on the relationship between Mark and paleo-Christian meetings. I have argued that especially this First Gospel demonstrates the mutual coherence between Gospel book and Christian assembly. Thus, the "houses" of the narrative were intended by the author to evoke the house churches and small gatherings where the book would be primarily read; Mark meant to call those assemblies away from the "yeast of the Pharisees and the yeast of Herod" in their meal practice; and by means of this book those gatherings were brought to be "in on the secret" of Jesus' identity and of his continued presence. The stories were told so that the community might know that "Jesus-then" was indeed "Jesus-now." More: I have said that I believe that the ancient title of the book is found in its first verse, "The beginning of the gospel of Jesus Christ, the Son of God,"[1] and that this title intentionally subverted imperial religious meanings. The book itself, the account of the revelation of the identity of Jesus in his preaching and healing as also in his suffering and death, was to be the grounds for the preached and enacted gospel in the assembly. This gospel, like the imperial "gospels," those imperial announcements of accessions and births and military victories, invited its hearers to a communal celebration. However, here the celebration was not to be marked by sacrifice, social hierarchy, and negotiations of power, but by faith and mutual service, by

---

1. The argument remains the same if the title reads only "The beginning of the gospel of Jesus Christ." The textual evidence is strong for the omission of the phrase "the Son of God," but it is equally strong for its inclusion. Major manuscripts disagree: Codex Sinaiticus contains the omission and Codex Vaticanus the inclusion. Irenaeus can be quoted to support both. The NRSV follows the evidence for the inclusion. However, even without the phrase "Son of God," the title stills reveals that Jesus is the Messiah and still presents this remarkable ἀρχή.

the presence of the crucified risen one and by the wholeness and healing that he brings.[2] The gospel of which this book is "the beginning" criticizes religion in its malformations, the religion of the imperium as well as any religion that works in a similar way. This "beginning of the gospel," this Gospel book, was meant to ground and continually reform Christian meetings.

Still, we need to test several of these assertions. The idea of the "secret" of Jesus' identity is an obvious trait of Mark. But can it be shown more clearly what this secret had to do with the assemblies that may have read the book? Can both the secret and the image of the house be further explored? Another obvious trait, seen by even a casual reader, occurs in the repeated use of frames in telling a story—the fig tree both before and after the cleansing of the Temple (Mark 11:12-25), for example, or Jairus both before and after the woman with the flow of blood (5:21-43). These frames may also be called *chiasms* or circular compositions, and they are a trait of some classical writings of great weight and communal significance.[3] Are they also of significance to the Christian communities? Finally, I have argued that the book of Mark itself was meant to be the means of the community encountering the presence of Jesus in the assembly, to be the resurrection appearance promised by the end of the story. Is this true? How so?

As a way of further exploring the relationship of Mark to Christian meetings, we turn to secrets, houses, circles, and the resurrection appearance.

Secrets Revealed

Many first-time readers of Mark are puzzled by the fact that Jesus, as presented in the story, repeatedly urges silence on anyone who begins to know who he is. First-time readers are not alone. For long-time readers and biblical scholars as well, the question of the "messianic secret" is unavoidable. What is it about?

Look at the texts again. In the first miracle story of the book, the healing of a man "with an unclean spirit" in the synagogue at Capernaum (1:21-28), the spirit possessing the man cries out, among other things, "I know who you are,

---

2. It is immensely suggestive that the unclean spirits that torment the man living among the tombs are called "Legion," and that this Legion is then identified with the unclean swine and drowned in the sea (5:2-15). "Legion" unavoidably implies the Roman imperial army. Health, then, includes freedom from the fear induced by this Legion as well as from the cult of death.

3. See especially Mary Douglas, *Thinking in Circles: An Essay on Ring Composition* (New Haven: Yale University Press, 2007).

the Holy One of God!" In response, Jesus says, "Be silent, and come out of him!" Were this simply an independently circulating miracle story, that "Be silent!" would be no surprise. Other exorcists, in other stories besides those about Jesus, conventionally silence the demons or spirits they are opposing. But, at the head of the series of stories gathered in Mark and responding to an assertion that Jesus' identity is known, this "Be silent!" introduces a theme. Indeed, it is not at all impossible that this pericope was originally an independently circulating story, and that the author of Mark, in collecting the story, added to the speech of the unclean spirit the sentence, "I know who you are," precisely in order to introduce this theme.

In any case, the theme does continue. In the closely following summary report about healing (1:32-34), the event is repeated. Jesus does "not permit the demons to speak, because they knew him." But it is not only the demons who are silenced. In healing a leper, Jesus says to him, "See that you say nothing to anyone . . ." (1:43). The characteristic and intense Markan double negative is used here: say μηδενὶ μηδέν, absolutely nothing to anybody at all. But then, because Jesus' fame does spread, he "could no longer go into a town openly" (1:45). For the moment he stays "out in wild places," ἔξω ἐπ᾽ ἐρήμοις τόποις,[4] in the wilderness that occurs elsewhere in the book as a location of his solitude (cf. 1:13, 35; 6:31; 8:4). The unclean spirits are then again silenced in a further summary report, this time because they shout, "You are the Son of God!" (3:11-12). And, again, though it seems to be especially the evil spirits who know who he is and what a threat he is to them, the silencing does not only target them; those who see the raising of Jairus's daughter are also "strictly ordered . . . that no one should know this" (5:43). When Jesus goes to the region of Tyre, he goes into a house and does "not want anyone to know he was there" (7:24). Returning toward the Sea of Galilee, he heals a deaf and mute man and orders that no one be told (7:36). Against this background, when he tells a healed blind man, "Do not even go into the village," (8:26) it seems like more silencing.

The fascinating thing about these silencings and withdrawals in the narrative is that they do not work. The truth about Jesus breaks out of the silence. His fame spreads (1:28). The healed leper freely speaks "the word," as the truth about Jesus is called (1:45). The more Jesus orders silence, the more zealously he is proclaimed (7:36). As Joel Marcus says, "paradoxically . . . the silencings serve

---

4. The NRSV says "out in the country" but thereby loses the verbal connections to other wilderness locations.

the purpose of revelation."[5] The same paradox accompanies the withdrawals. He goes to a deserted place, and Simon and the others come, while everyone is seeking him (1:36-37). He stays in the deserted places, and people come to him from every quarter (1:45). He is alone, yet paradoxically there are those who are around him (4:10). He takes the disciples to the wilderness to be alone, and the great crowd runs toward them, finally to be met by Jesus' great compassion (6:30-34). He goes into a house, not wanting anyone to know, and he cannot escape notice (7:24).

A dialectic of strong concealing and strong revealing has been set up in the story. Indeed, this dialectic comes to characterize the entire Gospel book.[6]

So when Jesus then engages his disciples in a discussion of his identity and Peter confesses, "You are the Messiah," Jesus responds. First he once again sternly orders them "not to tell anyone about him" (8:30). But then he takes charge of the revelation. He speaks the first "passion prediction," the first of the three announcements Jesus makes in Mark about his coming rejection, suffering, death, and resurrection. Paradoxically, after silencing any speech about his identity, he himself speaks about his death boldly, openly, παρρησία. It is as if the silencing and the death are tied together. Even more, it is as if the open proclamation of his suffering and death, like the word about him breaking out of the silence or like his hiddenness becoming a place for gathering, corresponds to the resurrection from the dead. The truth of his identity is both hidden and revealed, especially in the open proclamation of his suffering, cross and resurrection, an open proclamation called here "the word," τὸν λόγον (8:32).

In the immediately following narrative of the transfiguration (9:2-8), the linking of silence with death and of open proclamation with resurrection from the dead grows even clearer. Or, rather, that linkage becomes evident when we see that the author of Mark has added several words from Jesus (9:9-13) to what was probably first an orally circulated story of the event. In those following words, Jesus orders the three witnesses of this powerful enacting of his identity "to tell no one about what they had seen, until after the Son of Man had risen

---

5. Joel Marcus, "Identity and Ambiguity in Markan Christology," in Beverly Roberts Gaventa and Richard B. Hays, *Seeking the Identity of Jesus: A Pilgrimage* (Grand Rapids: Eerdmans, 2008), 136.

6. Thus Martin Dibelius famously called Mark "the book of secret epiphanies." See W. G. Kümmel, *Introduction to the New Testament*, 14th rev. ed. (Nashville: Abingdon, 1966), 67.

from the dead" (9:9). What they "had seen" was the content of the original story. They saw the presence of Moses and Elijah, the very two figures from the Hebrew scriptures of whom it was said that at their deaths they ascended to God. These two become signs for the resurrection. The disciples also saw the shining of Jesus' garments, as if they were the garments of the risen one ahead of time,[7] and they saw the overshadowing glory of God. They heard God's own voice, declaring Jesus "my Son, the Beloved," and adding, "Listen to him!" They thus saw and heard the strong revelation of Jesus' identity, as if that revelation were correlated with his resurrection already.

But the strong concealing follows, first of all because they now see "only Jesus," this mere and mortal human being.[8] Then there is explicit concealing in the prohibition of speaking until the time of the resurrection, a prohibition that makes quite clear that this Jesus is to die. His death and the secret go together. But the concealing also occurs in the mysterious evocation of John the Baptist as himself "Elijah," who does indeed come first, before the coming of the Lord. "Elijah" is a powerful biblical metaphor for the identity and function of John the Baptist.[9] In Mark, Elijah has come in the vision of the transfiguration. Even more, however, he has come in John. But now, this is an Elijah to whom "they did whatever they pleased." The phrase is chilling, horrible. The eschatological prophet of God's arrival has been brutalized. A figure from the glorious revelation scene has been killed. This Elijah's death has come as a down payment on what will be the contempt for, killing, and thus ultimate concealing of the Son of Man (9:10-13).

The transfiguration story narrates a strong revealing and a strong concealing, images of the risen Jesus as the crucified one. Rudolf Bultmann and many other twentieth-century scholars have long argued that the transfiguration account was likely first of all an account of a resurrection appearance of Jesus.[10] This judgment seems correct. Moses and Elijah bore witness to the risen one, one who is "hidden

---

7. Cf. the image in Rev. 1:12-16.

8. If the author of Mark largely maintained the language of an originally oral story of the transfiguration, when it was gathered into the Gospel book, he or she might have added the words "but only Jesus" or "but only Jesus with them."

9. I believe that the author of Mark does not agree with the superstition of Herod and those around Herod (6:14-16), nor with the rumors reported by the disciples (8:28). Jesus is neither Elijah nor John *redivivus*. Just so, John was not Elijah *redivivus*. "Elijah" is a biblical metaphor.

10. See Rudolf Bultmann, *Die Geschichte der synoptischen Tradition*, 7th ed. (Göttingen: Vandenhoeck & Ruprecht, 1967), 278.

in God" as they are but with an identity even closer to the divine, as first the shining clothing and then the voice testify. Christian tradition had it that Jesus "was declared to be Son of God with power . . . by resurrection from the dead" (Rom. 1:4), and so he was in this story. The church leaders saw this and they were called upon to attend to his remembered words. The author of Mark, however, added the following words of Jesus to the largely traditional story. He or she thereby gathered this story under the secret and placed it in the section of the narrative that turned toward Jerusalem and the cross, in order to make utterly clear a matter that this narrative in its original form did not make clear: the risen one is the crucified one. For Mark, the resurrection appearance story could otherwise be misunderstood, as if it primarily licensed the authority of the church leaders and as if the resurrection were a way to forget about Jesus' death.

Then, finally, at the second passion prediction, the text reads:

> They went on from there and passed through Galilee. He did not want anyone to know it; for he was teaching his disciples, saying to them, "The Son of Man is to be betrayed into human hands, and they will kill him, and three days after being killed, he will rise again." (9:30-31)

From this point on in the Gospel book, the secret no longer exists. The second passion prediction seems to mark a central turn in the narrative. Withdrawing or hiding on Jesus' part no longer occurs, nor is there any further silencing. The disciples' misunderstanding of Jesus does continue, a misunderstanding that could also be construed as a kind of hiding of his identity.[11] But the third passion prediction (10:32-34) has no word about silence attached to it. By that point, the story has moved out of Galilee into Judea (10:1) and is going up to Jerusalem (10:32). Jerusalem is the place where Jesus will be killed, and the threat of that death, which has already been suggested,[12] reaches out increasingly to surround

---

11. Already his family and his hometown misunderstand him (3:21; 6:2-3), then the disciples and Peter follow (8:16-21; 8:32-33). The theme continues most clearly in 9:32, but also in 9:33-34; 9:38; 10:13; 10:35, 41. In 9:10, the three witnesses of the transfiguration have no idea what "rising from the dead" means. In the rest of the book, the theme then becomes the betrayal of Judas, the denial of Peter, and the flight of all of the disciples.

12. "The Pharisees went out and immediately conspired with the Herodians against him, how to destroy him," 3:6; cf. Herod's murder of John, told in a way that evokes the question of the identity of Jesus, 6:14-29, and the painful image of John as Elijah, who "comes first," and "they did to him whatever they pleased," an image combined with the suffering of the Son of Man, 9:11-13.

him.[13] Misunderstanding and death may cover him, but Jesus himself no longer hides his identity. Now, it is those who are seeking to kill him who want to hide Jesus and their actions toward him. They look "for a way to arrest Jesus by stealth and kill him" (14:1). The strong dialectic of concealing and revealing now moves from words to the actions those words evoke. The second part of the book tells of the concealing of Jesus by his execution. Yet it also tells of the revealing of Jesus in the midst of that very killing: in the paradoxical testimony of his murderers, in the cross as the beginning of the arrival of the day of God, and in the promise that the community will see the crucified one as the risen one.

We thus stand before the meaning of the secret. The first two passion predictions and Jesus' words after the transfiguration, recalling the impossible murder of "Elijah" and yet enjoining silence until after his resurrection, give us a clear key to all of the instances of the secret. Used only in the first half of the book, it functions as the presence already there, in the Galilean narratives, of the truth of Jesus' sufferings and death, even in the midst of the breaking out of the truth of his identity. He is indeed the "Holy One of God," the "Son of God," and the "Messiah," as figures in these stories say. He is also the one who defeats the demons, heals the deaf and blind, and raises the dead. But he is that one in the same way that he is "the one who comes in the name of the Lord" while riding on a colt, without weapons (11:1-11), the same way that he is anointed Messiah by being anointed beforehand for his burial (14:3-9), the same way that he drinks the new cup of the arriving dominion of God by drinking sour wine when they are killing him (15:36). He is all of these things in a surprising way, hidden, killed, and now proclaimed as risen. The secret in Mark is not so much a historical report of Jesus' humility, though it may contain something of that memory within its use. Rather, it is a narrative symbol that seeks to say something very much like what Paul wrote to the Corinthians: "When I came to you, brothers and sisters, I did not come proclaiming the mystery[14] of God to you in lofty words or wisdom. For I decided to know nothing among you but Jesus Christ and him crucified" (1 Cor. 2:1-2). It is the crucified, for Paul, who is the source of life and wisdom and the power of God (1 Cor. 1:30). This truth is the mystery or secret of God. And it is the crucified for Mark who casts out demons

---

13. So the death comes to expression in the phrases "with persecutions," 10:30; "looking for a way to kill him," 11:18; "wanted to arrest him," 12:12; "looking for a way to arrest Jesus by stealth and kill him." 14:1; and then, of course, in the passion story itself, 14:3—15:47.

14. Or "the secret." The word in Greek is τὸ μυστήριον.

and gives life. It is the crucified to whom those astonishing titles that fill the first part of the Gospel book apply.

Houses Reformed

The Gospel book itself gives a further key to the meaning of this secret. In the midst of its collection of the parables of Jesus (4:1-34), it sets out several passages on secrets and revelation. First, while he speaks these parables, especially the parable of the seed, to "a very large crowd" (4:1), Jesus explains them "in private to his disciples" (4:34) or when "he was alone" and yet others are with him (4:10). Parables themselves are intended to hide, but "to you," that is, to the gathered disciples, "has been given the secret [τὸ μυστήριον] of the kingdom of God" (4:11). Even more, Jesus says that there is nothing hidden or secret except to be disclosed and come to light, like a lamp being pulled out from under a basket or a bed (4:21-22). With these texts we may begin to see how the secret relates to the assemblies, the "houses" of the church, who would see themselves in the disciples gathered around Jesus here.

It seems that a Markan understanding of the parables of chapter 4 must involve the death and resurrection of Jesus. Ultimately, the hiding and secrecy indicate his death. The "coming to light" and the "disclosure" denote the resurrection and the word of the resurrection alive in the community of disciples. Just so, tiny, seemingly weak, virtually dead seed springs up to a huge harvest secretly, surprisingly (4:26-29).[15] Just so, an annual bush, one that inevitably is cut down and dies, is the very promised tree of life giving shelter to all (4:30-32). This word about the death and resurrection of Jesus, about Jesus' identity hidden by death and yet bursting forth with life, is the very word (cf. 8:31) that is scattered throughout the world, small, vulnerable to loss and neglect, yet capable of the hundredfold harvest (4:3-9, 13-20).

But then the parable of the seed comes as a reforming word to the assemblies where this book will be read. The point is not that the hearers should work hard to make themselves into "good soil." Rather, the communities are urged to hear the gospel, called here "the word," and make it the center of their meetings. "Let anyone with ears to hear listen!" (4:23).[16] This word is a small, seemingly

---

15. Cf. Paul's metaphor in 1 Cor. 15:36-37, 42-43. Also here there is a link between Mark and Paul.

16. Such listening to the word is evoked again in the very command of God at the

insignificant thing, easily brushed away or lost or ignored in the face of other more powerful things or in the face of persecution. It is the word about a cruci-fied man, crushed under the power of Rome. But it is also the very "secret of the kingdom of God." The assemblies that hear this book have heard its title, its hidden revelations of the identity of Jesus, its recounting of his death and its promise of his resurrection. They are to know that they are the place where the one who was hidden by death is now to be openly proclaimed. Their meetings continue the gatherings of the disciples with Jesus, in the houses or when he was alone (4:10) or when he made his explanations (4:34). With this book and with those who will preach the gospel with this book as its beginning, those explana-tions arrive in local assemblies. Because of this very book, their gatherings hear of the event, for example, that only Peter, James, and John saw (9:2-8). Now, in their meetings, the time "after the Son of Man had risen from the dead" (9:9) has arrived. Now the lamp comes out from under the basket or the bed. Indeed, the silence comes to an end in an assembly in the very narrative pattern of Mark itself. After the second passion prediction, after the last imposition of the mes-sianic secret (9:30), a paradigmatic meeting of the assembly takes place (9:33-50).[17] In assembly, in the house, the crucified risen one is openly encountered in the welcoming of little ones (9:37) by a serving leadership.

Interestingly enough, the one place in the first part of the book where there is no silencing—where, rather, Jesus tells someone to tell about him—is found in the story of the man who had been possessed by the Legion. Jesus sends the healed demoniac, now clothed and in his right mind, to his home and to those who are with him there,[18] to tell them "how much the Lord has done for you, and what mercy he has shown you" (5:19). The word for "Lord" here, of course, is κύριος, a title that the church applied especially to the risen one and that Mark uses for "the Lord of the house" (13:35), and the word for "home" is οἶκος, "house," one of the words that evoked the ancient Christian meetings. The truth about the risen crucified Lord is to be told in the houses.

---

transfiguration (9:7). The concealing and revealing of the Son of God, his death and resur-rection, is to be heard as a *word*.

17. See further below.

18. In the NRSV, Jesus sends the man "home to your friends." But the Greek for "your friends" is simply τοὺς σούς, "your own." What may be evoked here are those who are together in a house gathering, reminding us of the familial expressions for the various gather-ings in Rome that Paul uses in Romans 16.

If the secret is functioning in the narrative in this symbolic way, for the sake of the centering and reform of the assemblies, then it is right to see that several other narrative features of the first half of the book also may carry similar symbolic meaning. For example, it is fascinating to note that the direct articulations of the identity of Jesus are not the only places in the narrative where his identity is expressed. Jesus does forgive sins, even though only God may do so (2:7). Is he, then, God? Indeed, this one who goes in the boat, "just as he is," is the very one who commands the wind and the sea (4:39). His being called, surprisingly, "son of Mary," with no mention of his father, leaves the reader to remember that he is also called "Son of God" (6:3).[19] And when he appears as if a "ghost," perhaps as if dead, he assures the fearful disciples by using the divine name: ἐγώ εἰμι, "I AM" (6:50), which also can be understood more ambiguously as simply "it is I." In each of these cases, the divine identity of Jesus breaks out of something like a secret—a misunderstanding, a threat, his mere humanity, even what seems like death—especially for the hearers of the book. In this man, according already to this Gospel, we are dealing with God.[20] The reading community is to hear and see.

Something like the same thing is enacted when Jesus is accused of being possessed by Beelzebul and when he is thought mad by his family. He is hidden in this slander, but then a crowd is around him. His house, full of these people, is not divided against itself (3:19-35). The "spirit" he "has" is the very Spirit that descended on him in his baptism, and that Spirit gathers and enlivens the people in his house. The reading community is invited to come into that house.

Furthermore, the first half of the book is filled with questions from others about Jesus' identity: "What is this?" (1:24); "Who can forgive . . . ?" (2:7); "Who is this?" (4:41); and, finally, the fourfold questions of his hometown: "Where did this man get all this? What is this wisdom that has been given to him? What deeds of power are being done by his hands?[21] Is not this the carpenter, the son

---

19. The assertion that Jesus is the "carpenter," the τέκτων, in 6:3, may hide a reference to Jesus being the eschatological builder of the new Temple (cf. 14:58). The same or a similar word is used in other Greek texts to describe both Bezalel, the builder of the tabernacle, and Hiram, the builder of the first Temple. And Bezalel is sometimes called, in ancient Jewish literature, the "son of Miriam."

20. The Christology of Mark is, thus, already a "high Christology," not unlike that of Paul. In encountering Jesus "as he is," we are encountering God. The idea that Mark represents an "early," "low" Christology is as vacuous as the idea that the book is an early, primitive, and simple "report."

21. The NRSV understands this question as an indicative statement.

of Mary . . . ?" (6:2-3). To the reading assembly, these questions have an answer, remembered from the very title of the book, or from the voice at his baptism, or from the cries of the demons, or from the implications of his forgiving sins and stilling the storm. This is the Son of God. This, indeed, is God among us, since in Mark the title "Son of God" does not only carry the old metaphoric kingship meaning, known to us in the psalms, but is an actual indication of a mysterious divine origin and divine presence. Jesus is seen as far more mysteriously and essentially "son of God" than was David, in Israelite history, or than is Caesar, in the time of the Gospel. But the questions here have the effect of the secret, hiding him, and the effect is redoubled by the hometown community being scandalized by him and by his being brought, at the end of this whole section of questions, to utter weakness, a kind of down payment on his death. Mark's intense double negative once more appears: he is not at all able to do there any mighty deed whatsoever, οὐκ . . . οὐδεμίαν (6:4). Except that he heals a few sick people. With that word *except*, the leaking out once more occurs, the down payment on the resurrection. The assemblies are not to be like the assembly in the hometown, not to take offense at the humanity of Jesus, nor be afraid of his weakness and death. The crucified one is the risen one.

Then, after 6:6, the identity questions essentially stop. Herod has opinions about his identity but not questions (6:14-16). As the story goes on, there are questions about his authority or tricky questions about his teachings. But the next question about identity is from Jesus himself: "Who do people say that I am?" (8:27), the question being answered both by the confession of Peter and the first passion prediction, together. After that, the next and final identity questions from others occur when Jesus is about to be killed and the high priest asks, "Are you the Messiah, the Son of the Blessed One?" and Jesus answers with that astonishing, open ἐγώ εἰμι, "I AM" (14:61-62); and when Pilate asks, "Are you the King of the Jews?" and Jesus answers with his ambiguous "You say so," as if the title is inadequate (15:2). More is said about his identity after this point, but it is paradoxically in the mouth of those who are killing him (15:9-13, 18, 26, 29-32, 39), and yet it is essentially true. This one they are killing, who cannot come down from the cross, is Messiah and King, does save others, is the Son of God, precisely at the cross. Furthermore, Bar-Timaeus, the blind man whom Jesus heals on the way to Jerusalem, cries out openly to the "Son of David," which is to say, to the Messiah. Others try to silence him, but Jesus does not. Instead he calls him (10:47-49). Then, at the entrance into Jerusalem, many people call out,

"Blessed is the one who comes in the name of the Lord," and no silencing occurs (11:9). Furthermore, Jesus says that the anointing act of the woman, an act that reveals both his death and his messiahship, will be told wherever the gospel is proclaimed in the whole world (14:9). In the midst of his death, Jesus takes charge of the questions, and the truth of his identity is revealed. The dialectic of hiddenness and revelation continues, but now others are hiding him in death and he himself is putting together the gospel that will be preached as a sign of the resurrection. The second half of the book enacts the boldness and openness with which Jesus speaks the passion predictions at the center of the book.

We should note again: the houses where Jesus explains everything to his disciples evoke the assemblies of the church that would have been intended to hear this book. The image of gatherings around him where the secret is revealed call for readers of the book to see their own gatherings. To the extent that readers of Mark's own time are also "clothed and in their right mind" (cf. 5:15) by the encounter with Jesus, they, too, are sent to their houses and to the ones who gather there. The "messianic secret" points to those assemblies. The secret exists in the book, then, to ground those assemblies in the word of that crucified one, the one hidden now from the life and power of the world, the one whose death still haunts Christian memory as a scandal and an overwhelming shame, yet the one who is the Holy One of God. Indeed, his death is the very dawning of God's day of judgment and of healing.

But if this Gospel book is indeed, like the letters of Paul, a reforming proposal to paleo-Christian assemblies, then the idea that the secret was for the sake of these assemblies must carry an edge. In the view of the writer, the assemblies must have been saying and doing something else than is proposed in the book. I do not think that we can easily construct what that something else was. But we can make some responsible guesses. One possibility we have already entertained. Some of the meetings may have been holding meals as if those meals were already the arriving feast of God, but doing so only for a limited group and doing so while hiding the horrible death of Jesus from their conscious memory. The Eucharist reflected in the *Didache* could be an example of such practice. But there are other possibilities. The meetings of Christians might have devolved into clubs that were mutually supportive, interested in old scriptures, and even pious, but trying hard to hide from persecution. They could have known and told stories of Jesus' miracles and of visions of him risen, but without the cross. Such persecutions as they had seen were profoundly frightening. The Neronian treatment of Christians in Rome had been appalling. The traumatic death of Jesus himself was a matter of shame, and some Christians were indeed ashamed (cf. 8:38). So the temptation would be to become private, even secret clubs, and to suppress the story of Jesus' death. As many scholars have suggested, the first readers of Mark may have been themselves persecuted and afraid of further persecution. Then the narrative secret of Mark and its connection to the suffering of Jesus would have drawn them in, evoked their own situation, called up their identification with the story. The explicit references to persecutions would have been similarly intended.[22] But the powerful revelation of the secret would have called them to bold openness, to not hiding from themselves or from the world itself the truth of the crucified. Following Jesus on the way was no longer to be secret.

In any case, the mention of houses in the narrative of the book does continually suggest reform. Even Jesus' own house needs its roof removed to welcome those who cannot get in to forgiveness and life (2:1-12).[23] Indeed, his own house can be a place of misunderstanding and refusal to hear the word (3:19-21; 6:4); better the open crowd sitting around him, who are to him brother and sister and mother (3:31-35). Jairus's house, a place of mourning and fear, needs to be turned into a place of the word of resurrection and the resurrection meal (5:39-43). The house where the little, weak ones are forbidden access needs to welcome them (10:10, 13-16). The model house seems to be like that of Simon, where a woman is healed and is a deacon, a server of the communal meal (1:29-31), or like that of Levi, where sinners eat and drink with Jesus, regardless of the offense (2:15-16), or like that in Tyre, where Jesus' hiddenness is revealed and where a Gentile woman also eats the crumbs from the table (7:24-30), or especially like that of Simon the leper as it becomes the place of the witness of the anointing woman to Jesus' death and of his call to remember the poor. This house is a place of the secret revealed (14:3-9).

Then there is the house at the very center of the book (9:33), the house of gathering after the final injunction to secrecy. It is a house in Capernaum, perhaps again Jesus' own house, in any case the house that marks the last gathering in

---

22. See 4:17; 8:34-38; 10:30; 13:9-13.

23. It is fascinating to note that virtually all of the actual physical remains of structures that we can currently identify as ancient "houses of the church" show traces of remodeling. Ancient buildings had to be worked on to meet the needs of assembly. See my *Holy People: A Liturgical Ecclesiology* (Minneapolis: Fortress Press, 1999), 41; and L. Michael White, *Building God's House in the Roman World* (Baltimore: Johns Hopkins University Press, 1990).

Galilee before the turn to Judea and Jerusalem. This house is also to be reformed. In accordance with the content of the revealed secret, those who gather in the house need to serve if they wish to lead (9:35). But they also need to welcome the little ones, the powerless ones, as if these little ones were Jesus himself, and thus as if they were God (9:36-37). They need to renounce competition and mutual prohibitions among the followers of Jesus and the users of his name (9:38-41). The house that finds its center in the revealed secret of the suffering of the Son of God will also find itself continually called to openness toward the little ones and toward all the others.

Still, for all of these calls to reform, the word of this Gospel does not itself cast out the unreformed or the misunderstanding. "Reform," here, does not turn into idealistic tyranny. The gospel of which the book is the beginning, after all, is good news, not bad. The houses addressed by this Gospel remain houses of the movement. In Mark, Jesus has mercy on the crowd, calls the crowd "brother and sister and mother." In Mark, the misunderstanding disciples are still included in his community, still invited in each of the passion predictions to share his way, still expected to pass out the fragments of his meal (6:37, 41; 8:6, 19-20). When Jesus withdraws or is alone, they are with him, until the last "withdrawal," his death, when they themselves run away. As Joel Marcus says, "in spite of everything they remain Jesus' chosen companions up until the end of the story, and . . . even their abandonment of Jesus there cannot annul his promise that after his resurrection they will be reunited with him in Galilee (14:27-28; 16:7)."[24]

But that promise leads to a further puzzle. The final verse of the book demonstrates once again the Markan double negative. While the women are sent to tell the disciples again of the promised meeting in Galilee, they instead flee and say οὐδενὶ οὐδέν, absolutely nothing at all to anybody at all. The secret is back, as if to cloak the whole story. But the readers may follow the directive of the young man—and of Jesus!—back to the "Galilee" with which the narrative has begun and the meeting in Galilee that forms its center. The readers may realize that the book itself is breaking out of this silence, is telling everything, especially everything about the mystery of God in the cross, to everyone. But then we start to suppose that we have to do here with a narrative circle and with another conception of "resurrection appearance" than we may have expected.

---

24. Marcus, "Identity and Ambiguity in Markan Christology," 135.

Circles Constructed

Even before we note the Galilee-Galilee connection, we see circles in Mark. We have already said that even a casual reader of Mark may observe the occurrence of small circles in its composition. Material about Jesus' house and family both precedes and follows the accusation of the scribes that he is casting out demons by the ruler of demons (3:19b-35). Similarly, the response of Jesus to the death of a twelve-year-old girl frames his healing of a woman who has suffered with a twelve-year-long hemorrhage (5:21-43). Again, the account of Jesus' encounter with a barren fig tree surrounds the story of the cleansing of the Temple (11:12-21).

From these examples, it becomes clear that the use of this circular mode, this A-B-A structure of narrative, does not only convey a passage of time. It intends to convey important meaning by its juxtapositions. The Temple, on the temple mount (cf. 11:23), with all of its religious transactions, is for Mark as an unfruitful tree. Furthermore, all women, young and old, in life and in death, are welcome to the ministry of Jesus. None are "unclean," or, if they are ritually unclean—as both the dead and the menstruous are considered—then he is unclean with them. And the accusations of his family and the accusations of the scribes are associated with each other, and both are contrasted with his "real" mother and brothers and sisters, the crowd around him in his house who do the will of God simply by being there, listening. The *chiastic* or circular shape in the narrative clearly means to be a poetic way of making sense, a rhetoric of parallelisms. Its employment here helps to make clear that Mark is a complex literary work, not a simple report, and that the book means to convey its theological proposals through poetic constructions, one thing significantly next to another.

We are not used to noting such literary methods as we read. Many times we miss them altogether or they seem to us to be evidences of clumsy narrative. Mark itself has been commonly regarded as "clumsy," primitive, repetitive, or artless in its composition.[25] But recent scholarship has urged us to see that the chiasm was a common literary figure in ancient writing. Already in 1969, John Bligh noted the symmetrical structure Paul utilized in Galatians and, especially, in the centrally located and chiastically structured passage in Galatians 4:1-10.[26]

---

25. On such accusations being directed toward "ring compositions" more generally, see Douglas, *Thinking in Circles*, 8–9, 11.

26. John Bligh, *Galatians: A Discussion on Paul's Epistle*, Householder Commentary (London: St. Paul, 1969), 37–42. Perhaps, also in literary structures, Mark was a follower of Paul.

Robert Alter has rightly pointed out that parallelism—of which, the chiasm is an especially strong example—is the Bible's dominant literary tool.[27] Recent scholarship has also invited us to note that many important ancient works employed circular construction generally in a much larger way.[28] The *Iliad*, for example, is such a composition.[29] For us to ignore these constructions is to ignore one major ancient way of proposing meaning and one very great clue to the intentions of the author of such a work.

Indeed, once we note the occasional small use in Mark of both the circular method and its construction of meaning by juxtaposition, we begin to note also larger circles in the book. The section containing the three passion predictions (8:27—10:45) is, in fact, framed by two accounts of the healing of men who are blind (8:22-26; 10:46-52). Again, the juxtaposition suggests that healing of deepest blindness, the blindness that "may indeed look, but not perceive" (4:12), the blindness of those "who have eyes, and fail to see" (8:18), is to be found in the word of Jesus' death and resurrection so clearly central to this section.

A looser frame may be found in the section 6:6—8:21. This section begins with its own small circle: the sending of the Twelve without bread, the deadly meal of Herod, and then the return of the Twelve (6:6-32). This little circle functions as a prologue to the feeding of the five thousand (6:33-44). It also signals to us that we ought to pay attention to circles in the narrative. So, the section concludes with the feeding of the four thousand (8:1-9) followed by a conflict, now not with Herod but with the Pharisees, and with the summarizing speech to the disciples about the yeast of Herod and the yeast of the Pharisees, about the seven and twelve baskets-full of bread fragments (8:11-21). The frame of the section, the beginning together with the end, both of which can be said to be about the disciples and sending and bread, invites us to understand the content of the section, a content that is almost entirely about meals: the meal of Herod, the feeding of the five thousand, the disciples who do not understand the

---

27. Robert Alter, "The Characteristics of Ancient Hebrew Poetry," in Robert Alter and Frank Kermode, eds., *The Literary Guide to the Bible* (Cambridge: Harvard University Press, 1987), 611–24. See also the discussion of proposals by Harold Bloom in chap. 8 below.

28. See, especially, Douglas, *Thinking in Circles*.

29. Already, W. A. van Otterloo, *De Ringcompositie als Opbouwprincipe in de Epische Gedichten van Homerus* (Amsterdam: Noord-Hollandsche Uitgevers Maatschappij, 1948). On the possible influence of Homer on the writing of Mark, see Dennis R. MacDonald, *The Homeric Epics and the Gospel of Mark* (New Haven: Yale University Press, 2000); and my *Holy Ground: A Liturgical Cosmology* (Minneapolis: Fortress Press, 2003), 31.

walking on the sea because "they did not understand about the loaves" (6:52), purity rules for eating, the declaration of all foods as clean, the Syrophoenician woman eating crumbs at the table, the feeding of the four thousand, and the warning about the yeast of Herod and the yeast of the Pharisees. We have already considered the importance of this latter warning.[30] As we look more closely, this entire section then seems to have a circular character. Jesus' walking on the water follows the first feeding of the multitude. His *"ephphatha"* healing precedes the second. It slowly begins to appear that the entire section might be outlined as a great chiasm:

A Sending of the Twelve without bread—6:6b-13
  B Herod's meal, return of the disciples—6:14-30
    C Feeding of the five thousand—6:31-44
      D Walking on the sea and healing—6:45-56
        E *Controversy with Pharisees on purity*
        . . In the house: all food clean
        . . In the house at Tyre: crumbs from the table
        for all —7:1-30
      D′ Ephphatha—7:31-37
    C′ Feeding of the four thousand—8:1-10
  B′ The Pharisees seek a sign from heaven—8:11-13
A′ The disciples have no bread: the yeast and the baskets full—8:14-21

Such a reading of the section helps to make clear not only that the entire section stands behind the warning about the yeast of Herod and the yeast of the Pharisees, but also that the center of the section, surrounded by the four miracle stories, bears a great interpretive weight. Purity rules are a distortion of religion as it is in Jesus Christ, and the outsider woman is welcome to the table. Indeed, she is herself a model of faith, hands reaching out for the life-giving crumbs.

We also begin to note one further thing about this chiastic construction. The juxtapositions that propose meaning do not occur only side by side. They occur also across the circle, in this outline C with C′ for example, and they occur by the relationship of all the members of the outline to the importantly accented center. So the bread of Jesus is to be distributed not only to the five thousand

---

30. See above, chap. 2.

men (6:44), who may represent a kind of Jewish eschatological assembly (6:39),[31] but also to the crowd of the four thousand, undifferentiated by gender, many of whom come "from a great distance" (8:3), who may represent the nations coming from the four corners of the earth, all men and all women.[32] In Jesus Christ, the eschatological meal is to be available to all, the Jew first, but also the Gentile, indeed—remembering the center—also the Syrophoenician woman and her child.

Awakened by this structure in 6:6b—8:21, we look at the section 11:1—13:37. Again we may discover a circle, a larger chiasm. The section begins with the entry into Jerusalem (11:1-11) and concludes with a discussion of the coming of the Son of Man (13:3-37). Already we may see that those two passages bear a certain relationship with each other through their accent on the eschatological coming. Even more, in a certain parallel to the complex frame of 6:6—8:21, we can see that the beginning of this section includes both the coming of Jesus and the small circle[33] of fig tree and Temple (11:1-26), while its final section involves the destruction of the Temple, the fig tree as a sign (13:28-29), and the coming of the Son of Man. In between, there are seven controversy accounts. One might argue that the result is simple: frame, seven stories, frame. But the stories might also be seen as chiastic, with the consequent outline as follows:

---

31. Besides the organization of the thousands in companies—"symposia," actually!—on the grass of the blossoming wilderness, note also the numbers *five* (the books of the Law) and *twelve* (the tribes of Israel).

32. It is fascinating to note that the twelve and seven baskets-full of remaining pieces, accentuated in both stories and repeated in the summary (8:19-20), correspond exactly to the numbers of those who seem to be serving the tables of the Jewish-Christian and Hellenist-Christian widows in Jerusalem, according to the story of Acts 6:1-6. There may have been a memory that associated these numbers with the earliest Jewish and Gentile (or, at least, Hellenizing) Christians. In any case, in Mark the baskets still remain, as if the bread and fish are still to continue to be distributed. See above, chap. 2.

33. Like the small circle of the sending of the disciples, Herod's meal, and the return of the disciples, this circle may once again be alerting us to the following larger circular composition.

A Entry, fig tree, Temple—11:1-26

  B Question: By what authority?—11:27-37

    C Parable of the vineyard: killing the beloved son—12:1-12

      D Giving to the emperor and to God—12:13-17

        E *God is God of the living*—12:18-27

      D′ The great commandment—12:28-34

    C′ Question of Jesus: Is the Messiah son of David?—12:35-37

  B′ Beware the scribes—12:38-44

A′ Temple, fig tree, coming—13:1-37

Written out in this way, we are invited to follow the juxtapositions across the circle, the parallelisms of sections. We are invited to see the mysterious authority of Jesus as utterly other than the overbearing, widow-devouring authority of the scribes, to see the one who cannot quite be the son of David as nonetheless the beloved son of the vineyard owner,[34] and to see the giving to God and the emperor next to the commandment to love God and the neighbor. The circle works, stunningly. But then the weight-bearing center of the circle, the crossing point of the chiasm, the primary text of the whole section, is this: "God is God not of the dead, but of the living" (12:27). The religion being enacted by the coming of Jesus is not an extended legalistic argument about inheritance and the regulation of marriage, nor is it fawning before the emperor. It is, rather, the religion of the burning bush, and the truly living one is the risen one around whom the community gathers. While the whole section, situated in Jerusalem, intensifies the threat to Jesus' life, this central passage is an affirmation of the resurrection.

If these circles work, if they actually aid us in interpreting the book, then we ought to look again at 8:22—10:52, the section closely framed by the stories of healing blindness and more largely framed by these two circular sections. It is apparently the very central section of Mark. It might be outlined as follows:

---

34. One might note that, while the "secret" is no longer being exercised, the identity of Jesus is still being revealed in these texts in hidden ways: he will not say the origin of his authority, though the readers know. If he is not the son of David, then the reader nonetheless knows whose son he is.

A The blind man at Bethsaida—8:22-26

   B First passion prediction and way of the cross—8:27-38

      C Transfiguration—9:1-13

         D Healing of a child; in the house on prayer—9:14-29

            E *Second passion prediction*

              and the child in the house—9:30-50

         D´ Divorce; in the house; welcoming children—10:1-16

      C´ The rich man and inheritance in the kingdom—10:17-31

   B´ Third passion prediction and the way for leaders—10:32-45

A´ The blind son of Timaeus—10:46-52

The very fact that we have already discovered circles functioning in Mark and, in addition, the clear parallels we see here between A and A´ and B and B´, between the stories of healing blindness and the accounts of the first and third passion predictions, suggest two things to us. The second passion prediction functions as the center of the section. And we ought to be helped in interpretation by reading C and C´ and D and D´ side by side. In fact, it turns out that C and C´ are verbally linked: the transfiguration account is presented as, in some sense, the three disciples seeing "that the kingdom of God has come with power" (9:1), and rich man has difficulty entering "the kingdom of God" (10:23). Still, all things are possible for God. The kingdom comes as God's gift, and the hundredfold family and the hundredfold houses are given to those who gather with Jesus as part of that gift (10:30). The story of the transfiguration, told after Jesus' death and resurrection, goes together with those houses and that new family. The houses and the new sorts of family are the places where the secret is to be told, after the resurrection. Furthermore, the *houses* where both the need for prayer (9:28) and the equality of men and women both in marriage and in marriage failure are explained (10:10) link the two stories, D and D´, and underline the importance of the house in E, the central story (9:33). The child healed (9:27) and the children received (10:14), besides underscoring the reason for the importance of marriage and emphasizing once again the Markan interest in the welcoming and/or healing of the outsiders and the powerless, also function to underline the child in the midst in the central story (9:36). Furthermore, B and B´, besides including the first and third passion predictions and their paired discipleship sayings, also include the specific misunderstandings of Peter (B: 8:32-33) and of James and John (B´: 10:35-40). Though these misunderstandings link to the general misunderstanding of the central E (9:32), it is B and B′ that are exactly parallel. Then, the discipleship sayings that are part of B and B′ address all who wish to be followers of Jesus (8:34-38) and all who wish to be leaders in the community (10:41-45). Those sayings call the more attention to the house in E, where both leaders and the whole community, including a child, are together. The central text is for the assembly itself. This circle also works.

Mark as a Ring Composition

Once we have discovered such a use of chiasms or circular constructions, however, our eyes slowly open to the structure of the entire book. Mary Douglas, in her 2003 Terry Lectures at Yale University, argued that important ancient literature, not least, for example, the *Iliad* and the biblical book of Numbers, made use of what she calls "ring composition." In her analysis, she helpfully articulated the primary characteristics of such writing:[35]

1. It generally has an introduction or prologue, one that anticipates the midturn of the work and its ending.
2. It is split into two halves.
3. It works with parallel sections that emphasize this two-sided construction.
4. It has indicators, often key words or images, that mark individual sections.
5. It is "centrally loaded." The meaning of the work is found especially in the middle, in the turn between the parallel sides, for example in the C of the pattern A B C B′ A′.
6. It utilizes rings within rings.
7. It concludes by joining up with the beginning and by evoking some of the meaning with which the work began, meaning that also recurs in the center.

All seven of these characteristics may be seen to be true of Mark. We have been exploring some of them. When we add what we have noted above, that the "Galilee" of the conclusion (16:7) clearly links us back to the "Galilee" of the introduction to the book (1:9, 14, 16), when we further note that this same Galilee shows up in the central turn of the book (9:30), and when we thus observe the working of the two halves of the book ("in Galilee" up to the turn, 9:30-50, and "in Judea," the trans-Jordan and Jerusalem thereafter, 10:1), we must begin

---

35. Douglas, *Thinking in Circles*, 36–38.

to see that the Gospel of Mark as a whole is a ring composition. Its outline, after the title (1:1), would then be as follows:[36]

A Introduction—1:2-20

    B Synagogues, houses, the word—1:21—6:6a

        C Meals—6:6b—8:21

            D *Seeing the crucified risen one*—8:22—10:52

        C′ Coming, controversies, coming—11:1—13:37

    B′ Two meals and the passion—14:1—15:47

A′ Conclusion and return to the beginning—16:1-8

We have already seen that C and C′ in this outline are themselves minor rings, "rings within rings," as Mary Douglas says.[37] They surround D, the central section of the book, which is also itself a ring. It is less likely that we can discover B and B′ to be rings, even though B begins with the sequence synagogue-house (1:21-24) and concludes with the sequence house-synagogue (5:35—6:6a). It may be better to see these two sections side by side as largely being developed linearly.[38] Indeed, one might suggest that these two sections serve in a linear way to pull in the readers or hearers of the book, evoking what they know of God and of Jesus, including both miracle working and the suppressed knowledge that Jesus was shamefully killed, in order to make this knowledge then available to the reversals and transformations of the circles at the center of the book. The introduction (1:2-20) and the conclusion (16:1-8) and the very center section of the book (9:30-50) are linked to each other by Galilee (cf. 9:30, 33) and by the disciples (1:16-20; 16:7; 9:30, 35, 38), but also by the central theme of the identity of Jesus of Nazareth, the crucified, the risen, the Messiah, the Son of Man, the Son of God, and the very content of the gospel. At the center of the book, this identity, this gospel, is to be seen, proclaimed, encountered, and enacted in the house, the place where the disciples gather.

Reading Mark with this outline in mind yields several astonishing fruits. We become further aware of the power of the book as a constructed composition, a

---

36. For a slightly different but similar outline, see Bas van Iersel, *Reading Mark* (Edinburgh: T&T Clark, 1989), 18–26.

37. Douglas, *Thinking in Circles*, 37.

38. The synagogue-house/house-synagogue frame may again be functioning to call the attention of the reader or hearer to the following circles.

testimony indeed from one of our four Beasts. We learn that the very intention of the book is to proclaim the meaning and presence of Jesus by the use of strong symbols and images juxtaposed within a quite formal structure. Because of the parallelisms across the circle, we see several small things: the two houses in B′, the house of Simon the leper, where the meal of the anointing woman takes place (14:3), and the providentially provided house of the Last Supper (14:14) may be seen to recapitulate the many houses of B, recalling again the meetings of the Christian community in the time of Mark. The houses of both B and B′ may then relate to the house at the center of the book (9:33) and to the several houses, indeed the hundredfold houses of section D. The many questions about Jesus' identity that occur in part B, culminating with the list of questions in 6:2-3, are rightly set side by side with the two questions about his identity in B′, that from the high priest and that from Pilate (14:61 and 15:2), from the collaborating religious establishment and from the empire. The charge of blasphemy against Jesus in B (2:7) parallels the same charge in B′ (14:64). Both concern the identity of Jesus as God or as the Son of God. The man who in B finally is healed and is "sitting there clothed and in his right mind" (5:15) may rightly be set beside the "young man" who in B′ loses his clothing at the arrest of Jesus (14:51-52) and likely recurs clothed in the conclusion (16:5) as the proclaimer of the resurrection and the indicator of Galilee as the place of seeing. Both tell of Jesus, the former in his house, the latter sending the women to the disciples who gather in the houses. Indeed, the very passion account of B′ gives content to the "word" of B (cf. 4:33), openly revealing the secret that was so important there. Furthermore, both C and C′ end with a charge to "beware!"[39] "Beware the yeast" (8:15) in C; "beware" the scribes (11:38), the false gods ("many will come and say I AM," 13:6), the persecutors (13:9), and the coming of the day of God itself (13:33) in C′. It is helpful to interpret all of these passages by juxtapositions across the circle.

Because of the parallelisms across the circle, we also see one very large thing. It is a thing that the motif of the secret already showed us. The one who is killed in the story of the passion is the very one whose acts of healing and authoritative teaching fill the ministry in Galilee, the ministry narrated in B. This teaching and healing continue in the life of the churches gathered around the risen one, and the risen one is the crucified one. The Markan narrative of the passion

---

39. The English "beware" translates the Greek βλέπετε, which is a verb for "seeing." In English, we miss the connection between these warnings to see the danger in C and C′ and the healings of the blind which frame the central section, D.

makes the story of the suffering of the Son of God available to the assemblies as their core story, as the root and meaning of their life. The circular construction links the passion story and the continuing ministry in the assemblies. Now Jesus' death is not simply an appalling and degrading shame. It is the source of communal identity. It is the source of life. The circle, B across from B′ and centered on D, makes this clear. In Mark, one cannot read B′ without B and vice versa.

The very existence of the sections of this circular, chiastic outline helps us to see also the frequently contrasting linkages that are established between the sections. These linkages themselves carry important meanings. The weakness of Jesus at the end of B (6:5), out of which healing nonetheless comes, links to the beginning of C, to both the powerful success of the Twelve as they are authorized by this same powerless Jesus (6:7, 13) and to the outreaching shadow of murderous violence in Herod killing John, the book's "Elijah," a down payment on the killing of Jesus. This killing is both the final weakness of Jesus and yet also his final authority over the demons. Then, the blindness of the disciples at the end of C (8:18) yields to the healing of blindness that frames D. The son of Timaeus, healed at the end of D, follows Jesus "on the way" (10:52) and thus into the comings of C′ and the passion story of B′.[40] And, perhaps most importantly, the times given at the end of C′, the times at which the community should watch for the coming of the Lord of the house—"in the evening, or at midnight, or at cockcrow, or at dawn" (13:35)—correspond exactly to the times that occur in the immediately following passion story of B′: for Mark, the eschatological coming of the Lord does indeed occur at evening at the supper (14:17), at midnight in the garden (where the disciples are again to "watch," 14:34), at cockcrow when Peter denies him (14:68,72), at dawn when they begin to actively kill him (15:1), at evening again when they are burying him (15:42), and again at the dawn of the resurrection (16:2). Even here we find a circle, and we find one that is open: the resurrection is revealed in the second dawn, the dawn beyond dawn. For Mark, the crucified risen one is already now the coming one of the eschaton,

---

40. If I am right about the name of this blind man playing on the name of the principal speaker in the *Timaeus* of Plato, then this important and central hinge story in Mark also contains a reference to the introduction to the Gospel. In the *Timaeus*, truth comes from philosophers using their eyes to following the courses of the stars in the perfect heaven, itself called "the only-begotten of God." In Mark, the gospel truth is found in Jesus Christ, the Son of God who shares our lot under the torn-open heavens (1:10), and a healed blind man, a symbolic descendent of Plato's Timaeus, follows Jesus into his passion, death, and resurrection. Philosophy itself is healed. See my *Holy Ground*, 25–38.

and the passage of each day bears witness to him. It is this one who is "the Lord of the house" (13:35). And the story of his passion is a faithfully constructed pattern of symbols to help us see him.

But the two most important insights given us by the awareness of Mark as a ring composition are (1) a new attention to the central turn of the book as carrying its most basic meaning and (2) a new sense of the purpose of the book at all.

When we are used to reading a book in a linear way and when we then discover that the book is, in fact, a ring composition, we need precisely to look once again at the center of the ring, the turn in the chiastic construction, to rediscover the meaning of the book.[41] In Mark, that turn is signaled not only by its central position, not only by its recapitulation of themes found in both introduction and conclusion, but also by its being flanked by several pairs. The rings of the C and C′, of 6:6b—8:21 and 11:1—13:37, flank the central section D, 8:22—10:52. But then the center of D, 9:30-50, is flanked by the two healings of blindness, two other accounts of healed or welcomed children, two other occurrences of "the house" for teaching the disciples, and especially the two other passion predictions and their paired discipleship sayings. These latter, in fact, form a triad with the central section—the *three* passion predictions—that serves to underline this center.[42] Furthermore, the central turn here is recognized because it is the last occasion for the "secret" and the final event recounted as occurring in Galilee. From these considerations, we can see again that the whole section of the passion predictions and the transfiguration, the little ones and the hundredfold houses, carries the burden of meaning in Mark. But we can see especially that the "second passion prediction" and its appended actions and sayings are at the heart of that burden. The content of this center of the book, once again, is the truth about the death and resurrection of Jesus and the concern that the life of the "house" be formed by this truth: that this word be spoken openly and centrally there; that it be served by a serving leadership; that the house be a

---

41. So Douglas, *Thinking in Circles*, 58: "a ring composition condenses the whole burden of its message into the mid-turn. What has been seen through straight linear reading has to be read again with a fresh eye for the message that is in the mid-turn."

42. Thus, Douglas writes: "It is common in ring compositions for the mid-turn to be flanked by two sections that are nearly the same. The parallels before and after the mid-turn form a triad that helps the reader to recognize the significance of the piece in the middle" (ibid., 55–56). This insight also helps us to see that, in Mark, neither the confession and misunderstanding of Peter nor the ambitions of James and John are central. They are flanking questions. The child in the midst of the house, put there by Jesus, is at the center.

place of welcome to the littlest ones; that it refuse competition with other communities acting in the name of Christ; that it boldly let the fear of persecution go;[43] and that it be a place of peace. The content of this center—and thus the burden of the Gospel—is both the "gospel" of which it is the "beginning" and the ongoing reform of the assemblies in that gospel.

Once again, we may be seeing, from the point of view of the author of Mark, what was lacking in the assemblies being addressed: they did not regularly speak of the death and resurrection of Jesus at the heart of their meetings. They knew a domineering, hierarchical leadership, vying for influence and power. They did not welcome the littlest ones. They were competitive with and judgmental of other Christians. They were afraid. They were not at peace. The center of the Gospel book makes clear its reforming intention.

In any case, this center of the book is further reinforced by noting the centers of the two flanking circles. At the center to C, the section so devoted to meals, the house at Tyre becomes the place of enacting the availability of the table to the ritually unclean, to the Gentile woman (7:1-30). At the center of C′, the burning bush is seen. God is proclaimed as the God of the living, of the resurrection (12:18-27). Both of these texts support the central text of D: the house gathered around the gospel is to be a place welcoming the rejected and the nations, as it is also a place for the encounter with the risen one. Mark seeks to make the gathering places of the churches into just such places as are evoked by these three juxtaposed, flanking central texts.

Something like the same point can be seen when we ask why the evangelist chose to use the ring form. Of course, ring structure with its parallelisms and marked sections did recommend itself to communities accustomed to the oral performance of their principal texts. Even if an actual written text was being used in a gathering—a codex in the hand of the reader—the very fact that ancient Greek was written without any word or sentence or paragraph breaks means that a reader would be immensely helped by knowing and memorizing the structure of the book.[44] The ring in Mark is memorable, and that reality already suggests

---

43. The advice to "cut it off" probably reflects hyperbole in the face of a potential torturer who would be pushing a Christian toward apostasy or worse by applying torture to hand or foot or eye. Cf. 2 Macc. 7:1-41, especially 7:4, 7.

44. On the oral performance of Gospel texts, see Richard Horsley, *Jesus in Context: Power, People, Performance* (Minneapolis: Fortress Press, 2008). On the utility of the ring or chiasm to oral performance, see esp. 106–7 of this book.

the communal intention of the book. Furthermore, the ring is clearly intended to be repeated, and that repetition suggests the ritual of a regular meeting by the assemblies using the book. But most of all, when we realize that the author of Mark was creating a new genre, at least as far as we know, then the ring form gave weight to the book. A ring composition was "an elegant form of writing for reciting at important events"[45] and "the common form for reciting myths of origin."[46] Indeed, when well crafted, the words of such a composition function as their "own authentication,"[47] as reliable words amid the vagaries of fragile communities.[48] The chiastic ring structure tells us this: Mark seems to have been intended to be read in assemblies as authoritative, origin-telling, gospel-founding scripture. Mark means to make of the story of Jesus a weighted classic text, presenting central images worthy of constant repetition and reinterpretation, enabling communities constantly to rethink their understanding of God and their experience of the world. Mark seems to be written to be sent around to the assemblies as an important, foundational book.

But we are told also something else by the Markan use of the circle in narration. The book is not finished and closed by itself. It remains open, open especially to what is to happen in the assembles where it is read. It is the "beginning," the ἀρχή, of the gospel that is to occur there. It is thus no surprise that the double negative of the last lines of the book—"they said nothing at all to anyone at all"—seems to renew the secret as the readers are sent back to the beginning and back to Galilee, as the circle is rounded. But then we come to what the book means by "there you will see him" (16:7), what it understands to be the resurrection appearance of Jesus.

Mark on Worship: The Resurrection Appearance

According to the conclusion of the book, recapitulating the narrated promise of Jesus at the Mount of Olives (14:28), the crucified and risen Jesus is to be seen "in Galilee." There is no further resurrection appearance reported in the book, at least not in what now appears to have been its original form. Along with the disciples, the readers of the book are sent to "Galilee." Indeed, since the women

---

45. Douglas, *Thinking in Circles*, 131.
46. Ibid., 27.
47. Ibid.
48. Ibid., 27–30.

have not carried out their mission, especially the readers of the book hear the promise of seeing the risen one in Galilee.

Where is "Galilee"? Some readers of Mark have presumed that the reference is to one or more actual Galilean appearances in the earliest days of the Jesus movement, like the appearances that are narrated in Matthew (28:16-20) and in the appendix to John (21:1-23). But these events are not in Mark, and, in fact, this Gospel concludes with the silence of the women, the renewed secret. Other readers assume, nonetheless, a literally geographical reference, but to events in the time of the Gospel writer. By this understanding, the original Gospel would have been intended for communities of Christians in Galilee, more or less at the time of the destruction of the Temple in Jerusalem. The promise would be one of encountering Jesus risen in the midst of the daily life of these communities. Such a reading is possible, but given the Pauline character of Mark and the distinct possibility that Mark was written elsewhere, perhaps even at Rome or in Syria, and that it was intended for a widespread set of Christian communities, perhaps even all of them that existed at the time, this interpretation seems rather limited. Furthermore, the symbolic cast of so much of the Markan narrative, its construction of meaning by image juxtaposed to image, seems to suggest that this important word—"Galilee"—should also be read symbolically.

The ring composition of Mark brings us to see that the concluding promise, the concluding *secret*, should be read next to both the beginning of the book and its central turn. Galilee is the location of the second passion prediction, the central announcement of Jesus' death and resurrection, and of the house which is to be ordered in accord with that announcement, the house where the content of the secret is revealed and enacted. It seems that Mark indicates that the risen Christ is to be encountered in the midst of such a house. Welcoming the child in this house, welcoming the powerless one, is welcoming Christ, and welcoming Christ is welcoming God. The verb δέχεται—welcome, receive—is repeated, in one form or another, four times.[49] Suddenly, we see with new eyes that Jesus has already told us, at the center of the narrative, at least one way that we will see the risen crucified one in Galilee.[50] Furthermore, Galilee is the location of

---

49. Elsewhere in Mark, that verb is found only at 6:11, about the welcome of the Twelve on mission, and at 10:15, about receiving or welcoming the kingdom of God as a little child does. The latter is one of the texts marking the circle around this central text.

50. When the ring composition brings us to see Mark 9:30-50 as the center of the book and when thus the conclusion (16:1-8) is related to this center, 9:37 comes to stand out as a

the narrative of the first half of the book, beginning at 1:14. I suggest that Mark indicates that the risen one is to be encountered in the reading of the book itself, the book that begins in Galilee.[51] The book is both the communication of the message that the women failed to bring—telling everything to everyone—and the very resurrection appearance itself. Reading this book in the house, reading of Jesus then, the gathered community sees the risen one, sees Jesus now, in the book and the words of the book come alive in the community and so in the powerless ones all around and in the community. The Gospel of Mark, the book itself, means to be communal scripture. We see that in its ring structure. But more: it means to be the beginning and grounds of the gospel occurring in the house. If the author of Mark knew of the traditional catalog of resurrection appearances known to Paul (1 Cor. 15:5-8), he or she is here going beyond that catalog, making the resurrection appearance available to all the present community. Or, rather, if he or she knew of the memory that the communities of the Jesus movement began to understand and "see" that Jesus was risen in their meal gatherings in the months and years after his execution, then he or she is here building on and correcting that memory. The resurrection of Jesus is indeed known in the assembly, but it is especially so known as the secret is proclaimed openly, as the story of his death is proclaimed, as the community is anchored in that gospel and patterned, in service and openness and welcome to the least, according to it. The risen one is the crucified one.

Thus, what the First Gospel has to say about the ancient Christian assemblies is central to the book itself. It is the reason for the secret and the center of the circular construction. Indeed, I propose that the discoverable ring composition and its burden-bearing center are decisive to our question about the Gospel's interest in and address to paleo-Christian assemblies. For Mark, the resurrection is encountered in the gospel of the crucified alive in the house, reorienting the house.

---

way in which the risen one is to be "seen in Galilee" (16:7). Just so, protecting the little ones becomes more important than whatever the persecutors may do to hand or foot or eye (9:43-48), and the salty courage of such a community is a response to the fear of the women (16:8). For this understanding to be clear, it is important that we not sentimentalize the image of the child in ways marked by modern consciousness. The child, in ancient society, was among the expendable and marginal and powerless ones, and the child, here, stands as a symbol for all such people: "these little ones."

51. See my *Holy Things: A Liturgical Theology* (Minneapolis: Fortress Press, 1993), 29.

That is a start. But in thinking about what this first Gospel has to say about the Christian assembly, we might add yet more. There are small things, interesting things. If I am right about the "houses" of the narrative, we might think about how ancient Christian assemblies may have heard the story of the blocked access and the removed house roof in Mark 2:1-2, for example. Could the story have called for Christian communities to make actual architectural changes, real room for others in whatever place they used for a meeting? Or, could the call to repentance in 1:15 be seen as reflecting an ancient Christian baptismal invitation? Indeed, might the book itself also be understood to have functioned as baptismal catechesis, and could the stripping of the young man before the passion of Christ and his white robe as he bears witness to the resurrection, perhaps like the clothing of the healed man of the "Legion" (5:15), also reflect ancient baptismal clothing practice? Then, for Mark, as well as for Paul, one is baptized into the death of Jesus (cf. 10:38; Rom. 6:3-4) in order to be raised with him, and in baptism one is clothed in Christ (Gal. 3:27; Rom. 13:14).[52] These hints are tantalizing but not the central point. They serve to remind us that any account of such a rich ancient book and its meanings cannot be exhaustive.

For now, it is enough to see the function of the secret and of the circles and the nature of the resurrection appearance here. The book had a critical purpose in the assemblies. We will need to ask how the edge of this book, its call for reform, meets our assemblies. But first we must consider the rest of the four.

What, then, did the other Gospels do with such a book?

This inquiry into the structure and original meanings of Mark also raises questions for our liturgical assemblies: Are we helping our meetings benefit from the layered symbolic meanings that are so important in this book, that are so like the layered meanings of healthy Christian liturgy? More: How similar to the gatherings that the author of Mark may have been critically addressing are our meetings? Are the challenges at the central turn of the book also challenges to us? Are our liturgical decisions driven by fear or by the avoidance of honesty about death and suffering? Is the word of the cross at the center of our meetings? Is it enacted there by a serving leadership,

---

52. I have also elsewhere argued that the very shape of Mark—baptism, leading to a long section of Jesus' teaching, leading to the two meals of chapter 14 that sum up the meaning of the passion, leading to the sending to see Jesus in Galilee—might be regarded as reflecting the already developing pattern of the ancient Christian meeting, a pattern fully seen later in Justin's *1 Apology* 67. Cf. my *Holy Ground*, 132.

a welcome to the least, a renunciation of Christian competition, an end to fear, an enacting of peace? And yet do we avoid turning a word of reform itself into tyranny? Does this Gospel of the welcome to sinners and outsiders welcome us? Is our meeting the primary place where we encounter the risen one who is himself the beginning of the healing of all things?

4

Matthew and Luke in Detail

Word and Meal in the Churches

The writers of the Gospel books "According to Matthew" and "According to Luke" knew and used Mark. That much is clear. Their books largely follow the outline established first in Mark. In Matthew and Luke, as in Mark, the narrative of the ministry of Jesus begins with his baptism, continues with stories located throughout greater Galilee, and then, after the second passion prediction, goes up to Jerusalem, where the passion story occurs. Indeed, the specific order of many of the discrete narratives found in Mark is largely maintained in the other two Synoptics, even though additional material has been inserted here and there. Furthermore, passages from Mark that could have had no independent existence as oral traditions, passages such as the summary reports of Jesus' healing and preaching activity, are taken up almost word for word into the new books.[1] In addition, some passages in Matthew and Luke look like intentional smoothing out of Markan formulations, formulations that the later authors might have experienced as rough or theologically awkward.[2]

Of course, these later books added more than "smoothing out" to what they received from Mark. In both cases, the story of Mark has been filled out with more extensive accounts of the teaching of Jesus, several unique stories of his activity, and new details in the passion narrative. In each case—most obviously in Matthew but

---

1. For example, Mark 1:32-34 and Luke 4:40-41, Mark 1:39 and Matt. 4:23.

2. See, for example, how Matt. 13:54 simplifies the questions of Mark 6:2-3 and how 13:58 eliminates the "awkward" double negative and its exception in Mark 6:5, giving instead a reason for the absence of powerful deeds. Matthew thereby loses the dialectic of concealing/revealing as it is expressed in Mark here. Luke also gives a reason for the absence of deeds of power, providing probative scriptural quotations and turning the whole story into the programmatic narrative of Jesus at Nazareth at the outset of Jesus' ministry (Luke 4:16-30). It is clear that Jesus' weakness in Mark (οὐκ ἐδύνατο . . . ποιῆσαι οὐδεμίαν) was troubling to the other writers and, from their point of view, needed to be corrected.

also importantly in Luke—more references to passages from the Hebrew scriptures are added to the book as evidence of the fulfillment of scripture in Jesus and the events of his life. In both cases, narrative accounts of appearances of the risen one are added to the conclusions of the books. And in each case, the book is begun by an account of Jesus' birth and one of two differing versions of his genealogy. The "beginning" of Mark (1:1) has been expanded to include the birth story of these later Gospels, the γένεσις (birth as beginning or origin) of Matthew (1:18) and the τεκεῖν (birth as in childbirth, child bearing) of Luke (2:7). It seems quite likely that these birth stories were added not only under the influence of the general pattern of Hellenistic *bioi* but also in an intended contradiction to those Roman "gospels" that could celebrate both imperial accessions and imperial birthdays. It is fascinating that the emperor Augustus appears in the Lukan account (Luke 2:1) and the Roman client-king Herod appears in Matthew's story (Matt. 2:1ff.). Jesus is presented as quite other than either of these rulers from the beginning.[3]

Most likely, each of the books was written to supersede what had gone before it and to become the churches' only necessary book about Jesus. That at least was what Luke clearly implied in its opening prologue (1:1-4). This book was not to be simply another "orderly account" but the most reliable account, the one from which Theophilus and others might know the truth. Those earlier "orderly accounts," referred to, used, and probably intended to be superseded by Luke, would have included at least Mark, perhaps the source now widely called Q or, as some would argue,[4] even Matthew itself. And, since the text of Matthew had embraced nearly all of Mark, as if in an expanded edition, it seems likely that it, too, was originally intended to replace the smaller book.[5]

But our question is whether and to what extent these later Gospels caught and carried on the Markan intention for use in and reform of the assemblies. Did these Gospels also address the Christian gatherings? Did they join the critical purpose of Mark? To the extent that my argument for the Markan purpose has been based upon the First Gospel's use of the messianic secret, its ring composition, and the idea that the book itself is a "resurrection appearance," the answer must be *no*. In both Matthew and Luke, there are narratives of resurrection appearances. The ring composition of the whole seems to have disappeared. And the accent on the "secret" has been much diminished.

---

3. See above, chap. 1.
4. See above, chap. 1, n.71.
5. See above, chap. 1, n.82.

Still, that observation has not yet fully answered the question. It may very well be that the ring composition of Mark had succeeded in establishing the scriptural character of a Gospel book, its function as a "myth of origin." A new Gospel book could build on that reception and could go on with a further elaboration of the Jesus story in assemblies now willing to receive such a book, now accustomed to such a book as new scripture, now hungry for more words about Jesus. The ring structure was no longer needed and could yield to a new structure and its accents. It may also be that the judgment of the authors of these new Gospels was that the subtleties of Mark, including the detailed subtleties of its circular compositions, were largely misunderstood or missed entirely by its hearers. Matthew, for example, not only reduces the references to the "secret." He also gives a reason for the secret, a reason preeminently and openly congruent with his constant insertion of the fulfillment-of-scripture motif. For the author of Matthew, Jesus was the very "servant" of the Isaian songs (Matt. 12:15-21). So, he did not "cry aloud . . . in the streets," exactly as the prophet said. Jesus' secret is thus to be understood as the reticence of the servant of God, in conformity with the promise of scripture.[6]

The question is not whether Matthew and Luke continued the Markan methods of addressing the assemblies but whether they were speaking directly to the assemblies at all. I propose that they were. The books carry on the communal authority of Mark, in Matthew especially an authority in extended teaching addressed to the church, in Luke an authority as if this book and its second volume, Acts, were together the new and reliable epic of the churches. Both books continue to lead their readers to the passion story, that remembrance of the crucified one which Mark had already proposed as the central concern of faithful

---

6. Matthew also reduces the hidden references to Jesus as God, so common in Mark and seemingly expected to be understood by Mark's hearers. For example, in Matthew, when the paralytic is forgiven and healed, the scribes do not say, as in Mark, "Who can forgive sins but God alone?" Indeed, at the end of the story in Matthew, the crowd glorifies God "who had given such authority to human beings" (Matt. 9:2-8; cf. Mark 2:1-12). In Jesus' hometown, unlike in Mark, his father is mentioned (Matt. 13:55), by changing the reference to "the carpenter" or "the builder" (cf. Mark 6:3). And, in Matthew, when Jesus is before the high priest, he does not say, "I AM" (Matt. 26:64), as he does in Mark (Mark 14:62). One could argue that besides a flattening of the Markan subtleties Matthew also represents a somewhat "lower" Christology. Nonetheless, Matthew introduces its own subtleties, as when the four women in the genealogy before Mary are also suspect women used by God (Matt. 1:3, 5, 6) and as when the vacillating Peter is called "the rock" (16:18).

assemblies. Furthermore, in both books, the resurrection appearances of Jesus occur as ecclesial events. We have said that Mark 16:7—together with Mark 9:30-50, the central turn in Mark's ring—points to a church seeing the risen one in its midst, in the welcomed little one, in the word of the crucified, and in the book itself. Both Matthew and Luke have caught that idea, though they represent it differently. For Matthew, the risen crucified one is always with the churches, even the smallest assemblies (Matt. 18:20; 28:20), in their gathering, teaching, and baptizing. For Luke, the risen crucified one himself is the interpreter of scriptures read in an assembly and himself is seen in the practice of the assembly's meal (Luke 24:13-35). These matters are addressed to the churches, to the communities that will read these books.

It is clear that, like Mark, these books are not eyewitness accounts or newspaper reports. Indeed, the author of Luke says directly that the book is not an eyewitness report, though the author has received such reports, but an "orderly" writing (Luke 1:3). Then, according to Luke (1:1), the other, earlier books that the author knew—including, as we have said, at least Mark and either Matthew or "Q"—were also "orderly accounts," dependent on handed-down stories. We would say that this "order" is a symbolic and theological one. The books are symbolic and theologically weighted words about Jesus as Jesus is to be known in the assemblies. They are Jesus-then becoming in the assemblies Jesus-now. Indeed, the Jesus of these books is the crucified and risen one, now proclaimed in the churches. When we read these books today, we will indeed encounter the story of Jesus. We will also encounter, woven throughout that story, some intimations of the assemblies for which these versions of the story of Jesus were intended.

But neither book is Mark. They each go about a new presentation of the genre we and the later churches have called "Gospel" with unique accents. Can we identify some of the most central of these accents? And can we inquire more carefully if these unique characteristics are at least partly intended for the reform of the assemblies?

Matthew: Reforming Discourses for the Assemblies

The most obviously unique trait of Matthew encounters us in the extended discourses that make up a great part of the book. Besides the birth narrative at the beginning and the resurrection appearances at the end, it is especially these discourses that fill out the outline of Mark as that outline is reworked in this Gospel.

Indeed, many current commentators on Matthew use the discourses to make the book's outline clear, arguing that the author has intentionally divided his writing into five "books," as if the Gospel were now the authoritative companion and the interpreter of the Torah, the five "books of Moses," the basic scriptures of the people of God, and as if Jesus were a new Moses, greater than Moses.[7] Here we begin to catch something of the "order" of Matthew's orderly account.

The discourses themselves are readily discovered by their repeated concluding words: "when Jesus had finished . . ." (Matt. 7:28; 11:1; 13:53; 19:1; 26:1). Using this marker, we find:

5:1—7:29	First discourse: the Sermon on the Mount, Jesus' inaugural preaching
9:35—11:1	Second discourse: instructions to the Twelve for mission
13:1-53	Third discourse: a collection of parables
18:1—19:2	Fourth discourse: instructions for the assemblies
24:1—26:1	Fifth discourse: instructions concerning the last things

There are as well other, somewhat lengthy collections of sayings that are not marked by these concluding words, for example, the "woes" addressed to scribes and the Pharisees (23:1-39).[8] But, by means of these final words, the author himself seems to underline the key importance of especially these five discourses and the symbolic importance of there being five. In any case, following the indications of these important discourses, the Gospel book may be outlined as follows:[9]

---

7. See Dale C. Allison Jr., *The New Moses: A Matthean Typology* (Minneapolis: Fortress Press, 1993); and idem, "The Embodiment of God's Will: Jesus in Matthew," in Beverly Roberts Gaventa and Richard B. Hays, eds., *Seeking the Identity of Jesus: A Pilgrimage* (Grand Rapids: Eerdmans, 2008), 119–21. Other scholars argue for Matthew's organization echoing the *hexateuch*, the six books of Genesis through Joshua, the birth narrative being Matthew's Genesis and the final discourse together with the passion being Matthew's Joshua. See Austin Farrer, "On Dispensing with Q," in D. E. Nineham, *Studies in the Gospels* (Oxford: Blackwell, 1955), 75–77.

8. Still, Matthew 23 may rightly belong to the fifth discourse which would then be taken as including Matt. 23:1—26:1 and be regarded as a discourse on the judgment.

9. Cf. John L. McKenzie, "The Gospel According to Matthew," in Raymond E. Brown, Joseph A. Fitzmyer, and Roland E. Murphy, eds., *The Jerome Biblical Commentary* (Englewood Cliffs: Prentice-Hall, 1968), 66. McKenzie calls the five discourses, "The Sermon on the Mount," "The Missionary Sermon," "The Parables of the Reign," "The Sermon on the Church," and "The Eschatological Sermon."

Prologue: Genealogy and Infancy Narrative—1:1—2:23
Book One: Opening Proclamation of the Kingdom
    Narrative—3:1—4:25 (beginning of ministry)
    Discourse—5:1—7:29 (Sermon on the Mount)
Book Two: Ministry in Galilee
    Narrative—8:1—9:34 (ten miracles)
    Discourse—9:35—11:1 (instructions to the Twelve for mission)
Book Three: Controversy and Parables
    Narrative—11:2—12:50 (incredulity and hostility)
    Discourse—13:1-53 (a collection of parables)
Book Four: Formation of the Disciples
    Narrative—13:54—17:27 (stories before the journey to Jerusalem)
    Discourse—18:1—19:2 (instructions for the assemblies)
Book Five: Up to Jerusalem
    Narrative—19:3—23:39 (stories on the journey and at Jerusalem)
    Discourse—24:1—26:1 (instructions concerning the last things)
The Passion—26:2—27:66
The Resurrection—28:1-20

If "According to Mark" made the burden of the book clear by the central turn in its ring construction, then "According to Matthew" accomplished the same purpose by the structure of these five discourses. The author of Matthew had a great interest in accentuating the teaching of Jesus and calling people to obedience to that teaching. The entire book is summed up in the final words of the risen one who calls upon the disciples to make disciples everywhere, baptizing them and "teaching them to obey everything that I have commanded you" (28:19-20). That "everything" is gathered together, in Matthew, especially in the discourses.

What is more, in regard to our question, these discourses are not so much historical reports of "what Jesus said" as they are addresses to the churches—to the assemblies—in the time of the Gospel book itself. The risen one is still with these assemblies (28:20; 18:20), where they are baptizing and teaching and even where only a few are gathered. A quorum—or a *minyan*, to use the term from the synagogue—for holding these assemblies is as little as two or three. There are, after all, relatively few Christians. Then, each of the discourses has some reference to those assemblies within it. The *Sermon on the Mount*, for example, is interested in how they are being persecuted (5:11-12), as also in their existence as salt and light for the world (5:13-16),[10] in their teachers (5:19; 7:15-20), in their practice of almsgiving, prayer, and fasting (6:1-18), in their not judging (7:1-5), and in their discipline and their difference from ordinary religion (5:20; 7:6, 21-23). It makes a text of the Lord's Prayer available for their common practice, a practice in the house, in the assembly, not alone, and not on display in public.[11] And when it calls for "the house" to be built on the "rock" of Jesus' teaching (7:24-27), it probably is imagining the very house of the church. Jesus was a teacher, in Matthew's perception, and also here Jesus-then has become and is constantly becoming Jesus-now.

All of these sayings are more appropriate to the late first century than they are to the time of the preaching of the historical Jesus. Even though many of them may have roots in the earliest memories of what Jesus actually said, placed in their current form in the history of Jesus, the sayings are anachronisms. Persecution of Jesus' followers, for example (cf. 5:11-12), took place later in the first century, not during the time of the ministry of the historical Jesus. But placed in the midst of the assemblies of the late first century, these sayings represent Jesus-then becoming Jesus-now. For Matthew, the crucified risen one is present in the churches, teaching. While narratively located in the time of Jesus-then, the discourses are nonetheless words into the present of the current gatherings of Christians.

Similar examples of address to the assemblies can be found in all the other four major discourses of the book. While the *address to the Twelve* (9:35—11:1) and their restriction to the "towns of Israel" presents itself as material from the history of Jesus, in Matthew it represents the author's interest in the responsibility of the current leadership of the church and Matthew's interest in a Christianity that is first of all for the Jews, and only then for the nations. In any case, we hear of "houses" that are to receive the missionary preachers (10:12), and we hear of Jesus himself as "master of the house" and his followers as "those of the household" (10:25). The theme sounds like a continuation of the Markan image of the church. The characterization of preaching as the open declaration of the

---

10. The "you" here is plural.

11. The singular "you" of 6:6, which contrasts with the plural of 6:5, is drawn in a direct quote from the Septuagint of Isa. 26:20, a passage that is nonetheless addressed to "my people" as a singular, collective noun. Matthew's Jesus is speaking about prayer in the house of the church, for which "your room" is a metaphor drawn from the scriptures.

secret (10:26-27) seems similarly Markan. On the other hand, for Mark, whoever receives (δέχεται) a little, powerless one, receives Jesus and so God (Mark 9:37). Here, whoever receives the missionary preacher—perhaps with those preachers even regarded as continuing to carry the authority of the Twelve—receives (δέχεται) Jesus (Matt. 10:40). The difference is striking. In any case, these themes belong to the time of the late-first-century assemblies, as do the words about persecution and familial division (10:16-25, 28-39). Over the shoulders of the Twelve, the assemblies are being addressed.

The *collection of parables*, the third discourse, continues the Markan themes of the revealed secret (Matt. 13:10-17) and of explanation in the house (13:34-36) as images for preaching in the current assemblies. But Matthew adds several parables to the Markan collection (Mark 4:1-34), two of which may have to do with the book's conception of the church. The wheat-and-tares parable and its explanation (13:24-30, 36-43) urge setting aside the community's judgment of who is righteous or not and waiting for the judgment of God. In a book so fiercely interested in increasing the righteousness of the followers of Jesus (cf. 5:20), this is a wise and needed counsel, almost surprising to find in Matthew. And the parable of the woman hiding leaven in three measures of flour (13:33) is similarly critical of too strict an observance.[12] Three measures of flour is a huge amount, an *ephah* in fact, about a bushel, the amount to be baked by priests, unleavened, as an offering in Ezekiel's new Temple (Ezek. 46:5-11, 20). It is the amount that was baked unleavened for God by Abraham at Mamre and by Gideon at Ophrah. In the assemblies, the old strictures about priesthood and leaven and male leadership need to be put aside. The assembly around the gospel of the kingdom is radically different; its meals with God use ordinary, daily bread. Its leaders include women. The kingdom of God, as Jesus preaches it here, reverses much religious expectation: it is like leavened holy bread, baked by a woman. Given these two parables, Matthew's words for the assembly may be more complex and nuanced than we might have thought if we had only read the Sermon on the Mount.

The fourth discourse *addresses the assemblies* directly. Indeed, in this discourse (18:17) the word *assembly* (ἐκκλησία—the word most commonly translated as "church") is used twice. It is, in fact, a word that occurs only in this

---

12. For what follows, see my *Holy Things: A Liturgical Theology* (Minneapolis: Fortress Press, 1993), 24–27.

Gospel among the four.[13] Here, as in Mark 9:36, a child is placed in the middle of the assembly and the word about welcoming little ones and so welcoming Jesus is repeated (though nothing is said about God; Matt. 18:2-5). Here the Markan counsel against the assembly's fear of persecution is repeated (18:8-9). Here the Christian assembly language of "brother" and "sister" is used,[14] while words about the discipline of direct conversation (18:15-18), about the church's authority to bind and loose (18:18-20), and about mutual forgiveness (18:21-22) are spoken. Two parables are added to this collection of sayings (18:12-14, 23-35), and both of them urge mercy in the community and the high valuing of the sinner. Again, Matthew's rigorous calls to obedience are nuanced. Obedience here involves, rather, a rigorous attention to mercy and forgiveness. Perhaps most important, this discourse includes an actual image of the assembly: those two or three gathered together in the name of Jesus, among whom the crucified risen one is always present (18:20).

Even the fifth discourse, *the eschatological sermon*, has been turned at several points into direct address to the assemblies and their teachers. Not only are there again words, developed from Mark, about the persecution of the community and the reality of false teachers (24:4-26), but there is also a direct charge to the leaders of the community to serve as responsible stewards in the house (24:45-51), faithfully distributing food and avoiding practices that dominate and abuse the others. The presupposition of this text, a presupposition that we have seen is shared by current scholarly estimations,[15] is that early Christian gatherings were house-based meal associations. The image of the assembly leader as a servant and a steward in the house meeting, an image so important to both Paul and Mark, has then been developed here, directly evoking the church's meals and the dangers of an imperious leadership. But not only the leaders are addressed. The parable of the last judgment (25:31-46) images another way that the crucified and risen one continues to be present to all those who call on him as Lord: in the suffering other. Here those Markan words about one who receives a little one actually receiving Christ or one who gives a cup of cold water not losing the reward (Mark 9:37, 41) are given a striking and unforgettable narrative shape.[16]

---

13. Two out of its three occurrences are here. The other place is Matt. 16:18.

14. The NRSV translates "brother" here as "member of the church."

15. See above, chap. 2.

16. In Matt. 25:35 and 43, the "stranger" in whom Jesus is to be received is to be "welcomed." The verb is a form of συνάγω, "to gather," as into a house or an assembly.

Of course, there are other places in the Gospel according to Matthew that make a clear address to the churches.[17] But these five discourses play such an important role in the book that they serve especially to help us see a reforming Gospel also in Matthew. We can find yet further evidence. The materials out of which the burden-carrying, central turn in Mark was constructed all return in Matthew in these five discourses.[18] We can argue that the discourses were for Matthew what Mark 9:30-50 was for the First Gospel. So, in Matthew, the second passion prediction (17:22-23)[19] comes shortly before the discourse of chapter 18, the instructions for the church. But it comes without paired disciple-ship sayings, as are found in each of the other passion predictions. Instead, the discourse of chapter 18 takes the place of the Markan sayings and actions in the house (Mark 9:33-50) that were paired with the second passion prediction in that First Gospel.

Then all of the other discourses also join in that replacement. One can trace most of the contents of Mark 9:33-50 as they appear in the five discourses. The house (Mark 9:33) occurs in the Sermon on the Mount (Matt. 7:24-27), in the mission instructions (10:12, 13, 14), in the collection of parables (13:36), and in the eschatological discourse (24:45). The question about the greatest (Mark 9:34), now made into a direct question to Jesus, begins the instruction to the assemblies (Matt. 18:1), but it also appears in another, more Matthean form in the Sermon on the Mount (5:19). The word about the leaders of the assembly as servants in the house (Mark 9:33-35) has been developed into the warning to be stewards of the food for the assembly in the eschatological discourse (Matt. 24:45-51), recalling that the Markan word for "servant" here is διάκονος, "table server." The child is set in the midst of the assembly and the word about wel-coming (Mark 9:36-37) is repeated in the instructions to the assemblies (Matt. 18:2-7) and echoed in another way in the mission instructions (10:40). The Markan warning about competition (Mark 9:38-40), however, is omitted from any of the discourses, perhaps because the author of Matthew thought such admonishments to other Christians were often justified. The Markan cup of

17. The Matthean versions of the first and third passion predictions and their associated discipleship sayings (16:13-28; 20:17-28), for example, or the remarkable speech of Jesus as if he were Wisdom personified, "Come to me, all you that are weary" (11:28-30).

18. Indeed, the presence of this central material of Mark in the five discourses of Mat-thew helps us to see that the author of Matthew understood its centrality in Mark.

19. Cf. Mark 9:30-32.

water (Mark 9:41) appears in the missionary instructions (Matt. 10:42). Indeed, that cup of water and the welcome to Christ in the little one both stand behind the Matthean parable of the last judgment in the eschatological sermon (25:31-46). The warning against setting up a stumbling block (Mark 9:42) occurs in the instructions to the assemblies (Matt. 18:6-7). The word about boldness in the face of torture (Mark 9:43-48) is found in both the Sermon on the Mount (Matt. 5:29-30) and in the instructions to the assemblies (18:8-9), though in the former it has been changed by its context to become a warning against sexual lust. The fire of Gehenna, in Mark found only in this central passage addressed to the assemblies (Mark 9:43, 48, 49), recurs repeatedly in Matthew, in all five of the discourses (Matt. 5:22, 29, 30; 7:19; 10:28; 13:40, 42; 18:8, 9; 25:41), and only there.[20] And the community as salt (Mark 9:49-50) shows up in the Sermon on the Mount (Matt. 5:13). Matthew's five discourses can be seen to be direct descendants of the central passage in Mark. In fact, tracing what happens to the Markan materials here can give us some sense of the ways in which the gospel tradition continued to develop as the narratives about Jesus grew.

In any case, the author of Matthew was clearly concerned about what was occurring in the Christian assemblies of his time, wanting for them to be different from other associations and meal groups in the surrounding culture. This concern for reform was then set out in the Gospel book by a heightened accent on the teaching of Jesus in the midst of an expanded narrative account. It seems that the book itself responded to the ancient Christian need for more material about Jesus. But, in the midst of that added material, one can see something of the author's conception of the failings of the churches and their leaders by attending to the matters that occupy the five discourses. This author understood the centrality of Mark 9 and its appeal for reform but transferred that centrality to the discourses with their fierce calls for a rigorous obedience. Still, one needs to be careful here. Again and again, rigorous passages in Matthew are followed by passages of great mercy and forgiveness for sinners. The wrath of God is taken quite seriously in Matthew, and punishment is presented in images of hyperbole. But if the fire is to come, it is not to be administered by the members of the church themselves, nor by their leaders. The wheat and the tares are to be left for the Son of Man and his angels to separate, and self-righteousness is considerably worse than forgiven sin.

---

20. With the exception of the mention of "hell" (*Gehenna* in the Greek)—but not fire—in the woes to the scribes and Pharisees (23:15, 33).

Matthew on Worship

We might say the matter in another way. Looking at these discourses as addresses to the assemblies, we can catch some glimpses of what those assemblies known by the author of Matthew were actually doing when they met. They were, of course, gathering, as is clear, for example, from the exhortation about who should be welcomed (18:5) or from the images of the welcoming and nonwelcoming houses (10:11-14). They were primarily gathering for a shared meal, as is imaged in the urging that those who serve these meetings in the house should fairly distribute the food (24:45). At these meal gatherings, they were listening to preachers and teachers, as is clear in the Sermon on the Mount (5:19), perhaps preachers who arrived as travelers, as the mission instructions indicate (10:7, 12-14). That these preachers also had responsibility for healing is similarly indicated in these instructions (10:8). Then, the assemblies were praying, as the assumption of the Sermon on the Mount demonstrates ("and whenever you pray," 6:5). They may have been bringing alms for the poor and perhaps even something like the old temple taxes, as the counsel about how to do almsgiving and about "offering your gift" might indicate (6:2-4; 5:23-24).[21] And they were most likely baptizing, as we can guess from the final instructions of the book (28:19). For us, this is a remarkably contemporary list: assembly, preaching and teaching, prayer, healing, common meal, collection for the poor and for communal support, and baptism as the way to be part of the assembly that does these things.

---

21. Of course, the "altar" of Matt. 5:23-24 must be metaphorical. After the destruction of the Temple, this passage, which might indeed contain the remembrance of an historical utterance of Jesus about temple worship, would not be heard as counsel for behavior in Jerusalem but as counsel for people attending the assemblies of Christians. It is fascinating to note that the fourth discourse, the instructions to the assemblies (18:1—19:1), is immediately preceded by the story about the temple tax (17:24-27). It is possible that there was a debate in some assemblies known to Matthew about whether the temple tax was still to be paid. Perhaps the reference is to the *fiscus Iudaeus,* the Roman tax collected from Jews, after the destruction of the Temple, as reparation for the Jewish war. See L. Michael White, *From Jesus to Christianity: How Four Centuries of Visionaries and Storytellers Created the New Testament and Christian Faith* (San Francisco: HarperSanFrancisco, 2004), 246–47. The house meetings (cf. τὴν οἰκίαν, 17:25) could have been a place of its collection in Jewish-identified Christian circles. The coin that is mentioned here, after all, is a Greek coin, in circulation in the Hellenistic cities. Then Matthew's instruction about freedom in this matter would be part of all of the instructions to the assemblies that follow upon the second passion prediction (17:22-23).

Perhaps these things were especially practiced in assemblies of Jewish Christians, and perhaps Matthew was addressed primarily to such assemblies. Or, perhaps the book really was intended to be read everywhere among the Christians, even and especially with its interest in asserting a vigorous and Christian reinterpretation of Torah. Then the author would be assuming that gathering and meal keeping, preaching and praying and baptizing were found everywhere in Christian communities.

The purpose of the book becomes clear as these practices are addressed with counsel for reform. Here is something of what I think the book may have been saying:

Let the gatherings in the houses listen clearly to the teaching of Jesus, represented by this Gospel and expressed centrally in its discourses. Thus, let the house be shaped by this word. Let it be built upon the rock (7:24-27). And, as it listens to the heart of that teaching and to the story of the suffering of this teacher, let the members of the assembly welcome the excluded and little ones (18:5-7, 10), indeed all those who are strangers (25:35). Let them work on the permeable boundaries of this meeting. Let them not be surprised by the collection of sinners or the straying lost sheep who may come (13:47; 18:12-14). Let them understand that the kingdom of God is like leavened holy bread, made by a woman (13:33), not pure, unleavened temple bread, baked by male priests. Furthermore, let the assembly eschew third-party gossip. Rather, let them engage in direct speech with each other and in reconciliation and mutual forgiveness in their gatherings (5:24; 6:12; 18:15-20). Indeed, according to the word of Jesus, forgiveness given here is forgiveness from God.

Of course, they will keep a meal. Like all the associations around them, that is why they gather. But, let them remember that life is more than food and drink (6:25). Let them hunger and thirst for righteousness (5:6) and for the kingdom of God (6:31-33). Let them share their food with the hungry (25:35). Still, let them know in confidence that God gives them today the bread of the kingdom (6:11), the "foretaste of the feast to come,"[22] as their meal becomes a place to proclaim the gift and presence of the crucified and risen one (cf. 26:26-29). The meetings of the assembly are already the day when Jesus is drinking with them the new cup in the kingdom. That drinking carries within it the very forgiveness

---

22. This phrase probably accurately translates the original intention of τὸν ἄρτον τὸν ἐπιούσιον in the Lord's Prayer. See my *Holy People: A Liturgical Ecclesiology* (Minneapolis: Fortress Press, 1999), 33–34, 76–78.

of the multitude, of "the many" (26:28), of all the needy world. Indeed, the meal of the community is to be the way in which the assembly is inserted again and again into the meaning of the passion story with which the Gospel concludes. Furthermore, let those who preside in this assembly meeting, in this "household," do so as stewards and servants of the community, carefully and justly distributing the food to all. Let them avoid imperious and judgmental behavior, and let them avoid making the meal a place for their own importance and their own drunken excess (24:45-51).[23]

Let the preachers and teachers in the assembly proclaim the gospel (10:7), bring out old and new from the scriptures (13:52), tell openly the secrets of the kingdom (10:27; 13:11), keep and teach the commandments (5:19), and yet, paradoxically, not be called "my teacher" or "father" or "instructor" (cf. 23:8-10), there being one teacher, the crucified risen one still present in the assembly. In short, let their teaching be "this gospel of the kingdom" (24:14), a phrase that may be the very title of this Gospel book itself. If we join the content of the Matthean discourses to the passion and resurrection story of Jesus, we will be seeing a summary of what the author of this book thought should be preached in the assemblies.[24]

As for prayer, let the assemblies pray earnestly and confidently for the coming of God's day and God's justice for all the earth (5:9-10). But let them do it humbly, not ostentatiously, in the house of the meeting (5:6), as if they are enacting there the counsel of Isaiah 26:20, waiting for God's wrath to pass in these last times (5:13). Even more, let them know with assurance that God is even now answering their prayer for the bread and mutual forgiveness of the end times and doing so in the assembly itself. In Matthew, especially the petition for forgiveness in the Lord's Prayer is accented in the gloss that Matthew adds to the prayer. The members of the assembly are invited to live with each other as they pray (6:14-15; cf. 18:15-22).

In almsgiving, let the members of the assembly not look for public praise (6:2-4). But let them reflect that the very judge of all the earth identifies himself

---

23. This counsel sounds a great deal like Paul in 1 Cor. 11:11-22.

24. It is true that the passion story in Matthew has become less integrated with the material that precedes it than is the case with Mark. Matthew has actually become that "passion story with the long preface" that Martin Kähler discussed. Nonetheless, the clear accent on the presence of the risen one in the church states definitely what is so strongly implied by the structure and poetic method of Mark.

with the hidden recipients of the food, drink, money, clothing, hospitality, and care that they give away (25:31-46). Indeed, for Christians, this "Son of Man," this Human Being as a heavenly figure, is none other than the crucified Jesus Christ seen by faith as having become the arbiter of all that is good.

In baptizing, let the assemblies teach those coming to join the assemblies all the contents of this Gospel book. The discourses themselves may be seen as catechesis, as that "everything that I have commanded you" (28:20) which should go paired with baptism.

And, in all of this, let the assemblies know that the crucified and risen one is always with them, present in their midst (28:20; 18:20).

But there is a problem here. Such a list of proposals to local assemblies might often have been read as the beginning of a Christian legalism. Especially if the sayings of the discourses were taken on their own, without the context of the passion account, without the promise of presence of the risen one, and without the repeated urging of forgiveness and mercy, they could be read as simply harsh injunctions. In that sense, they would have been a good deal like the injunctions of the letter of James.

The letter of James provides an apt comparison. Very likely also arising, like Matthew, from one version of Jewish Christianity (see James 1:1) and very likely also written in the late first century, this letter is similarly interested in the behavior of the assemblies.[25] Like the Matthean discourses when taken on their own, it, too, is made up of loosely connected sayings or aphorisms, directing the behavior of the hearers. Indeed, many of those directions in James sound a good deal like Matthew:

Take persecutions as a joy (1:2; cf. Matt. 5:10-12).

Be perfect (1:4; cf. Matt. 5:48).

Ask in faith, not doubting (1:6; 4:3; cf. Matt. 7:7 and 21:21).

Do not be angry (1:19; cf. Matt. 5:22).

Do the word; do not simply hear it (1:22, 25; cf. Matt. 7:21-26).

Note that the poor are rich in faith (2:5; cf. Matt. 5:3).

Do not turn away the wretched poor with nothing (2:15; cf. Matt. 25:35).

Understand that the tongue works iniquity, staining the whole body (3:6; cf. Matt. 12:36f; 15:11, 18f.).

---

25. See especially James 2:1-7 and 5:13-16. The assembly is called here both συναγωγή (2:2) and ἐκκλησία (5:14).

Know that a fig tree does not bring forth olives (3:12; cf. Matt. 7:16ff.; 12:33).

Be peacemakers (3:18; cf. Matt. 5:9).

Do not judge (4:11-12; cf. Matt. 7:1-5).

Understand that riches rot (5:2; cf. Matt. 6:19).

See that the true judge is at the door, about to come (5:9; cf. Matt. 24:33).

Know that the prophets, too, were persecuted (5:10; cf. Matt. 5:12).

And do not swear, but rather say simply yes and no (5:12; cf. Matt. 5:34-37).

This is a stunning list of similarities. For all that such admonishments may have been needed in some assemblies, however, there is nothing particularly Christian about the list. It is not wrong to see, with some ancient and Reformation-era estimations of James,[26] that such a list of scriptural sounding exhortations could lead simply to harsh mutual judgment in an assembly, in spite of the warning to avoid judgment. One such judgment is in the book itself: "Come now, you rich people, weep and wail for the miseries that are coming upon you" (5:1).

James was probably saved for Christian use by its pseudonymous character, its presenting itself as a letter from the brother of Jesus. One might hope that it was also saved by its images of the open hospitality of the assembly, its calls for healing in the community, and its attempts to correlate these things to the name of Jesus Christ (e.g., 2:1). Still, for the actual content in that name—as also for content of the "word" of which the letter speaks, as well as for anything at all about forgiveness—one would have had to look elsewhere. Indeed, for a far deeper correlation of the crucified and risen Jesus Christ with care for the wretched and the poor, one might have looked at the parable of the last judgment in Matthew (25:31-46).

While Matthew shares some of the moral intensity of the letter of James, many of its concrete exhortations, and many of its dangers, it does place those exhortations in a clearer Christian context. Thus, while the basic Matthean proposals to the assemblies are quite differently expressed and considerably less paradoxical than what we have found in Mark, they do not have to be seen as substantially differing in content. The Matthean counsel to the assemblies, especially that central word about the presence of the risen crucified one and the implications that follow from that presence, can be read as carrying on and developing the counsel of the Gospel according to Mark, at least if one holds

26. Werner G. Kümmel, *Introduction to the New Testament* (Nashville: Abingdon, 1966), 285.

together Matthew's fierce admonitions with its equally fierce and sometimes contradictory defenses of mercy to the sinner and help for the poor. The author of Matthew may intend to urge the assemblies to keep Torah (5:17-20). He also urges them to know that the God of the Torah, encountered in Jesus Christ, in his death, resurrection, and teaching, is the God of forgiveness (6:14-15).

Luke: Meals on the Journey and the Assemblies

But what about Luke? How does Luke envision the assemblies? We have already seen that the Lukan interest in meals can be interpreted as addressed to meal-keeping communities of Christians in the late first century, with an interest in deepening the experienced meaning of those meals.[27] But it is important to look yet further at the extensive importance these meals have to the structure of Luke. Such a survey may help us to estimate more clearly the reforming purpose of this Gospel, the ways in which this Gospel was also addressed to its contemporary assemblies.

Begin with structure again. As with Matthew, the Markan outline is also followed here, with similar additions of an introductory birth narrative and concluding resurrection appearance accounts.[28] But in Luke, unlike Matthew, the significant addition of other narratives and of extensive accounts of Jesus' teaching is not found in insertions placed at intervals throughout the Markan outline. Rather, such additions are primarily found in a single central section, the so-called Lukan travel narrative. The outline of Luke thus looks like this:[29]

Introduction:
Prologue	1:1-4	
Infancy narrative	1:5—2:52	
Preparation for ministry	3:1—4:13	
Galilean ministry	4:14—9:50	
Travel narrative	9:51—19:28	
Passion narrative	19:29—23:56	
Resurrection narrative	24:1-53	

---

27. See above, chap. 2.

28. It may be that Luke's similarity to Matthew here belies Luke's *knowledge* of Matthew.

29. Cf. Joseph A. Fitzmyer, *The Gospel according to Luke (I–IX)* (Garden City: Doubleday, 1981), 134.

Perhaps the most unique characteristic of the third Gospel then is to be found in that "travel narrative." While Luke otherwise carefully follows the order of the Gospel according to Mark, with only three major exceptions between the infancy narrative and the resurrection accounts,[30] the book significantly interrupts that flow after Mark 9:40. At that point Luke introduces a long account of Jesus' journey to Jerusalem, stretching from Luke 9:51 to 19:28, from Jesus setting "his face to go to Jerusalem" (9:51) to his reception by Zacchaeus at Jericho (19:1-10) and his speaking of the parable of the pounds (19:11-27) "because he was near Jerusalem" (19:11). The passage ends just before the Lukan account of the entrance into the city (19:29ff.) or, rather, the long journey of Jesus connects to that entry. Toward the conclusion of this material, Luke resumes drawing from the Markan outline, with Mark 10:13-52 (welcoming the children; the question about inheriting eternal life; the hundredfold family and houses; the third passion prediction; and the healing of Bartimaeus) standing behind and altered in Luke 18:15-42. But, for the most part, this long passage at the center of Luke's Gospel consists of stories and other material that are quite unique to Luke or, especially, of sayings shared with Matthew—thus, either "Q" material or material actually taken from Matthew and reused and rearranged at this place by the author of Luke. Here are most of the Lukan sermons. Here, indeed, are also many of the characteristic Lukan narratives: the good Samaritan; Mary and Martha; the Lukan Lord's Prayer; the lost sheep and lost coin; the prodigal son; the rich man and Lazarus; the Pharisee and the publican; and Zacchaeus.

Many scholars have read this travel narrative as simply a catch-all construct for Luke to collect together a disparate body of material that is otherwise unconnected. More recently, however, a strong case has been made for the unity of the section around the theme of the "Lord" (as Jesus is repeatedly called here) traveling and being both received and refused.[31] Woven through all of this material are continued references to Jesus journeying (9:52-53, 56-57; 10:1, 38; 13:22, 33; 14:25; 17:11; 18:31, 35; 19:1, 11). Indeed, both traveling and hospitality given or refused to the traveler also appear as themes present in many of the narratives and parables

---

30. Mark 6:1-6, the rejection in Jesus' hometown, is moved to the beginning of Jesus' ministry in Luke 4:14-30; Mark 6:45–8:26, sometimes called the "great omission," is skipped at Luke 9:17; and Mark 9:41—10:12, sometimes called the "little omission," is skipped at Luke 9:50.

31. See, especially, David Moessner, *Lord of the Banquet: The Literary and Theological Significance of the Lukan Travel Narrative* (Minneapolis: Fortress Press, 1989).

here. Emissaries are sent ahead of Jesus' own journey (9:52; 10:1). Individuals, groups, and crowds travel with Jesus (9:57; 14:25; 18:28, 31). Parables are told of travelers (10:29-37; 11:5-8; 12:35-38, 42-48; 15:11-32; 19:12-27). Travel and accommodation to the traveler are matters woven throughout the whole section.

The fact that this unique passage is inserted at the very place we have identified as the center of Mark's Gospel underlines its importance to Luke. Of course, this Markan center provides the place in the Markan narrative where Jesus leaves Galilee and begins to go toward Jerusalem, and Luke can be understood as simply expanding that theme. But it may also be that the author of Luke could read Mark's intention of weighted centrality here and chose to place this new book's interpretive center at the same place. In any case, in the great outline of the two-volume work Luke-Acts, the story moves up to Jerusalem for its climax and then away from Jerusalem in mission to all the earth (cf. Luke 24:47; Acts 1:8). This Jerusalem-bound journey of Jesus thus matters to Luke's purpose and strongly helps to establish that Lukan geographical schema.

But the reason for the central importance of the travel narrative in Luke may not only be that it corresponds to this intentional geographical schema. It may also intend to interpret "travel" theologically. It appears that the ἔξοδος that Moses and Elijah discuss with Jesus at the Lukan transfiguration—"his departure," indeed, in a term unique to Luke's account of the story, his *exodus* (9:31)—gives special weight and direction to the narrative. For Luke, this long account of Jesus' journey to the city and to his death and resurrection already enacts this exodus, this journey like the journey of Moses and the people to the new land.[32] The transfiguration account, positioned close to the beginning of the travel narrative, provides one of its major themes. And, if this is so, then for Luke the risen Lord is still the journeying one, still gathering people into the kingdom, still being refused and opposed, but also still the one coming to be received by the current assemblies of Christians—like the stranger in the Emmaus account (24:15-16) and like the traveling preachers. These travelers are imaged twice in Luke, as the Twelve and as the Seventy (9:6; 10:1ff.), traveling preachers who are to be listened to as to the Lord himself (10:16). Welcome to the crucified

---

32. Moessner argues, indeed, that Jesus is presented by Luke as the "prophet like Moses" promised in Deut. 18:15 and his journey is thus a new exodus, with extensive parallels to the book of Deuteronomy (ibid., 45–71, and passim). On the parallels between the travel section and Deuteronomy, see already Farrer, "On Dispensing with Q," 75–77, and C. F. Evans, "The Central Section of St. Luke's Gospel," in D. E. Nineham, ed., *Studies in the Gospels*, 37–53.

and risen Lord and welcome to those who journey in his name would then be a way that this Gospel images the healthy Christian assembly. Just as in Mark and Matthew, the image of the houses welcoming traveling preachers and healers is an image that belongs to the late first century, to the time of the evangelists more than to the time of the historical Jesus. More: as the travel narrative shows the community of followers moving with Jesus, the author of Luke may be indicating his sense that the assemblies themselves are metaphorically on the exodus way. In the culture that surrounds them, they are sojourners. They are journeying with God's new prophet into the new age.

Such a unifying theme inevitably turns one's attention to *meals*, as the preeminent sign of joyful welcome or as the thing refused by inhospitable refusal. In fact, it is not only the transfiguration and its discussion of the *exodus* of Jesus that sets a theme for the travel narrative. It is also the account of the feeding of the five thousand (9:11-17). In the Lukan reordering of Markan material, the so-called great omission (Mark 6:45—8:26)[33] makes it so that the feeding of the multitude is drawn much closer to the travel narrative. In Luke, the feeding miracle is followed directly by the confession of Peter and the first passion prediction, the transfiguration, the healing of the epileptic boy, the second passion prediction (with its attendant sayings to the assembly), and so the beginning of the travel narrative. Luke has then added to the Markan and Matthean versions of this story an indication of Jesus' own hospitality: "the crowds . . . followed him; and he welcomed them" ($\dot{\alpha}\pi o\delta\epsilon\xi\acute{\alpha}\mu\epsilon\nu o\varsigma$ $\alpha\dot{\nu}\tauo\grave{\nu}\varsigma$, 9:11). Such hospitality ordinarily indicates a welcome to shared food, and that food here miraculously follows. Food is given in the wilderness (9:12), like manna and quail in the exodus. If the "exodus" of the transfiguration leads us to the meaning of Jesus' journey, then the hospitable wilderness meal that Jesus provides just before that journey also signals to us that we should attend to the meals that will occur in the narrative of the journey that follows.[34]

And the travel narrative is full of meals. Messengers are sent to a Samaritan village "to make ready for him"—thus, to arrange for him to be welcomed to eat

---

33. See above, n.30.

34. We should also attend to the many occurrences of verbs with the -δεκ- root, used here for welcome to table. The repeated use in Luke of words for welcome may very well come from the intention to make "benefaction" a theme (see below). But it may also arise from the centrality of the "welcome of the child" image in the central text of the Markan circle composition. It is fascinating that Simeon "takes" or "welcomes" ($\dot{\epsilon}\delta\acute{\epsilon}\xi\alpha\tauo$) the child Jesus into his arms, at the outset of the Gospel, in 2:28.

(9:52)[35]—but the village refuses to welcome him (οὐκ ἐδέξαντο αὐτόν, 9:53). The Seventy are told to eat and drink whatever is provided them in the houses (10:7-8), thus setting aside the kosher rules around which much primitive Christian conflict took place. In the parable of the good Samaritan, the hurt traveler is brought to an inn, and the Samaritan tells the innkeeper to "take care of him" (10:35), a care that would have included meals. Martha welcomes Jesus to her house (ὑπεδέξατο αὐτόν, 10:38) and she undertakes to serve him (διακονεῖν, 10:39, 40), that is, she undertakes to set food before him. While Mary is indeed listening to the word of the Lord, Martha here plays the role of host and provider at table, a role that Luke-Acts elsewhere gives to the apostles and the "seven" (Acts 6:2-3). The Lukan Lord's Prayer prays for tomorrow's bread (Luke 11:3), as does the Matthean version, but Luke underlines this petition in the gloss that follows in this Gospel. The Matthean version is followed by words about mutual forgiveness (Matt. 6:14-15), but the Lukan prayer is followed by reflections on asking for bread (Luke 11:5-8) and other food (11:11-12) as paradigmatic of all prayer. Indeed, in the first such reflection, it is an arriving traveler who occasions the request for three loaves of bread. Jesus is twice the meal guest of a Pharisee (11:37; 14:1), and both events give occasion for meal teaching: against purity rules (11:30-37), about humility at table (14:7-11), and in favor of the invitation of outsiders (14:12-14). The first occasion then leads Jesus to warn against the "yeast of the Pharisees,"[36] which is here identified as "hypocrisy" (12:1). The second meal at the house of a Pharisee is followed by a dinner guest calling out, "Blessed is anyone who will eat bread in the kingdom of God" (14:15) and then by the Lukan version of the parable of the banquet, underscoring the call of Jesus to invite "the poor, the crippled, the blind, and the lame" (14:21). In between these two meals, Jesus teaches that life is more than food (12:22-23, 29), against those who store up wealth that they might "eat, drink, be merry" (12:19).

But then, astonishingly, in a passage that carries what may be the heart of the travel narrative, Jesus urges his followers to be like slaves waiting for their Lord to return from a wedding banquet. Here, however, the journeying Lord himself comes in to serve the slaves at table (12:35-38), reversing the patterns of service. Now the journeying Lord acts like the good Samaritan, only he cares for

---

35. Cf. 22:8-13 on "making ready" for the Passover meal.

36. The Markan warning against the yeast of Herod and the yeast of the Pharisees has been one of the passages otherwise left out of Luke in the "great omission." Luke is dealing with the theme of meals in another way.

an entire community and does so personally. This passage gathers up and reexpresses two "service" passages from Mark (Mark 9:35; 10:43-45) and anticipates both the serving Lord of the Lukan Last Supper (22:24-27) and the guest who becomes the host at Emmaus (24:29-30). It is at this important place (12:41-48) that Luke sets the instructions to the leaders of his followers that they should be faithful stewards, carefully and justly distributing "food at the proper time" (12:42) and avoiding abusive behavior and self-indulgent eating and drinking, instructions that Matthew included in the fifth discourse. Luke adds Peter here (12:41), as a symbol of these leaders, and indicates that the ones whom they lead are both men and women (12:45). Luke also seems to indicate that some leaders may not know the full weight of what the Lord wants to happen in the household, at the meetings (12:48), moderating in their case the dreadful punishment that is otherwise threatened. But then, this Gospel itself means to make those instructions to assembly leaders quite clear. It becomes evident that all of these instructions—the communal food, the serving Lord, and the serving leaders— belong to the time of the churches, the meal-keeping associations in the late first century, rather than to the time of the historical Jesus.

Among the parables with which the travel narrative then continues is the comparison of the kingdom of God to a woman leavening the holy bread (13:20- 21), a parable we have already met in Matthew. Furthermore, while some with whom the Lord ate and drank and in whose streets he taught as he journeyed will not enter the house because of its "narrow door" (13:24-27), nonetheless "people will come from east and west, from north and south" to eat in the kingdom of God (13:29). In the end, the great final feast of mercy will be for far more than the Israel of the time of the historical Jesus, for far wider a company than even the current meal participants in the churches, certainly for far greater a number than those religiously observant who scorn the outsiders and sinners who are to be welcomed there.

In the same vein, after the second meal in the house of a Pharisee, where Jesus goes to "eat bread" ($\phi\alpha\gamma\epsilon\hat{\iota}\nu$ ἄρτον, 14:1), and after the conjoined instructions on humility and on inviting the poor, Jesus is complained against: "This fellow welcomes [προσδέχεται] sinners and eats with them" (15:2). Here there then follow the unique Lukan images of the rejoicing of the neighbors and of the household of the man who found the lost sheep (15:6) and the woman who found the lost coin (15:9) and the father who received back the lost and journeying son (15:23-25). Most likely a shared meal is implied at the conclusion of the first two parables, just as it is concretely imaged in the story of the prodigal son. To the latter, there is added the image of the jealous older brother who is at the edge of refusing the feast. The welcome of the younger, deviant son has become a narrow door to him. Jesus then urges his disciples to learn from the dishonest steward who knows how to act corruptly so that he will be received (δέξωνται, 16:4, 9)—welcomed to table—by other corrupt people. As will become clear by the closely following parable of the rich man and Lazarus (the rich man "feasted sumptuously," 16:19, while Lazarus longed for what falls from the rich man's table, 16:21), the counsel is a counterimage: welcome the poor and the outsiders to your communal table so that, in God's great meal of mercy, they may be able to welcome you in return.

Then, in what seems like a warning appended to the promise of the Lord who will return and serve his own slaves (12:35-38), another image is set out: the slaves are expected to come in from the fields, serve the Lord his dinner, and say that it is only their duty (17:7-10). The surprising kindness of the Lord is not to be taken for granted. More warnings follow. In the days of Noah and the days of Lot, the people were "eating and drinking" and yet destruction arrived. So, one could eat and drink with the Lord, as in the meals of Jesus with the Pharisees, as in some meals that may be being held in the assemblies, and still miss the communal "duty" of hearing the word of the Lord and welcoming the least and the sinners. It seems that the meal which the whole travel narrative has been urging must always be a certain kind of meal: accompanied by the word of the Lord and open to the poor.

At last, as the travel narrative comes to a close, a final meal takes place. Jesus tells the sinful tax collector Zacchaeus that he must stay at his house, and Zacchaeus gladly welcomes him (ὑπεδέξατο αὐτὸν χαίρων, 19:6). The meal becomes a location both of the reformed beneficence of the tax collector and of continued complaints about the company that Jesus keeps. The meal signifies salvation arrived in the house.

This list of meals is striking. Especially of the Lukan travel narrative it may be said that Jesus seems to be always going to a meal, at a meal, or coming from a meal.[37] But the travel narrative may then be seen as evoking, in this regard, the introductory chapters of the Gospel, in which Mary sang of God filling the hungry with good things (1:53), Jesus resisted a misuse of bread (4:3), and Jesus' sermon at Nazareth provocatively pointed to the meal and the washing Elijah and

---

37. R. Alan Culpepper, "The Gospel of Luke," in *The New Interpreters Bible* 9 (Nashville: Abingdon, 1995), 26.

Elisha made available to Gentiles. Indeed, the Lukan account of the ministry in Galilee also carries central meal images: Luke makes use of the Markan accounts of the meal with sinners in Levi's house (5:29-32), of Jesus as the "bridegroom" in whose presence one must feast, not fast (5:33-35), and of Jesus' direction to give Jairus's daughter something to eat as sign of her coming from death to life (8:55). Then, one of the four Lukan beatitudes is "Blessed are you who are hungry now, for you will be filled" (6:21). Luke pulls the Markan account of the anointing woman out of the passion narrative and makes of it a meal story (7:36-50), a down payment on the two meals with Pharisees that will follow in the travel narrative. In this case, a woman called "a sinner" is forgiven. While she does not recline at table, is not welcome in that sense, Jesus does reorient the room by turning toward her (7:44). Finally, bridging to the travel narrative, Luke tells of the feeding of the five thousand, accentuating Jesus' "welcome" of the crowd (9:11).

All of these meals—in the travel narrative and in the first part of the Gospel—prepare us for the final meal accounts of the book: the Lukan version of the Last Supper (22:14-38) and the resurrection meal at Emmaus (24:28-33). In the Last Supper, besides the words at the gift of the first cup, of the bread, and of the final cup,[38] this Gospel uses the supper account to counter the argument about who is the greatest among the disciples, to call the leaders in the community to service at table, and to have Jesus say, "I am among you as one who serves" (22:24-27), material that in Mark followed the second and third passion predictions (Mark 9:34-35; 10:42-45). And this Gospel uses this place to have Jesus actually confer the kingdom of God on those who have followed him and are at table with him, "so that you may eat and drink at my table in my kingdom" (Luke 22:29-30), as if the promise of 13:29 were actually beginning to be fulfilled. Indeed, the realization of this very promise is then also extended by the crucified Jesus, as if he were indeed the reigning king, to the wretched and repentant criminal crucified beside him (23:43). The cross makes the feast of the kingdom open to wretched sinners and outsiders, just as the meals of the travel narrative have been repeatedly proclaiming. Then, in the Emmaus meal, the risen one, who has interpreted the scriptures to the travelers, stays with them—as he had stayed with Zacchaeus—becomes the presider and the server of the meal, and is known "in the breaking of the bread" (24:35). This meal seems to spill over into the eating of fish with the rest of the disciples, the "anything to

---

38. On the Lukan long text, see above, chap. 2, n.25.

eat" given to Jesus here like the food given to Jairus's daughter (24:41; 8:55) to celebrate life in the face of death. In spite of the "ascension" (24:51; Acts 1)—or, perhaps because of it—these final stories imply that the risen one continues to be present in the meetings of the churches.[39]

Perhaps the intention of the evangelist in using these multiple meal images, one after another, is to portray Jesus in a way that would be recognizable in Hellenistic culture. Jesus acts as benefactor, as the distributer of good things, as "lord" and patron of the house. Such patronage belonged to Hellenistic banquet ideology and marked the social organization of the first- and second-century Graeco-Roman world, with local officials and especially the emperor himself praised—as in the Priene inscription—as "benefactors." So Luke, in a phrase added to the Markan account (Mark 10:42), has Jesus say at the Last Supper, "The kings of the Gentiles lord it over them; and those in authority over them are called benefactors" (Luke 22:24). For Luke, Jesus is the great benefactor, the true and reliable benefactor, unlike pseudo-benefactors with which the cultural moment is filled.[40] He is so in his meals. He is so, finally, on the cross. Indeed, cross and meals go together: "I am among you as one who serves."

But it seems that even more is intended. The meals of the churches are themselves to continue to mirror the benefaction of Jesus. As Frederick Danker says, in Luke, "Israel's mission as Servant of the Lord and benefactor to the world finds fulfillment under the endowment of the Spirit through Jesus *and his followers.*"[41] The theme of Jesus as benefactor ought to continue in the meals of those followers. Or, as Alan Culpepper says, summarizing the theme of this Gospel,[42]

> After investigating everything carefully (1:3), Luke has found that he recognizes "the truth concerning the things about which you have been instructed" when memory of the actions and teachings of Jesus' ministry is enlightened by the Scriptures and reenacted in the hospitality and table fellowship of the community of believers.

---

39. Acts 1:1 can be translated to the effect that the first book, the Gospel, was about what "Jesus *began* to do and teach." That beginning, that ἀρχή, now continues in the life of the churches.

40. Frederick Danker, *Luke*, Proclamation Commentaries (Philadelphia: Fortress Press, 1987), v, 29–30. For pseudo-benefactors in Luke, see 4:5-7; 23:24; Acts 24:2-3, 27. For Luke, the Augustus of the Priene inscription should be considered a pseudo-benefactor.

41. Ibid., 7, italics added.

42. Culpepper, "The Gospel of Luke," 26–27.

Among other intentions, then, the meal stories of Luke can be read as urgent counsel to the assemblies.

Luke on Worship

How, then, does the Gospel according to Luke address those meal-keeping associations of its time that understood themselves as Christian? How does especially the travel narrative of the book envision what we would call the "worship" of those assemblies? We might say it like this. Several of the passages in Luke 9:51—19:28 can be considered counterimages, warnings against similar practice. So, for example, let the assemblies who read this book not be like the Samaritan village, refusing those emissaries who announce the presence of Jesus, nor like those meal events with the Pharisees where the accent is on purity or rank. Let them not mock or exclude those who are regarded as sinners or as unclean or as poor. Let them avoid this version of the "yeast of the Pharisees." Furthermore, let the meals of these associations not be about gluttony and drunkenness, as if food were enough for life and food *for me* the most important thing. Let them, like the people during Noah's time or like the people of Sodom or like the rich man who did not see Lazarus, not miss the signs of the time. Rather, like their Lord—like Jesus as the great benefactor—let then welcome sinners and eat with them.

But, then, many of the other stories of the travel narrative stand as direct models for Christian assembly life. Christians know that Jesus has himself been the good Samaritan: made an outsider and unclean in his death, he nonetheless is the one who lifts up the wounded and makes of his community an inn of refreshment for them. He still comes and serves that community. Let this word of his serving death be spoken and heard at the community's meals. Like Mary, let the community attend to this word as much as to the serving of food. Let them know the gift of God: in Jesus, crucified and risen, this bread already marks the beginning of the final feast of the kingdom, the bread of the morrow, the cup of the kingdom, the fish after death, with the nations already coming in to eat, paradise. So, let the community do its duty in serving their Lord by serving those he serves. Let salvation come to their houses, bringing with it forgiveness and a redirection of beneficence toward the wretched of the earth. Let the churches themselves act like the good Samaritan and like his inn. Let them pray for bread for the world. Let especially the leaders of these meal meetings distribute food justly and find their identity in serving, avoiding the abuse and misrule common among the pseudo-benefactors. Let the traveling preachers eat and drink the local food, abandoning the older Christian divisiveness of the controversy over clean foods, the kind of divisiveness we can see earlier in the first century in Galatians 2:11-14. Let their traveling take them into the streets and the lanes in order to bring surprising guests into the house. Let them not despair that even the older brother will find his way through the narrow door. Most of all, let them see that these meals carry the promise of the early part of the Gospel: God does fill the hungry with good things. God does provide bread for the outsider widow and washing for the Gentile leper. And let them see that their meals can carry the blessings of the final two meals of the book: the blessing of the serving crucified one—"I give you the kingdom"—and the presence of the scripture-interpreting, mission-establishing risen one. Blessed, indeed, is anyone who will eat bread in the kingdom of God.

I think that the Gospel according to Luke can be read as saying these things, in the late first century, to the Christian assemblies known by its author. But there is also a problem here. For all that this complex of ideas has a strikingly Christian center in its image of the serving Lord, it is also an overwhelmingly ideal set of proposals, with little irony or paradox or even realism to temper its earnestness. Many of its conceptions would be quite at home in the "banquet ideology" of the surrounding Hellenistic culture, similar to the ideals that many other meal-keeping associations in the cities would also themselves have espoused. Other associations would also have aspired to resisting an accent on rank, to avoiding gluttony, to a fair distribution of food, and to giving priority to stories about the gods or invocations of the gods to whom these associations were dedicated. Other associations would also have been devoted to the ideals of benefaction.[43]

It may very well be that the author of Luke intended to image a set of hopes that could be seen as understandable by the people of the cities and villages where Christian house assemblies found themselves in the very late first century. The author of Luke may also have worried about the Gospel according

---

43. Philip A. Harland, *Associations, Synagogues, and Congregations: Claiming a Place in Ancient Mediterranean Society* (Minneapolis: Fortress Press, 2003), 31, 181ff. On Greco-Roman religion, generally, as participation in the benefaction of the gods as mediated through benefactors, see Luke Timothy Johnson, *Among the Gentiles: Greco-Roman Religion and Christianity* (New Haven: Yale University Press, 2009), 50ff.

to Mark—and that according to Matthew, too, if he knew it—as most likely exacerbating the possibility of the persecution of Christian assemblies, and he may have intended with his latest "orderly account" to ameliorate this danger. Such intentions would cohere with other characteristics we can see in the Gospel as well. Jesus in Luke is portrayed in ways that would have been familiar: he is a patron and a benefactor, a holy man not unlike other Hellenistic holy men. His birth is peaceful and not conflicted.[44] His enemies are imaged as figures from the past—Pharisees and other Jews—not figures easily recognizable in the present culture, not really even the Roman authorities who, in this book, try to avoid hurting him. Here, his death is made gentler than it is imaged in Mark and Matthew, with the words spoken from the cross being words of confidence, forgiveness, mercy, benefaction even, as he gives to the dying criminal beside him, rather than words of dereliction. Furthermore, at a time when the full participation of women in social groups was sometimes possible but remained controversial,[45] the author of Luke suggests that it is possible for women to lead in the assemblies, like Martha (10:38), but it is better for them to be subservient and silent, listening like Mary (10:39), repenting like the anointing woman (7:37-38), and providing resources for the assemblies and the traveling leaders like the healed but wealthy women of Galilee (8:2-3). This attitude also would have been a conservative and recognizable stance in the Hellenistic culture of the late first century, intended to cause no offense.

This intent to avoid offense makes Luke quite similar to the first letter of Peter, probably a similarly late-first-century writing. In 1 Peter, a culturally recognizable "table of duties" appears (1 Pet. 2:18—3:12), among other things urging the submissiveness of women. Good behavior, recognizable as such, is counseled as the best defense against persecution (3:13-17). And the community is even urged to honor the emperor (2:17). Luke and 1 Peter might be regarded as texts that witness to the inculturation of the Christian community, the expected

---

44. In Matthew, the bloody search to kill Jesus and the flight into Egypt become both a foreshadowing of Jesus' suffering and death at the hands of the imperial authorities and a scriptural fulfillment: like Israel, Jesus comes out of Egypt. In Luke, this bloody opposition is gone. Imperial authorities are mentioned (3:1) and an implied contrast is set up, but there is no opposition to Jesus, except for that foretold by Simeon as he speaks of "the fall and the rising of many in Israel" (2:34-35).

45. See Kathleen E. Corley, *Private Women, Public Meals: Social Conflict in the Synoptic Tradition* (Peabody: Hendrickson, 1993), 6, 41, 141. See also idem, *Maranatha: Women's Funerary Rituals and Christian Origins* (Minneapolis: Fortress Press, 2010), 5–8.

use of cultural models and norms as Christianity spread and survived in the Mediterranean world. If, in the reform it urges for the assemblies, Mark sounds a note of resistance to imperial religion and imperial ideals, Luke makes use of Mark but tempers its image of empire-resisting assemblies.

Still, neither 1 Peter nor Luke become entirely acculturated. In both, we can see evidence of a complex process in which Christians, of course, continued forms they found around them—meal associations, for example—but also sorted, criticized, adopted, rejected, and adapted some of these forms and their mores.[46] In 1 Peter, in addition to counsel to avoid offense, we also find criticism of cultural practices, certainly of what the author regards as drunken carousing and idolatry, for example (4:3-5), both of which could characterize the meetings of meal associations. And the author does still expect persecution (3:14, 17-18; 4:1, 12-19), which he articulates as suffering like Jesus Christ, together with Christ. The imagery of being, in Christ, a people in "exile" (1:1), being a new temple and a new priesthood, built on the rejected cornerstone (2:4-8), provided ancient assemblies with a language with which to understand the Christian community's calling and its difference.

While the travel narrative's images for the assembly may echo with materials that would be recognizable and nonoffensive to other late-first-century Hellenistic supper clubs, Luke does push those materials to bear deeper Christian meanings. Not every such supper club would be an inn for the wounded or a place for forgiveness or a house for the redirection of beneficence. Not every such association would easily sing Mary's Magnificat with its reversal of values. And amid it all, there is that serving Lord—and this "benefactor," after all, is a crucified Roman criminal. Even Luke does not hide that fact. No wonder that his book, too, expects persecution (Luke 21:12-19).

Beginnings and Endings

Both Matthew and Luke can be read as addressed to paleo-Christian assemblies and as having reforming proposals for the worship—the structured meetings—of those assemblies. The authors of both books know of Mark's reforming ideas for these meetings: Matthew largely continues the Markan agenda, while presenting it more simply and with more direction; Luke slightly modifies it, concerned for the gracious or, at least, inoffensive presence of these meetings in

---

46. Harland, *Associations, Synagogues, and Congregations*, 198–99.

their current cities. Both books present more of the teaching of Jesus, as their authors had received it or as they have tried faithfully to construct it. But these are not simply reports of the teaching of "Jesus-then." For Matthew, this teacher is now present in the gatherings and his teaching is to be their foundation. For Luke, part of the teaching of Jesus deals directly with the meals of those supper clubs we call ancient "churches." Jesus' word and the word of his death and resurrection are to be heard at those tables.

The beginnings and endings of these Gospels reinforce our reading them as at least partly words to the assemblies, as coherent with the assemblies. The risen one, at the conclusion of Matthew, promises his presence in the midst of the baptizing churches in much the same terms as his promise to the small assembly in Matthew 18:20. Then, as the book concludes, there is no ascension, no parting. The risen Jesus stays with the church and its traveling emissaries. And, for Matthew, baptism itself—that Christian practice whereby people joined an assembly—is summed up at the end of the book (28:19-20) in terms that recall not only the teaching with which the discourses were full but also the baptism of Jesus with which, after the infancy narrative, the book began. People are to be baptized having been formed in the teaching of Jesus. People are to be baptized in the presence and power of God as God was revealed in the baptism of Jesus (3:16-17). The baptized are gathered into that same God: the crucified one in the water with us; the Spirit descending; the voice declaring Jesus to be the Son, the Beloved. Such presence and power are what the phrase "in the name of the Father and of the Son and of the Holy Spirit" means. The end of the Gospel intentionally makes both the baptism of its beginning and the teaching of its discourses available and central to the life of the assemblies around the continuing presence of the crucified risen one.

Like Matthew, Luke also begins with an infancy story, with John the Baptist, and with the baptism of Jesus. Interestingly, however, he weaves into the infancy story a small collection of hymns (Luke 1:46-55, 68-79; 2:29-32) that may have already been known and sung in some Christian assemblies. Then, by moving the account of Jesus' preaching in his hometown to the beginning of Jesus' ministry in Galilee (4:14-30), Luke creates an opening image of assembly—albeit a negative image, an image of an assembly that does not welcome Jesus in truth, like the later meals of the Pharisees—to balance the concluding assembly image of the book. Assembly frames the Lukan narrative. One can argue that the sermon of Jesus in Nazareth together with the sermon of the risen one on the way to Emmaus provided the ancient assemblies with a pattern of what the author of Luke thought belonged in current preaching.[47] The sermon at Nazareth includes scriptural references to what can be read as baptism and Eucharist: bread for the Gentile widow and a washing for the Gentile leper (4:25-27). And the Emmaus exposition of the scripture, the risen one interpreting his death in terms of the scripture, is finally burningly confirmed as the disciples' eyes are opened in the breaking of the bread (24:31-32). It seems that the meal at Emmaus was meant as a paradigm for the assemblies: the crucified and risen Christ was to be encountered in the scriptures interpreted in the meeting as also in the shared bread. Neither is to be neglected. Luke is interested in the meals of the churches. He is also interested in the presence of what he calls "the word" at those meals (10:39; 11:28; cf. 1:2). The beginning and the end of the book confirm that double interest.

Matthew and Luke are also still read in our meetings. It will be important for us, when we read these books, that we attend to several matters we have seen here. Matthew's fierce demands must not be turned into legalism or the grounds for self-righteousness, but always also balanced with his fierce calls for mercy. Luke's interest in inculturation must be seen as complex, as a matter of weighing what is needed to be present in current culture, while still maintaining the church as an inn for the wounded, as a place for the reversal of values. Luke, too, is not finally tame. And a reading from either book must be seen as carrying us readers toward the final narratives of the book, toward the death of the teacher and toward God acting to raise him up and make his presence in the Spirit the grounds of the churches.

But reading the ancient intention of these books, as we can glean that intention from the unique structures of both, will also raise questions to our assemblies. Here are a few: Do the charges that seem to be given to the ancient meetings by the discourses in Matthew and the travel narrative in Luke come also to us? Does our meeting balance judgment and mercy, inculturation and the reversal of values? Matthew accents the forgiveness petition of the Lord's Prayer, Luke the bread. Are bread and forgiveness central to our meetings? And, are our leaders stewards and servants? Is our meeting like that open, healing inn?

---

47. See my *The Pastor: A Spirituality* (Minneapolis: Fortress Press, 2006), 41–51.

5

John in Detail

Signs and Discourses on Sunday

In the very late first century C.E.—or, more likely, in the first decade or so of the
second century—the Gospel we call "According to John" was written. Perhaps,
as some scholars say also of the earlier Gospels, it was intended for a single
community, as *the* Gospel book for that community. The presumption of local
communal knowledge about someone called "the beloved disciple" as a guarantor
of tradition might speak for this intention.[1] On the other hand, the address to
those who have received "grace upon grace" through Jesus Christ (John 1:16) and
those "who have not seen and yet believed" (20:29) could also signal an intention
to be read by all the churches, as we have suggested may have been true for the
earlier three as well. We do not know.

The Fourth Book

What we do know, however, is that there is strong evidence that the author[2]
of John did know Mark and Luke and very possibly also Matthew. The book
certainly seems to presume that its readers/hearers already know the outline of
the story of Jesus and most of its central characters as those other books tell
that story.[3] In the Johannine account of the baptism of Jesus, for example, the

---

1. John 13:23; 19:26; 20:2; 21:7, 20; cf. 19:35 and 21:24. See especially Raymond E.
Brown, *The Community of the Beloved Disciple: The Life, Loves, and Hates of an Individual
Church in New Testament Times* (New York: Paulist, 1979).

2. Or, it might be, authors, a succession of writers who significantly shared the same
point of view. This discussion in Johannine studies need not concern us here.

3. See R. Alan Culpepper, *Anatomy of the Fourth Gospel: A Study in Literary Design*
(Philadelphia: Fortress Press, 1983), 224; L. Michael White, *From Jesus to Christianity: How
Four Generations of Visionaries and Storytellers Created the New Testament and Christian Faith*
(San Francisco: HarperSanFrancisco, 2004), 309; and idem, *Scripting Jesus: The Gospels in
Rewrite* (New York: HarperOne, 2010), 353.

baptism itself never actually occurs, though the Baptist's report that he saw the descent of the Spirit like a dove is given as a "testimony" (1:32), and the witness to this descent is preceded, just as in Mark's account of the full baptism, with John the Baptist proclaiming himself unworthy "to untie the thong" of Jesus' sandal (John 1:27; Mark 1:7). It seems like the Synoptic version of the event hovers behind this altered version. Furthermore, John presumes knowledge of the accounts of Jesus coming from both Galilee and Bethlehem (John 7:40-44), accounts present in varying ways in both Matthew and Luke. The saying of the Synoptic Jesus about a prophet being without honor in his home country (Mark 6:4; Matt. 13:57; Luke 4:24) is referred to in passing in John, as if it were a thing actually said in some other story (John 4:44). Similarly, in the Johannine passion account, as in the Synoptics, Jesus' final supper is narrated, followed by his going with his disciples to another place—identified in the Synoptics as "Gethsemane" and in John as "a place where there was a garden" (18:1)—though John reports neither the details of the arrangement for a room in which the supper could be held nor a reason for this journey to the "garden." The praying that functions as the purpose in the Synoptics has already taken place in John 17, and the agony of Jesus' facing death, the agony of the "cup" in the Synoptics, has already been replaced, in 12:27, by Jesus' "troubled soul" and the proclamation of his acceptance of the "hour." And when one notes that the Gospel according to Matthew narrates appearances of the risen one both in Jerusalem (Matt. 28:9) and in Galilee (28:16), while the appearances in Luke all take place in Jerusalem or its environs (Luke 24:13-49), it is fascinating to note that the book of John, including its epilogue (John 21), presents the appearances in both places (20:14, 19, 26; 21:1). In any case, the great outline of the Fourth Gospel generally corresponds to the pattern of the earlier three—a beginning and an account of the Baptist; the call of the disciples and a long account of the ministry of Jesus; then the account of his death and resurrection—though the Gospel according to John proceeds through this outline in its own unique way.

Nonetheless, important details from Mark and Luke do recur in John, albeit in new ways and new positions, indicating that the author of John most likely knew and used these books themselves and not only their outline. Mark's "beginning of the gospel" (Mark 1:1) has become the Johannine "in the beginning was the Word" (John 1:1). Mark's cleansing of the Temple (Mark 11:15-19) has been moved to the beginning of the story (John 2:13-22), where the idea suggested in Mark (Mark 14:58; cf. 6:3) that Jesus may be the eschatological builder of

the new Temple is reinterpreted with fresh force (John 2:19-21). The Johannine Jesus is accused of being possessed by a demon (7:20; 8:48; 10:20) as is
Jesus in Mark (Mark 3:22, 30). Mark's occasional and hidden use of the divine
name I AM for Jesus (14:62; cf. 6:50) has been taken over and strongly repeated
(John 18:5-6; 4:26; 6:21; 8:24, 28; 8:58).[4] The Markan Jesus speaks of his mes-
sianic identity only in a hidden way but speaks openly, boldly ($\pi\alpha\rho\rho\eta\sigma\acute{\iota}\alpha$) of his
cross (Mark 8:32).[5] Just so, Jesus in John paradoxically combines both hidden
presence (John 7:4, 13; 11:54—$o\dot{\upsilon}\kappa\grave{\epsilon}\tau\iota$ $\pi\alpha\rho\rho\eta\sigma\acute{\iota}\alpha$) and bold, open, revelatory
speech (7:26; 10:24-25; 16:25, 29; 18:20—$\pi\alpha\rho\rho\eta\sigma\acute{\iota}\alpha$), especially in face of his
proximate death. The use of the $\dot{\alpha}\rho\chi\acute{\eta}$, of the builder motif, of the demons, of
the divine name, of the dialectic between hiddenness and revelation, not to men-
tion the fact that the Johannine "realized eschatology" seems much like the way
Mark deals with the cross event—this all seems strikingly Markan.

Luke, too, has its echoes in John, though they have more to do with events
and names and less with themes. So, the Johannine Jesus, like Jesus in the travel
narrative of Luke, goes through Samaria (John 4:4; Luke 9:51ff.). More: Mary,
Martha, and Lazarus, presented as siblings in John (John 11:1-2), are figures that
have first occurred in Luke—Mary and Martha in that house that receives Jesus
on the way (Luke 10:38-41) and Lazarus as a named beggar who, in a parable,
dies and is taken to "Abraham's bosom" (16:20). It is as if their roles in Luke have
been narratively transformed to similar—though also quite different—roles in
John. Martha again serves table, exactly as she does in Luke (10:40)—or, she pre-
sides at the meal by distributing the food ($\delta\iota\eta\kappa\acute{o}\nu\epsilon\iota$, John 12:2). Mary has been
transformed from the one listening at Jesus' feet (Luke 10:39) to the one who
anoints his feet (John 12:3; cf. 11:2), eliding into one character the unnamed
anointing woman of Mark (Mark 14:3) and the woman weeping at Jesus' feet
in Luke (Luke 7:37-38), and thus newly recasting the Markan meal at Bethany.
And Lazarus becomes one who actually dies in the narrative, not just in a parable, one to whom Jesus paradigmatically gives life, partly thereby occasioning
his own death (John 11:43, 46-53; 12:10). Furthermore, the narrative of Jesus

---

4. Indeed, the many titles of Jesus in this Gospel may be understood as expansions of the
title I AM, as in "I AM the bread of life" (6:35, 51), "the light of the world" (8:12), "the door"
(10:9), "the good shepherd" (10:11, 14), "the resurrection and the life" (11:25), "the way, the
truth, and the life" (14:6), and "the true vine" (15:1, 5). See Rudolf Bultmann, *Theology of the
New Testament, vol. 2* (New York: Scribner's, 1955), 65.

5. This is the only occurrence of this word in the Synoptic Gospels. It is a word that
occurs several times in John.

washing the disciples' feet at the farewell supper in John (13:2-16) seems as if it is the Lukan saying at the Last Supper concerning the service of Jesus ("I am among you as one who serves," Luke 22:27) turned into a concrete story, an enacted image, a dramatization.[6]

There are at least hints that Matthew, too, was known by the author of John. The mixed quotation from Isaiah and Zechariah, found in the Matthean version of the story of the entrance into Jerusalem (Matt. 21:5), and found only in Matthew among the Synoptics, occurs also as a mixed quote in the Johannine account (John 12:15). Similarly, the quotation from Isaiah in Matthew 13:14-15 is echoed by the quotation in John 12:40. One might argue that John's author was simply using a collection of "testimonies" very like a similar collection that might have been used by the author of Matthew, but John's use of Matthew itself seems more likely. That is especially so when one also looks again at what happens to the Markan saying about whoever receives a child receiving Jesus and so receiving the one who sent Jesus (Mark 9:37), one of the sayings we have found to be at the weighted center of Mark's ring composition. Matthew has turned that saying into a promise to the Twelve as missionaries in his second discourse: "Whoever welcomes you welcomes me, and whoever welcomes me welcomes the one who sent me" (Matt. 10:40), while also keeping the word about the child separately, in the fourth discourse (18:5). In John, the child has disappeared, but the Matthean development of the saying seems to stand behind: "Whoever receives one whom I send receives me; and whoever receives me receives him who sent me" (John 13:20). Furthermore, one might find in John (8:19 and 14:7, for example) a development of the idea in Matthew (at 11:27) about it not being possible to know the "Father" except through the "Son." All of these connections make it conceivable that the structure of Matthew—its narratives interleaved with extensive discourses—could have contributed to the structure of John: narrative "signs" interleaved with and interpreted by lengthy discourses.

With the exception of the stories of the feeding of the multitude (John 6:1-14) and the walking on the sea (6:16-21),[7] however, those "signs" in John are unique to this Fourth Gospel and not a repetition of the miracle narratives found

---

6. Cf. C. H. Dodd, *The Interpretation of the Fourth Gospel* (Cambridge: Cambridge University Press, 1968), 393.

7. Also in Mark (6:30-52) and Matthew (14:13-27) these stories are set immediately side by side, though Matthew then adds the account of Peter's attempt to walk on the water.

in the Synoptics. Nonetheless, the water turned into wine at the wedding at Cana (John 2:1-11) does seem to echo the bridegroom of Mark 2:19 and the new wine of Mark 2:22, as if the Cana sign were a story form of those sayings and the Cana celebration already the beginning of the nuptials of God with the earth that will come when Jesus' "hour" arrives. The healing of the royal official's son (John 4:46-54) does seem much like the healing of the centurion's servant or slave (in Matt. 8:5-13 and Luke 7:1-10). The healing of the man at Bethzatha (or Bethesda; John 5:2-9) seems to echo the healing in Mark 2:1-12, including the command to "take up your mat and walk" (John 5:8; cf. Mark 2:9). The healing of the blind man in John (John 9:1-12) may owe something to the healings of Bartimaeus and of the anonymous blind man in Mark (Mark 8:22-26; 10:46-52). Jesus' saliva functions in Mark (8:22) as in John (9:6). And the Johannine blind man is healed in a pool that corresponds to Jesus himself as the "sent one" (John 9:7; cf. 3:17; 11:42; 17:3). Just so, Bartimaeus is healed and follows Jesus into the passion and resurrection story, as if being immersed in it (Mark 10:52; cf. 14:51-52). And, as we have seen, Lazarus raised seems to recall the Lazarus of the Lukan parable. The Johannine Lazarus may also owe something to the Markan demoniac, who is first found among the tombs, crazed and nearly dead himself, and then found clothed and in his right mind (Mark 5:1-20). Jesus' command in John—"Unbind him, and let him go" (John 11:44)—could be spoken of both of them. The Johannine signs take the miracle stories of the earlier books and mine them for the stuff of symbolization. Water, wine, temple, bread, sea, sight and light, and death and life themselves: these all are used to show forth the identity of Jesus.

It is as if the author of John is creatively ringing the changes on themes, ideas, and narratives that we know from the other Gospels. The author of John seems to have clearly understood how these books were symbolic constructions for the sake of speaking the meaning of Jesus in the present time, and this author has also gone to work to heighten the symbols and make explicit the theology used in such a construction. But one ought not easily assume a modern image of a scholar, sitting in a study, writing a new book with the three earlier books spread out on the desk. A more likely scenario is that the earlier Gospels were known in the community where the Gospel of John originated, that storytellers,[8] narrators, and readers had already mixed these accounts with other continuing

---

8. The work of paleo-Christian storytellers is especially envisioned by L. Michael White in his *Scripting Jesus*.

oral traditions, had already begun to "ring the changes" on their stories, and that the author of John intentionally put together a new account, drawing on these sources, which he knew thoroughly, but also creating new material with a new theological intention.

But once we have seen the way John has used Mark, Matthew, and Luke, we need to ask our questions again. Did this new account, so full of material from the Synoptics while also so different, nonetheless follow the earlier Gospels in their coherence with assembly? And was this new Gospel, like the earlier books, also interested in communal reform? I think that the answer to these questions is yes.

In fact, whatever other reasons there were for the creation of this new, theologically weighted, and symbolically rich Gospel, one of the reasons seems to be an address to the Christian assemblies of its time. The early second century found the house churches, the assemblies, newly engaged in sorting out their own identities, sometimes in conflict with the new identities of neighboring assemblies of post-Temple Jews who rejected Christian messianism, sometimes in conflict with world-denying movements that also considered themselves to be Christian, always in continuing differentiation from other clubs, cults, and communities of the Hellenistic world. The Fourth Gospel clearly addresses these conflicts. But in doing so, it puts "assembly" at the heart of its concern, even without using the word. It is likely that the author of John saw the function of the houses and the ring composition in Mark, of the discourses to the churches and promised presence of the risen one in Matthew, and of the accent on welcome in Luke's travel narrative, and that the author then decided to enact that function—that address to the assemblies—in a new and focused way, still telling the story of Jesus to the needs of the time. In many ways, intentional address to assembly is clearest of all in John.

Assembly in the Johannine Structure

Evidences of assembly appear in the Fourth Gospel from its beginning. It may very well be that the first words of the Gospel, its "prologue," have been crafted out of a communally known and sung hymn.[9] If that is so, then the assembly that so sang has already been evoked at the beginning of the book. The people who make up such an assembly, knowing the song, form at least a part of the

---

9. Raymond E. Brown, *The Gospel According to John (I-XII)* (Garden City: Doubleday, 1966), 20–23.

"we" in the Gospel's phrases, "we have seen his glory" (John 1:14) and "from his fullness we have all received, grace upon grace" (1:16).

Then the Gospel turns to its version of the call of the disciples. Although the phrase "follow me"—known to us from the Synoptics in their versions of these stories of call—also occurs in John (1:43), the more unique phrase in the Johannine form of those stories is "come and see" (1:39, 46). The disciples do come, first of all to see "where Jesus was staying" (1:38-39) and to remain with him. It is as if a small assembly is being convoked in this text. Later in the book, remaining or "abiding" with Jesus will become a primary directive to an assembly (15:4; cf. 14:2, 23).[10] Though no further account is given of what occurs or what is said in this little assembly that abides with Jesus, the idea of assembly is nonetheless suggested at this outset of the book.

In the stories that follow, one of the most characteristic Johannine narrative traits involves Jesus encountering and talking alone with an individual. Nicodemus (3:1-21), the Samaritan woman at the well (4:5-26), and the man born blind (9:35-39) are all such figures. So is Mary Magdalene in the account of the resurrection (20:11-18). The frequently recurring second- or third-person singular in Johannine commands and promises (for example, "No one can enter the kingdom of God without being born of water and the Spirit," 3:5, or "If anyone love me, that one will keep my word," 14:23) seems to pick up the existential force of these encounters. For John, faith seems to be an individual matter.[11] Still, frequently near to these words to individuals, there are summarizing words about a community (for example, "you" *plural* "must be born again," 3:7, or "the word that you" *plural* "hear is not mine, but is from the Father who sent me," 14:24). The same move toward community happens narratively. The Samaritan woman goes to her village to say, "Come and see" (4:29), and the people begin to assemble (4:30). Indeed, Jesus "abides" with them (4:40), and they hear and believe. The conversation with the man who had been born blind is followed

---

10. The verb both in 1:38-39 and in chaps. 14 and 15 is μένειν. Cf. also the small assembly in 4:40.

11. Perhaps the author of the Fourth Gospel is intentionally evoking the idea of the meeting between "the revealer" and an individual, an idea that was hugely popular in the kind of Hellenistic religion that was marked by an interest in transcending the world. See Luke Timothy Johnson, *Among the Gentiles: Greco-Roman Religion and Christianity* (New Haven: Yale University Press, 2009), 88. This idea, of course, is widely present in Christian Gnostic literature and already is found in the Gospel of Thomas. Unlike Thomas, however, the individuals in John are also gathered into communities.

directly by Jesus speaking of calling the sheep into "one flock" with "one shepherd" (10:16), as if this man had been one of those sheep. And Mary Magdalene is sent back to the assembly of disciples (20:17-18), apostle to the apostles. Even Nicodemus, who seems to get things so wrong in chapter 3, at last joins with Joseph of Arimathea in a small community to receive the body of Jesus in a manner fit for a king (19:38-42). The individual stories open toward the evocation of assemblies. For all of its interest in the existential encounter of individual faith, the book does have a strong coherence with assembly.

Then it is not surprising that throughout the book Jesus speaks not like the teacher we know from the Synoptic narratives but like an early-second-century preacher in a Christian assembly. Jesus' voice in John is not the voice of Jesus-then, perhaps not even the voice of a prophet speaking the word of the risen one as Jesus-now, but the voice that a preacher with the concerns of this author would use to speak about Jesus, to speak even in the name of Jesus, in the Christian house churches of the early second century.[12] Later in the same century, a tone very like the tone we find in John is used by the preacher and bishop Melito of Sardis, in a homily that we still have.[13]

Still, it is important to note that in the first eleven chapters of the book, no single narrative account of an actual assembly is given, with the exception of the multitude gathered around Jesus in the sign of the bread (6:1-14). Unlike Mark, no gathering takes place in a house. No significant withdrawn conversation with the disciples is reported.[14] The speaking of Jesus in John 1–11 is usually either public or addressed to individuals. Unlike Matthew, no discipline is described

---

12. Cf. Brown, *The Gospel According to John*, xxxv; and Harold W. Attridge, "Genre Bending in the Fourth Gospel," *Journal of Biblical Literature* 121/1 (2002): 7.

13. Dated to about 160 C.E., Melito's *On Pascha*, which may indeed be the remains of a mid-second-century house-church sermon, includes the preacher speaking with rhetorical intensity in the voice of Christ and saying (103: ll. 772-780), "I am the lamb slain for you; I am your ransom, I am your life, I am your light, I am your salvation, I am your resurrection, I am your king. I will raise you up by my right hand; I am leading you up to the heights of heaven; there I will show you the Father from ages past." The *you* and *your* of this passage is plural, addressing the present assembly. Stuart George Hall, *Melito of Sardis* (Oxford: Clarendon, 1979), 59.

14. Dodd, *The Interpretation of the Fourth Gospel*, 390. Dodd suggests that the calling of the disciples in 1:37-51, the brief conversation with the disciples at the well in 4:31-38, and the scene of Peter's confession in 6:66-71 may represent exceptions to the absence of "esoteric teaching" to the disciples in the first eleven chapters of the book. In none of these cases, however, is the imaged gathering quite like the Markan gatherings in a house.

for the churches. And thoroughly unlike Luke—as well as Mark—not a single meal is narrated, again with the exception of the sign of the loaves and fishes.[15] This change from the Synoptics seems intentional.

In order to understand how this absence might relate to our question, we need to consider the structure of John more deeply. We will discover that assembly and the Johannine structure are interwoven. A very wide consensus among scholars today regards the end of chapter 12 and the beginning of chapter 13 as a clear break in the book.[16] Those first twelve chapters are largely concerned with the series of "signs," as we have seen that John calls them, the miracles that manifest Jesus' "glory," calling people to faith in him even before he is "glorified." At the same time, those chapters are filled with a series of interleaved discourses, many of which take up symbolic themes proposed by the signs: bread, light, and new birth, for example. It is as if the discourses bring to expression in words what the signs are meant to show forth in action, calling to faith those who see the signs and hear the discourses. In the narrative, some people believe. Many do not, especially those whom John calls "the Jews."[17] Then, in the second half of the book, there is a single great discourse (13:31—17:26), held in a gathering of the disciples. It is the first full account of Jesus' teaching in John that is placed in the context of this group, seen as at table and withdrawn, as a group around Jesus, as an assembly. That discourse, often called the farewell discourse, intends to bring into words the meaning of the greatest sign of the Gospel, the one toward which all the others have been pointing: the death and resurrection of Jesus, recounted in the chapters that follow. Once again and by way of climax, discourse is juxtaposed to sign. In some ways, the foot washing, the narrative with which the section begins (13:1-30), also constitutes a proleptic sign, another kind of signing of Jesus' death and resurrection, which the farewell discourse then brings into words. The account of the resurrection concludes with the narrative of the disciples gathering as an assembly on the two successive Sundays after Jesus' death, an assembly in which the risen one sets out signs (his

---

15. A concrete meal is even directly refused—or, at least, spiritualized—in 4:31.

16. For the outline of the Gospel, see especially Brown, *The Gospel According to John*, cxxxviii–cxxxix.

17. This term, of course, reflects the late-first- or early-second-century communal conflicts within which John was embedded, as Christian communities struggled for identity. The use of the term is no report from the time of the historical Jesus, as we must frequently repeat, while we also continually repent of the antisemitic horrors that this very terminology has encouraged when it has been taken as historical.

appearance, his wounds, and his breath) and two brief discourses for the sake of bringing those who are there into faith. A prologue, probably reworking a communal hymn, and an epilogue, probably added later (20:30-31 seems already like a conclusion) and including yet another assembly around a meal, then frame this whole. In any case, the resultant structure of the book is as follows:

Prologue—1:1-18
The Book of Signs—1:19—12:50
    Signs and discourses interwoven (1:19—11:57)
    Anticipation: Bethany assembly, entry into Jerusalem, the Greeks, arrival
    of the hour (12)
The Book of Glory—13:1—20:31
    Assembly: foot washing and farewell discourse (13–17)
    The Great Sign and the two Sunday assemblies (18–20)
Epilogue—21:1-25

One should note that woven through the Book of Signs one finds repeated reference to the "hour" or the "glorification" or the "lifting up" of Jesus, as yet to be accomplished,[18] even though the glory is being manifested at the time in the signs themselves. Indeed, here the old Markan theme of the misunderstanding of the disciples has been remolded to point toward the time, after Jesus' resurrection (2:22), after he was glorified (12:16), when the events of the Book of Signs would be understood more clearly by Christians. Then, toward the conclusion of this Book of Signs, the hour begins to arrive (12:27-33). For John, Jesus' glorification is none other than his death, and this death is, just as in Mark, the arrival of the eschatological moment. Thus, Jesus' death, for John, is also, at the same time, the judgment of the world, the resurrection itself, the ascension, and the pouring out of the Spirit to create faith and new life. These things are recounted in the Book of Glory. The hour arrives (13:1). The glorification occurs (13:31). The Book of Signs has been leaning toward and pointing to the events of the Book of Glory.

The absence of assembly in the Book of Signs thus becomes quite clear. Just as the whole book moves toward the death and resurrection of Jesus, so also the whole book moves toward assembly. For the Fourth Gospel, the death and resurrection of Jesus implies assembly, grounds assembly, and the structure

---

18. See esp., 2:4; 3:14; 7:39; 8:28; 11:4; 12:32.

of the book intends to make that clear. In assembly Jesus is seen again by faith. There his death is encountered and interpreted. There the Spirit is poured out. In assembly, the signs and discourses all bear fruit, being presented to the assembly in the book of the Gospel itself (20:31) and thereby bringing people to faith and giving life, the very life signified by the signs.

The Gospel of John takes up a clear, schematic approach to assembly, bringing Mark's meaning and its reworking by Matthew and Luke to an even more intense expression. First, assembly is foreshadowed in the Book of Signs. Then, the Book of Signs closes with a small, actual, but proleptic assembly, one that gives a down payment on the greater assembly that will immediately follow. Then, in the Book of Glory, John "rings the changes" on the Synoptic Last Supper. As the Last Supper in Luke became the place for extended teaching from Jesus (Luke 22:24-38), so John extends the significance of the supper and its accompanying teaching even further. There Jesus signs the meaning of his death in the foot washing during the meal, and he speaks of that meaning—especially the meaning of his death for this assembly—in the farewell discourse. But even this great assembly is proleptic. It points toward the two Sunday gatherings with which the Gospel concludes, and those gatherings foreshadow the continuation of Sunday in the life of the Christian movement. Such an ending opens onto Sunday at the time of the reading of the Gospel book itself, onto any Sunday meeting where the signs of the book are read to enable faith and thus give life.

But we should say all this with more detail. Assembly is foreshadowed in the Book of Signs. It is foreshadowed by the "come and see" of the disciples and of the Samaritan woman, by the whole household of the royal official believing (John 4:53), by the multitude gathered around Jesus and the sign of bread, though not quite understanding (cf. 6:15), by the word about the Good Shepherd gathering the flock, by the Greeks wishing to see Jesus and so indicating that gathering beginning (12:21), even by the observation that the disciples would come to understand later. These intimations of assembly to come, woven through the first twelve chapters of the Gospel, indicate that the signs of Jesus will finally bear a greater fruit, when the Spirit has been given (7:39) and a community of the far and the near, of Gentiles and Jews, has been gathered by the Shepherd in his death (10:14-18). The coming of the Greeks, enacting "the world gone after him" (12:19) and all people being drawn to him on the cross (12:32), may well be intended to pull the current Gentile house-church hearers of the Gospel into the story. The Greeks disappear in the further narrative, as if they become all the hearers of the Gospel book gathered into the assemblies to come, where they will indeed see Jesus in faith (20:29).

Assembly is especially anticipated at Bethany. This first actual assembly around Jesus, this first meal in a house in John,[19] occurs toward the end of the Book of Signs, in the house of Mary and Martha and Lazarus, the house that had been a place of mourning (11:31), as part of the anticipatory and transitional material in chapter 12. The anointing at Bethany, the plotting of the priests, the entry into Jerusalem, and the coming of the Greeks—all of these show forth ahead of time the death and resurrection that will occupy the Book of Glory. But the house at Bethany also shows forth the assemblies that will be filled with the life-giving discourse and sign of his death: the assembly of the foot washing, first of all, and then the following assemblies of the two Sundays, and then all of the assemblies of the Christians that will follow on subsequent Sundays. Bethany is a down payment on Christian assembly. As it is filled with the fragrance of the μύρος that shows forth his coming death (12:3), so these following assemblies are also to be filled with word and sign, fragrant with life-giving meaning.

Then the Book of Glory begins with the longest Johannine assembly account. This is the assembly of the foot washing and the assembly of the farewell discourse. In the proleptic assembly at Bethany, Mary has anointed and wiped Jesus' feet as a sign of his death, a down payment on his burial. She is the preacher in this assembly, the sign giver. In the assembly of the Book of Glory, Jesus washes all of the disciples' feet and wipes them with a towel. The service that is represented is slave service, the service of washing the feet of the guests. This service, too, stands for Jesus' death, for his giving himself to the uttermost in loving care for the lost and needy world, dying as a slave would die in Roman executions. It, too, fills the house with its fragrance, only now the "fragrance" is both communal love and the knowledge of the meaning of his death from which that love proceeds.

The fascinating thing is that in the Fourth Gospel the foot washing virtually takes the place of the meal. The foot washing does not occur before the meal as the guests arrive, as one might expect but, rather, "during supper" (13:2b). Here the very content of the meal is Jesus' humble service. It seems as if the author of

---

19. Indeed, after the "house" of the Temple in 2:16-17 and the house of the royal official in 4:53, this is the first actual house in the Gospel. Only at this place does "house" appear in John as a potential metaphor for assembly. "House" is then implied by the words in 20:19 and 26. Cf. also 8:35.

the Fourth Gospel, not unlike Paul in the much earlier letter to the Corinthians and not unlike Mark against the "yeast of the Pharisees and the yeast of Herod," means to call the meal practice of the house churches to a deepening reform.[20] The church's meal is not to be a meal focused only on feeding its participants nor to be a meal of betrayal (after all, the only person who actually eats in the Johannine account is Judas; 13:26-27). In this meal, rather, Jesus serves the participants with his serving love, with his very death. The Fourth Gospel is probably not so much recommending an ongoing foot-washing rite[21] as urging that people see and hear the slave service of Jesus when they eat a common meal in church. The Gospel is urging that those who eat and drink then be formed to turn in slave service toward the others of the assembly and of the world. As at Bethany, "you always have the poor with you" (12:8).

The assembly of the Book of Glory then continues with the final discourse. If the food sharing (the *deipnon*) of this gathering has been essentially supplanted by the foot washing, then the *symposion* of the meal has now become this discourse. Here is the Johannine version of Jesus' words at taking the final cup of the meal. Jesus has served the disciples, astonishingly, knowing that all things had been given into his hands, that he had come from God and was going to God (13:3), that this was the hour of his "departure" (13:1). Now he brings that "departure" into words. In this discourse two things occur. First, the Markan motif of Jesus telling his disciples, in assembly, in the house, of his death, resurrection, and being seen again, is taken up in a Johannine way. This gathering has now become "the house" of Mark 9, and the discourse here has become the Johannine version of the Markan passion predictions together with the Markan promise, "there you will see him." The final discourse inherits the role of the central Markan words to and about assembly. Second, the themes of the Book of Signs, especially the life shown forth to faith in the signs and discourses of the earlier part of the book, now all are brought here, coming to fruition in this congregation of the disciples. Because of the death and resurrection of Jesus, the assembly becomes the place of showing forth and giving out the very life of God.[22]

---

20. See above, chap. 2.

21. Still, the churches that have maintained such a rite—perhaps in regular relationship to the celebration of the Lord's Supper or perhaps as part of the annual celebration of Maundy Thursday—can be seen as keeping the Johannine critique alive.

22. Both C. H. Dodd and Rudolf Bultmann, two of the very most important interpreters of the Fourth Gospel in the last century and two who otherwise agreed on very little, assert these two primary characteristics of the farewell discourse: redoing the Synoptic passion

Repeated again and again in the discourse we find this theme: "I am going away and I am coming to you" (14:28).[23] The death of Jesus, his "going away," directly brings about the resurrection; here, that resurrection is the promise that the disciples will see him in assembly. The death of Jesus also directly brings about the gift of the Spirit, enlivening Jesus' word remembered in the assembly (14:25-26).[24] It directly yields an assembly visited and dwelt in by "the Father and the Son" (14:20, 24b),[25] as the life-giving God has been named throughout the signs and discourses of the earlier part of the Gospel. Indeed, the assembly is gathered into Jesus to dwell in God and God's house (14:1-7).[26] For John, the faithful assembly gathers in what the later church will call the Holy Trinity. Then, to make clear that this discourse is indeed about assembly, there follows the image of the vine as a metaphor for the community dwelling in Jesus (15:11), a further urging to mutual love in the community (15:12, 17), a discussion of the potential persecution of the churches (15:18-21; 16:1-4, 33), and several calls to mission (15:8; 17:14-18) and to communal prayer (14:13-14; 15:7; 16:23-24). Above all, there is the concluding prayer of Jesus for the community and for its unity. All of this begins to happen in this gathering of disciples where the meaning of Jesus' death and resurrection is set out. "From now on" (14:7) these things are true.

But that "from now on" reaches beyond the gathering of the disciples in John 13–17. Also, this assembly functions proleptically, an image of what Christian assemblies are to become. The promises are for "now," but they are also

---

predictions and pointing to the themes of the Book of Signs as fulfilled in the congregation of the disciples. See Dodd, 394, 398–99, and W. G. Robinson, trans., "Rudolf Bultmann's Review of C. H. Dodd: *The Interpretation of the Fourth Gospel*," *Harvard Divinity Bulletin* 27/2 (January 1963): 20.

23. Indeed, this is what the disciples are told that they "heard me say." See also 14:3, 18-19; 16:16, 22; cf. 16:7.

24. See also 14:16-17; 15:26; 16:7-15. This gift of the Spirit, foreshadowed in 7:37-39 and promised here, actually flows, according to John, from Jesus' death (19:29, 34) and is encountered as his resurrection is encountered in the assembly (20:22).

25. Cf. 17:21-23. In the context of an accent on the assembly of disciples, the plural *you*, this promise is also given to individuals, in the characteristic Johannine way (14:21-24a).

26. The promise of 14:2-3 is also spoken to a plural *you*. I do not believe that this promise, in John, was originally about Christians "going to heaven" after death. Rather, it was about the assembly being gathered into being with Jesus in God, a gathering that was possible because of Jesus' death. It was thus about the assembly as a place where one could encounter the true "house of God," the one built by Jesus in his resurrection (cf. 2:19-21).

for the future, as the future tense shows: "You will see me" and "The Advocate will teach you everything." The image of assembly in these chapters appears to us as a kind of mix between a gathering already around the risen one, with the risen one speaking,[27] and a report of the night before they killed "Jesus-then." So, while Jesus speaks as if all has occurred "now" (13:31), this text also tells of Judas going out to betray him (13:30) and of how the disciples will all be scattered, leaving Jesus alone (16:32). The "now" includes Jesus' death. Even more, the prayer of chapter 17 prays not only for these church-founding disciples but also for the assemblies to come, for "those who will believe in me through their word" (17:20).

The assembly at Bethany has pointed to the assembly of the foot washing and of the final discourse. Now the assembly of the foot washing points to the Sunday assemblies.

Sunday: John on Worship

The Fourth Gospel enacts the fulfillment of the promise about seeing Jesus and receiving the Spirit in its concluding passage: the two Sunday assemblies (20:19-29). As individuals were called into assembly in the Book of Signs, so now Mary Magdalene and Peter, the beloved disciple and, finally, Thomas, also are sent there (20:17-18, 24-25). Then, if the assembly of the foot washing and its farewell discourse were developments of the Synoptic Last Supper account—ringing the changes on that story—these Sunday assemblies are a similar development of the Lukan resurrection appearances at Emmaus and Jerusalem (Luke 24:13-53). Here, unlike Luke, no report is given of what these assemblies are actually doing as they meet. We may be expected to presume Luke's image of the community interpreting texts and sharing a meal. In any case, the risen one appears, is seen, as he had promised in John 13–17. In a brief and striking way, this appearance continues the signs and discourses that have occupied the whole Gospel and thus presents itself as the culmination of the whole book. As signs, we find the appearance itself, the showing of the wounds of crucifixion—an action repeated for Thomas—and the breathing out of the Spirit. This risen one is the crucified one and, at the same time, the source of the Spirit. As discourse, as words that bring

---

27. Passages from this discourse are used as Gospel readings during the fifty days of Easter in the Western lectionary. That seems a brilliant choice, with words about the meaning of Jesus' death and resurrection for the assembly used to interpret the Easter season.

to expression what the signs mean and join them in doing what they do, we find the greeting of peace, the sending, the spoken gift of the Spirit and thereby the empowering to forgive sins, the invitation to faith, and the blessing on those who have not seen and yet believe.

Inevitably, that blessing reaches out to assemblies that will follow. It makes of this account of the first Sunday assemblies and the accounts of the assemblies before these, at Bethany and for the foot washing, to be what the author of John has to say about worship, that is, about what the assemblies are doing or should be doing when they gather. It may be that the locked doors and the shared fear (20:19) were intended to evoke the situation of the communities for which the Gospel was first written, communities in considerable agony and fear about their identity and their potential persecution. It is certainly true that by recounting a series of Sundays—"eight days later," as the Greek text has it (20:26), utilizing the old Jewish way of counting off weeks[28]—a continuation of the series is suggested. The communities first reading this book also met on a Sunday that was eight days and then eight days and eight days later, down to their own time. But it is also true that these communities were not "seeing" Jesus in quite the same way that the narrative says that Thomas did, and the blessing was thus for them.

The Sunday assemblies in the Gospel book thus point toward the later assemblies of the churches. The Gospel book wishes to address these later assemblies with a concern for their clarity of purpose, indeed a concern for their reform. The assemblies imaged at the end of the Gospel have Sunday in common with later Christian assemblies, at least with the assemblies for which the Gospel is intended. Now the Gospel writer wants them to know the content of Sunday. The Gospel book itself is made available to them, carrying to them the signs of the story of Jesus, intended to create faith and give life, and carrying forward the tradition of Bethany and the foot-washing assembly as witnesses to assembly content.

We do not know when Sunday began to be the Christian day of meeting. Already Paul, in his first letter to Corinth, calls for the collection in which he is so deeply interested to be made on the first day of every week (1 Cor. 16:2). That hope may suggest that he understood the Christians in Corinth to be regularly meeting on that first day. The Gospels of Mark and Matthew place the resurrection of Jesus after the Sabbath, on the first day of the week, and Luke has the gatherings that first saw him risen on that same day. The Synoptic Gospels may

---

28. That "eight days" contributed to the later Christian tradition of calling Sunday "the eighth day," the day within and yet beyond our week, fulfilling our week, saving our week.

reflect, in this use of Sunday, an already existing practice of widespread Sunday meeting. Such a meeting is described as taking place in Troas, in Acts 20:7. Perhaps the growing Christian practice of meeting on the day after the Sabbath led to the report that Jesus was known as risen on that day. This seems most likely.[29] Or perhaps there was an old tradition of the resurrection occurring on Sunday that brought Christians to hold their meeting then.[30] We do not know. In any case, it is probably to Sunday that the author of the Revelation refers, perhaps at a time not far from the time of the writing of the Fourth Gospel, when he speaks of being "in the Spirit on the Lord's Day" (Rev. 1:10), of seeing the risen one and being connected by letter to seven Christian assemblies. In ways that are very like the Fourth Gospel, he thus images Sunday as the day of assembly, the day of the Spirit, and the day of encounter with the risen Lord. From the Fourth Gospel itself, however, we can gather that the assemblies known by the author were indeed accustomed to Sunday gathering. Then the author of the Gospel wishes to urge the assemblies that receive his book to understand something like the same meaning for Sunday as that found in the Revelation.

Though the risen one may not be seen as the disciples and Thomas—and, for that matter, the seer of the Revelation—saw him, the Sunday assembly is still to be filled with signs of his death and resurrection. We may assume that the assemblies known by the author of the Gospel continued to gather, like the Christian assemblies we have considered in relationship to the other Gospels, as regular supper clubs[31] and as communities where stories were told or teaching occurred. But now the evangelist wants these assemblies to see that such teaching needs to carry the story of Jesus' death and that such meals need to carry

---

29. If some or all of the gatherings of the Jesus movement made use of Sunday as a day of gathering, that use could have had a variety of roots. The day may have been chosen in an act of distinguishing the movement from the synagogue and its Sabbath observance, for example, or an act to accentuate the orientation of the communities' prayers toward the rising of the sun as a sign of eschatological hope. Solar orientation and the keeping of a solar calendar, with an accent on Sunday, have been found among the Essenes of the early first century c.e.

30. This seems less likely. The early tradition maintained by Paul in 1 Cor. 15:3-7, for example, does not clearly place the resurrection event on Sunday. It speaks rather of "the third day," which might be a reference to a Christian reading of Hosea 6:2 or might be a recalling of ancient funeral practice and earliest ideas that mourning women had seen Jesus raised. On the latter proposal, see Kathleen E. Corley, *Maranatha: Women's Funeral Rituals and Christian Origins* (Minneapolis: Fortress Press, 2010).

31. See above, chap. 1. This was generally the mode of gathering available in Hellenistic culture.

the critical meaning of the foot washing. Thus, both communal word and communal meal may stand for Jesus' wounds shown to faith. More: the members of the community may greet each other in peace, with a sense that the risen one greets them through each other. Here is one continuing Christian liturgical practice explicitly mentioned in this narrative. Sins may be forgiven, and so the Spirit that flows from the crucified will be enlivening the meeting. And the community may be sent with witness for the world, as the disciples were sent. The concluding narrative of the Sunday assemblies seems to urge these practices or these interpretations of practices already present in the assemblies. When the practices of the assembly show forth the identity of Jesus Christ, the gift of the Spirit, and the promise of this house as the dwelling place of God, then those practices become yet further concrete signs and discourses, in continuity with the signs and discourses of the Gospel book.

Then one further practice is also passed on: the book of the Gospel itself may be read. The relationship we have been tracing between Gospel books and assemblies comes to its clearest expression here in the Fourth Gospel, a kind of culmination of the development that began with Mark. Here the book actually concludes with a small but lucid discussion of its own purpose (20:30-31). The Gospel book tells of the signs that Jesus once enacted in the presence of his disciples—not all of them, it says, but enough—and it does so that the hearers of the book may come to faith in the risen one and so receive the very life that has been signed. The book is intended for assembly, for that Johannine plural *you*. Indeed, if the book of Mark was meant to stand for the risen one in assembly, as we have argued,[32] then that purpose is nuanced and further developed here. Those who have not seen and yet have come to believe (20:29), have done so, at least in part, through the signs narrated in the book. In the faith that comes through those narrated signs, the assembly encounters blessing and life. John's Gospel thus also makes clear its conception of the dialectic between Jesus-then and Jesus-now. In Mark, Jesus-then *is* Jesus-now; the same story has both functions: Jesus healing in the story is, at the same time, Jesus healing now in the assembly. The story takes place as the resurrection appearance. Matthew and Luke separate these functions more clearly: they see a need at the end of the books, by means of actual resurrection-appearance narratives, either to promise or to enact the continuing presence of Jesus-now. John builds on Matthew and Luke but retrieves the purpose of Mark. In John, Jesus-then inhabits the narratives of the

---

32. See above, chap. 3.

142

Book of Signs, but these narratives lean forward toward the hour of Jesus' death and, through the succession of assemblies, also to the present Sunday gathering. The signs that are narrated in the book—the lesser signs of the Book of Signs and the great sign of Jesus' death and resurrection—bring the gift of all the signs into the present assembly. The book itself becomes, through faith, the communal encounter with the crucified and risen Jesus in the actual text.[33]

One can trace some of these linkages. At Cana, we are told that water for purification was made into the new wine of grace (2:6). Nicodemus is told that birth into the kingdom of God is by water and the Spirit (3:5). Jesus also promised the thirst-slaking new water to those who come to him, the water of the Spirit that will be given (4:10-14; 7:37-39). And great pools of water become the location of healing, especially when they are seen to symbolize Jesus himself as that pool (5:7; 9:7). But the Jesus who promises these things is himself thirsty (4:6-7) and, then, as all of these references to water lean forward toward the story of the cross, he is deeply, mortally thirsty (19:28). Still, from his death there flows forth the water of which he has spoken (19:34), and, at the same time, the Spirit (19:30). All those promises come to the assembly: the disciples will be given the Spirit (14:16; 16:7) and that Spirit will make Jesus and Jesus' word present and alive (14:25; 16:14). One of those words is the word about water. The Spirit will be the presence of the very water that slakes thirst and heals (cf. 7:39). Thus, in the Sunday assembly, when the risen one breathes on the assembled and speaks to them the gift of the Spirit, they also receive all the force of the water signs. The water of life comes here. Such a promise then continues into the ongoing Sunday assemblies as they read the signs in the Gospel book and come to believe in Jesus Christ. Indeed, we may further surmise that all the layered meanings of water as a sign of Jesus will now also interpenetrate with the baptismal use of water in communities that read this Gospel. "Lord, give me this water," one who is being baptized may pray with the Samaritan woman (4:15), entering into the sign.

By the Gospel book's own estimate of its purpose, the signs come into assembly. That is true of not only the water signs. The house of the Temple was destroyed (2:17-19). But the house at Bethany has shown us that the crucified risen one is building God's house wherever there is assembly around the fragrant meaning of his death (12:3). Also for current Sunday assemblies, the house of mourning may become the house of life. And the place where Jesus is, the cross in the first

---

33. Sandra M. Schneiders, *Written That You May Believe: Encountering Jesus in the Fourth Gospel* (New York: Crossroad, 2003), 10.

place but then also the assembly where the crucified risen one abides, has become the house of God with its many rooms (14:1-3), drawing all people (12:32). The first disciples remained with Jesus, abided with him (1:39). Now every assembly is invited to abide in him and in the one who sent him, to find their house there. They may see him in faith in the Gospel book that recounts these stories. The Gospel book itself helps to make the assembly into the house of God.

More: the manna has long since disappeared and, with it, those who ate it (6:49). But when the bread of the communal meal is taken with the sense of the sign of the foot washing, when it is eaten in faith as the very presence of the one whose flesh is given for the life of the world (6:51), then it gives life, the very life that was signified by the sign of bread. "Lord, give us this bread always" (6:34), the assembly may pray with the community of that sign.

It is not so much, in John, that the healing of the man born blind is about baptism or that Cana and the multiplication of the loaves are about Eucharist or that the discourses are about preaching or that the cleansing of the Temple is about house assembly. Rather, they are presented as signs and discourses enacted by Jesus then, but signs and discourses that come through the cross and by means of the words of the book to the present assembly. These words make of the assembly and its communal meal, its communal bathing act, its communal teaching, as well as its mutual signs of forgiveness and peace, something more than these otherwise would be. The critical presence of the promise of the signs, their reforming edge,[34] calls the assembly to encounter through faith the crucified risen one in the water and the bread and in each other. "You will see me; because I live, you also will live" (14:19).

The Fourth Gospel calls for the assemblies to read this book and, by the critical presence of its signs and discourses, to see the actions of their meetings continually transformed into testimonies to the crucified risen one and gifts of the life in God that is through him, into a continuation of signs and discourses on Sunday.

That the Fourth Gospel thus leads its readers into thought about current assembly has a confirmation in the epilogue that seems to have been added to the book after its completion. Here, too, another assembly is imaged (21:1-2) and assembly matters are addressed. Now it is a fish meal—ringing the changes on Luke 24:42 and recalling the fish of the Johannine bread sign (John 6:9)—

---

34. We can probably guess, from this reforming edge, that the author of John felt there were assemblies where the death of Jesus was not taken seriously, where world escape was a dangerous theme, and where meal practice lacked the spirit of the foot washing.

which becomes a sign of the resurrection and thereby a tool for reinterpreting the ongoing meals of the assemblies.[35] The epilogue, however, is largely concerned with settling matters that must have been of some concern to the second-century assemblies and that otherwise had received no attention from the Fourth Gospel itself: the matter of authoritative leadership and the question of the relationship of Peter and Petrine leadership to the Johannine "beloved disciple." Not unlike the account in Mark (Mark 8:34-35), Peter is told of his coming death. He is also forgiven and invited to service toward the others. The fate of the beloved disciple remains mysterious. But the epilogue concludes with yet a further reflection on the book itself, echoing 20:30-31. While this final note, 21:25, justifies including one more narrative about what Jesus did, it also subtly suggests that this Gospel book is enough. While the world might be filled with such books, this book that you have, this book based on the testimony of the beloved disciple, is all that you need.[36]

The Four Beasts

But the churches of the second century finally did not follow this counsel. They did not adopt only a single book. There were certainly temptations to do so. And, as we have seen, each of the four books seems to have presented itself as if it were sufficient. But that is not the way that the churches finally went. There were to be four witnesses, rather. As Irenaeus would say in the late second century, four Beasts were needed, bearing their untamed testimony around the Lamb.

There certainly came to be more than four. We will not trace those other books here, since they were largely uninterested in assembly. Indeed, it may very well be that John was conceived at least partly in opposition to the growing tradition of what became "The Gospel of Thomas," perhaps even to an early version of the book itself.[37] Then John's fierce materialism[38] and its refusal of a docetic

---

35. The number of the fish (21:11) has provided a source of endless speculation. But the very fact of the meal being *fish*—here and in Luke 24: 42—suggests that this is already a taste of the meal of the last day. Leviathan, the great image of chaos and death, has been conquered and is being served as food. Cf. Ps. 74:14.

36. On the intention of John to replace other Gospels, see Attridge, "Genre Bending in the Fourth Gospel," 19.

37. So Elaine Pagels, *Beyond Belief: The Secret Gospel of Thomas* (New York: Vintage, 2004), 39–40.

38. For example, note that Jesus' use of his own saliva to heal the man born blind, in

Christology[39] would be the more understandable, even as would its contradictory remaining tendencies to a kind of spiritualizing and to dualisms between flesh and spirit, world and God. John's Gospel is making its statement within that world of Hellenistic religious discourse. But also understandable would be John's interest in assembly. The Jesus of Thomas does indeed speak as a "revealer" to individuals but, unlike the dialogues with individuals in John, the characters in Thomas are never sent back to the assembly, never gathered up with the other sheep to be one flock, one fold. Thomas supports individual religious experience, in the end an experience that tends to escape or abandon the world. John is also interested in individual experience and in the criticism and judgment of the world. But finally, in John, God loves the world (3:16), the flesh of Jesus is given for the life of the world (6:51), and individuals are sent to real gatherings of others. As part of its ultimate *sarcophilia,* John is interested in assemblies.

So are the Synoptic Gospels, as we have seen. The circle construction of Mark brought us to see the assembly purpose of the book and, especially, the assembly at the center of the book, a touchstone for ongoing assembly reform. The discourses of Matthew were clearly addressed to assemblies, bringing calls for discipline but also for an awareness of the promised presence of the risen one. The meals of the journey narrative in Luke, as also the Lukan resurrection appearances, were meant to call assemblies toward benevolent hospitality. And John, clearest of all, shaped the whole movement of the book toward those Sunday assemblies that continued in the second century. Indeed, the whole book might be called The Book of Signs in Assembly. All four of the books, like our untamed Beasts, are fierce with this interest, with these reforming calls.

But it is good that we have all four. With Mark alone, we might think that the counsel to the assembly was overwhelmingly about death and preparedness for death, not life. Matthew alone might easily be turned into legalism. Luke alone can seem too close to cultural accommodation, to counseling only politically and socially inoffensive behavior. And John, as well, could be misused.

For one thing, that remaining presence of a spiritualizing tendency can be taken as the dominant way to interpret John. One might read, "The flesh is

John 9:6, is even more materialistic than Mark 8:23. The saliva is mixed with the earth to make mud.

39. The blood and the water of John 19:34, for example, make it clear that, according to John, Jesus really died. Cf. Udo Schnelle, *Antidocetic Christology in the Gospel of John* (Minneapolis: Fortress Press, 1992), 209.

useless" (6:63), and forget the lively contradictions of "The bread that I will give for the life of the world is my flesh" (6:51) or "The Word became flesh" (1:14). One might read, "Righteous Father, the world does not know you" (17:25), and forget "God so loved the world" (3:16). One might forget, thus, that much of the Gospel is addressed in paradoxical reforming critique to practicing assemblies, assemblies tempted by the proto-Gnostic tendencies of Hellenistic transcendent religious themes.

But there are other problems. For example, that child whom the Markan Jesus told the assembly to receive (Mark 9:36-37), promising that such reception would be reception of the risen crucified one himself, has been omitted by John. John does have the Matthean conversion of that charge into the promise about the reception of the missionary Twelve (John 13:20; cf. Matt. 10:40). But John does not maintain the welcome to the child, as Matthew does (Matt. 18:5). When we note, in addition, that there is relatively little interest in John for the poor[40] or for other outsiders,[41] and that the great prayer of Jesus in John is explicitly for the churches and not for the world (John 17:9), then we may see that John's deep interest in the identity of the community has pushed these other, earlier Christian themes aside. John's interest in the "beloved disciple," as if there were an insider to Jesus' love, may be a further indication of his early second-century concern with reinforcing the conflicted identity of the communities he knew.[42] But for the ongoing usefulness of this Gospel, this insider accent carries significant dangers. Ought not the assembly pray for the world? Are not all the disciples loved by Jesus, as the Gospel itself indicates (13:34)? Ought not the assemblies be hospitable, as Luke indicates? Is not Matthew to be heard about the imprisoned and the wretched and Mark heard about the poor and the outsiders? Irenaeus was right. We need all four. It is a good thing that the soaring eagle did not push the lion or the ox or the human figure aside. They do correct each other, as they speak to the assemblies.

---

40. With the exception of mention at Bethany, John 12:8; cf. 13:29.

41. With the exception of the Samaritans, who may be intended to signify the Johannine view of the community of Christians as outsiders to the current synagogues.

42. In regard to "the beloved disciple," the hypothesis of Sandra Schneiders is extremely helpful: the beloved disciple is a "textual paradigm" for the corporate authority of the Johannine school, embodied in the text itself by a number figures: the Samaritan woman, Mary Magdalene, Nathanael, Mary, Martha, and Lazarus. Finally, it may be especially the Samaritan woman who is a kind of textual alter ego for the late-first or early-second-century author of the book, regardless of that author's gender. See Schneiders, *Written That You May Believe*, 246.

The very existence of the four, their successive appearance in the Christian communities of the late first and early second centuries, demonstrates that reform in the assemblies was not a once-and-done affair. The diverse but converging reform interests of the New Testament Gospels show that the assemblies for which they were originally intended were complex communities, with differing challenges. They were made up of people who belonged to their age and were, in diverse ways, both trying to belong and trying to distinguish themselves from others. They were sorting out the meanings of their Christian faith, sometimes brilliantly, sometimes not. The Gospel books intended to help them with this sorting. And the Gospel books intended especially to help them understand the purpose and the practice of their assemblies.

There are, of course, other ways to read the Gospels, other questions to ask of them. Much of modern scholarship and modern preaching, for example, has been primarily asking what these books say reliably about the historical Jesus. But the inquiry about the original coherence of these books with later Christian house assemblies has shown itself to be a fruitful one. From the "house" of Mark to the Sunday meetings of John, assembly is found everywhere in the four. Their interest in Jesus-then has been found to be overwhelmingly an interest in the ways in which he is becoming Jesus-now in assembly. We have discovered that the Gospels can be read afresh and very fruitfully with this reforming address to the assemblies in mind.

But we are the ones who are so reading. We are the ones who have asked these questions. Many of us still read the Gospels in assembly. The reforming interest of these books in "worship," a reforming interest that even in paleo-Christianity could not be once-and-done, reaches out also toward us. Does this original purpose still address us? What do the Gospels say to our assemblies? How do we hear them? We turn to the second concern of this book, the Gospels on our Sundays.

Before we do so, we may pause long enough to let the Fourth Gospel itself also raise explicit questions to our assembly practice: Do we have a sense of the purpose of Sunday as day of encountering the Lord, day of the life-giving Spirit, and day of assembly? Does our meeting center itself on signs and discourses that bear witness to the death and resurrection of Jesus? Does the force of all the signs—Cana and the Temple cleansing, Bethzatha and the official's son, bread for the world, water for the Samaritan woman, sight for the man born blind, and life for Lazarus, and more—

come here, to our meeting, into our discourses and our baptisms and our meals, giving God's gifts now? Do we see what the reading of the Gospel book may be for? Does our sharing of the peace proclaim the content of John's Sundays? And, since so many of us are drawn to powerful individual religious experience, do we, like Mary Magdalene, also find ourselves sent back to the concrete, real, flesh-and-blood assembly?

Then, taught by second-century churches and in communion with them, do we see the dangers of reading only one book and asking only its questions?

Part Two

The Beasts on Our Sundays

Assembly according to the Gospel

6

Word, Sacrament, and Assembly according to the Gospel

The Gospels in Assemblies Today

Why does this inquiry about the coherence of the four Gospels with ancient Christian assemblies matter so much? What are the intentions of such a study? Much of our response to these questions has already been evident in the foregoing chapters themselves. The italicized questions at the end of each of these chapters have woven current concerns into our inquiry about the original functions of the Gospels. But so has the clear presupposition operative here: that our current Christian assemblies for worship live in continuity and even communion with the ancient assemblies that heard these books. If the books had a certain interest in and concern for those gatherings, if the books sought either to reform or to illumine those meetings, then that interest and concern, that reform appeal or illumination ought still be heard by us, even granting all of our differences from those old meetings.

The four Gospels of the New Testament still belong in an assembly where they are read and heard aloud. They come to life there. They come to their purpose. Of course they are read elsewhere, are found to be interesting elsewhere. But it is in an assembly that they seem to breathe the air of their origin and intention. In an assembly they seem both to hold out hope and to push for reform, to criticize practices and to enable faith. By their words, their narratives, their rhetoric, their structure, their symbols, their juxtapositions to other scriptures and to each other, they do a communal work that is both mysterious and critical.

To so read the Gospels is to discover again what sort of books they are. That discovery is no loss, but an immense gain. By actually working with the four texts, we have seen that the Gospels are not primarily historical reports about Jesus, not documents working out differing views of what Jesus may have been like in his life, not invitations to imagine what actually happened then. They are,

153

rather, announcements of Jesus-then becoming Jesus-now, especially Jesus-now in assembly. This makes them far more interesting than we had otherwise thought, intentionally engaging assemblies—and thus us—in their stories. Not unlike Jonah or Job, for example, they would be diminished if they would be construed as historical reports rather than as fascinating and profound poetic constructions around issues of immense religious import. But quite unlike Jonah and Job, they do give accounts of a real person who acted and who was cruelly killed in a real place and time. They evidence the faith that this person still remains encounter-able and that those actions and that death matter profoundly now, in the assembly where the books are being read. The books make their meanings available in words of powerful, layered symbolism and in interpretive quotations from the old scriptures. They do so through subtle juxtapositions that move across a circular construction as in Mark, through structured discourses as in Matthew, through a series of meal stories as in Luke, or through a forward-leaning narrative sequence of signs, discourses, and assemblies as in John. They ring the changes on stories of the teachings and actions of Jesus, seeking to make those teachings and actions available to the current hearers. In every case, the goal seems to be the proclama-tion of the presence of the crucified risen one in current assemblies, the presenta-tion of the Gospel book itself as either a means of or a witness to that presence, and the elaboration of the consequences that flow from that presence. "There you will see him," says Mark. "I am there among them," says the Jesus of Matthew. "The master will have his own slaves sit down and eat, and he will come and serve them," says the Jesus of Luke. And "these signs are written so that you may come to believe that Jesus is the Messiah, the Son of God," says John.

The liturgical developments in the churches, the practices with which this study began[1]—the carrying of the bound Gospels into the midst of an assembly, for example, and the singing around this book as if addressing the risen one encountered in the text—thus can be seen as having caught the intention of the Gospels themselves. The classic liturgical practices of East and West can rightly be taken as hermeneutical keys to understanding the books. So can the remark-able statement of Martin Luther:

> When you open the book containing the Gospels and read or hear how Christ comes here or there, or how someone is brought to him, you should therein perceive the sermon or the gospel through which he is coming to you, or you are

---

1. See above, chap. 1.

being brought to him. For the proclamation of the Gospel is nothing else than Christ coming to us, or we being brought to him. When you see how he works, however, and how he helps everyone to whom he comes or who is brought to him, then rest assured that faith is accomplishing this in you and that he is offering your soul exactly the same sort of help and favor through the Gospel. If you pause here and let him do you good, that is, if you believe that he benefits and helps you, then you really have it. Then Christ is yours, presented to you as a gift. After that it is necessary that you turn this into an example and deal with your neighbor in the very same way, be given also to him as a gift and an example.[2]

Luther's statement may be read as an existential rationale for the Gospel procession and the Gospel acclamation or for the "Lesser Entrance," as these practices are called in the East. In East and West, the reading of the Gospel is now one of the major moments of the liturgy, one of the moments from which much of the rest of the liturgy may be interpreted. In East and West, the Gospel book, read in assembly, stands for the presence of Jesus Christ in our midst.

Of course, our assemblies are different from the assemblies first addressed by the Gospels. Our ideas of liturgy and ordered sacraments, ecclesial institutions, professional clergy and church buildings would be largely unrecognizable to Christians of those meetings. Our ways of reading books, our ability (or relative inability) to perceive a narrative ring or to understand symbols, even our patterns for thinking about reality, may very well differ from those that would have been present in such assemblies.[3] But between those meetings and Christian assemblies in the present time grounds for a deep communion nonetheless exists. Our most central practices—our reading of scriptures, our prayers for the world and for healing, our meals, our use of the baptismal bath—have roots in the diverse practices of those old meetings. Our very use of the Gospel books themselves comes from them. Most especially, we share with them the practice of remembering and continuing to encounter Jesus.

---

2. Martin Luther, "A Brief Instruction on What to Look for and Expect in the Gospels," in *Word and Sacrament, I*, ed. E. Theodore Bachmann, Luther's Works, vol. 35 (Philadelphia: Fortress Press, 1960), 121, trans. altered. The original German of the phrase "for the proclamation of the Gospel is nothing else . . ." reads "denn Evangeli predigen ist nicht anders . . ." See *D. Martin Luthers Werke* 10.1.1 (Weimar: 1910), 13–14.

3. For example, see the comments on an older "soft literalism" in Marcus J. Borg, *Reading the Bible Again for the First Time: Taking the Bible Seriously but Not Literally* (San Francisco: HarperSanFrancisco, 2002), 11.

Assembly according to the Gospel

The Gospels thus can be read as having something to say about the meals of our meetings, as also about our scripture reading, preaching, baptism, prayer, leadership, collection for the poor, communal boundaries, and the meaning of Sunday itself. They do this not by directly addressing any of these topics, but by being concerned with the identity of the one around whom they wish to see the assembly and its practices centered. The books themselves, read in the assembly, intend to be one means of that centering. In the remarkable metaphor of Richard Burridge,[4] these books are not clear glass, through which we may look at the historical Jesus. Neither are they mirrors, however, through which we may look only at ourselves as we interpret or at the author or authors as they write of their communities. They are, rather, stained glass, like the great stained-glass images of Jesus Christ and those around him. They are interpretive and doxological texts, intending to enable an encounter with God. Of course, to press the metaphor, the place for stained glass is in the house of a church, in an assembly's space. The authentic, classic way of remembering Jesus, of encountering his identity, includes the practices of assembly, around and reflecting the Gospel books.[5]

We need to think further about those practices in the light of what we have found in the four books. The classic sixteenth-century text about the church, the seventh article of the Augsburg Confession, itself a document of reform like the Gospels, offers a tool that we might use in this further thought. That article reads, in part: "The church is the assembly of all believers among whom the gospel is purely preached and the holy sacraments are administered according to the

---

4. Richard A. Burridge, "Who Writes, Why, and for Whom?," in Marcus Bockmuehl and Donald A. Hagner, eds., *The Written Gospel* (Cambridge: Cambridge University Press, 2005), 113.

5. Marianne Sawicki, *Crossing Galilee: Architectures of Contact in the Occupied Land of Jesus* (Harrisburg: Trinity International, 2000), 160: "Remembering Jesus occurs authentically in various places and practices, among which are liturgy, charity, teaching, and healing, as well as disciplined study of the Gospels. Scholarly historical investigations of who Jesus was and of how he was remembered by the paleochurch comprise a vital component in the contemporary discernment of who Jesus is. This is the position of Catholic and Orthodox Christianity." Sawicki sees this position confirmed by the fact of the four Gospels being maintained, side by side, in the "paleochurch," and contrasts the position with what are essentially Burridge's "mirror" and "clear glass" as well as with a scholarly process which rejects cultic and devotional memories as reliable keys to the identity of Jesus.

gospel (*lauts des Evangelii*)."[6] That Reformation-era assertion, written by Philip Melanchthon, subscribed to by several German princes, and proposed in 1530 as a grounds for Christian unity, perhaps meant to urge that the sacraments of the church should be celebrated in ways that conform to such original Christian practice as was discoverable in the texts of the Gospel books themselves. If so, the assertion was dependent on Renaissance conceptions of the recovery of ancient and "pure" practice, of the "original" and the old that could transcend current distortions. Such conceptions of the original, of course, were themselves liable to distortions, to the fallacy of origins, to idealizations of the past, and to unacknowledged projections from the present time. Nothing in paleo-Christian practice as evidenced in the Gospels, for example, was called a "sacrament."

But the assertion of the Augsburg Confession ought not be read in this way. The singular "gospel" recalls the singular used by Paul and points to the singular in the second-century titles for the books: "The Gospel according to . . ." The books are witnesses to a single gospel, like Paul and like the Beasts around the Lamb.[7] The assertion of the Confession also and especially points to the Pauline and Lutheran idea that the gospel is a word that occurs in the assembly, an event, a means of grace,[8] a witness to what God is doing in Jesus Christ for the life of the world, even itself the very presence of Christ. Then the Confession would be read now to indicate that our practices in worship should not so much strive to mimic ancient or "original" practices as that they should be evaluated according to whether they are filled with the one gospel, whether our preaching and our sacraments join the witness of the Beasts, whether they, too, are locations for the encounter with the presence of the risen crucified one and for the faith that comes to birth through him. More: "according to the gospel" could be read also as calling forth a critical reading from the four books. Our interest then would not be to have assemblies act like the Markan or the Johannine assemblies but to let the critique that the Gospels brought to the assemblies they knew come also to our assemblies.

We also continue to have our own versions of the paleo-Christian "clubs." We ourselves have assemblies that meet for a great variety of reasons, making

---

6. The Augsburg Confession, in Robert Kolb and Timothy J. Wengert, eds., *The Book of Concord* (Minneapolis: Fortress Press, 2000), 42. Cf. *Die Bekenntnisschriften der evangelisch-lutherischen Kirche* (Göttingen: Vandenhoeck & Ruprecht, 1963), 61.

7. And like the angel of Rev. 14:6: "Then I saw another angel flying in midheaven, having an eternal gospel to proclaim to those who live on the earth."

8. See Augsburg Confession, article 5.

use of our own cultural materials to understand how and why we meet.[9] Our congregations play societal roles in our own times. What we call "churches," placed under sociological consideration, might be thought of in the first place as religious audiences or ethical and religious interest groups or ethnic societies or romantic pageants or extended families or local chapters of international organizations or simply people seeking genuine community. Of course. These are the models of understanding available to us. But then, just as with the Hellenistic-era gatherings addressed by Paul and the Gospels, our assemblies are also invited, in the reading of these books, to sort through the purposes and rituals of our meetings and to inquire how they might be reformed "according to the gospel." The result will not necessarily be assemblies that all look alike. It may be assemblies that find their unity, across significant diversity, in shared principles for reform.

It has come to be common to understand that the Gospel narratives give new content to religious titles used to describe Jesus. "Christ," "Lord," and "King" all are significantly revalued when they are held against the narrative of the one who was crucified. This is a messiah who joins the lot of the unclean, a lord who serves, a king who reigns from the cross. Several years ago, Edward Schillebeeckx pointed out how many of those names might be regarded as the projections of our own religious hopes.[10] He might also have noted how each of these names can be and has been misused, pressed toward religious malformation and religious oppression. But such names do not finally determine who Jesus is. Rather, in the Gospels, who Jesus was and is redetermines the names. There is a negative theology, a critical theology, at work in the New Testament in regard to the names. One can see it, for example, in the first chapter of John. There, in succession, Jesus is called Word of God, Life, True Light, Lamb of God, Son of God, Rabbi, Messiah, Prophet, King of Israel, Son of Man, and even Bethel or House of God. Yet, there John the Baptist also says, "Among you stands one whom you do not know" (1:26). It is as if the *more-than-the-names* or the *other-than-the-names* that is in Jesus—the narrative reversals in the Gospels of the expectations present in the names but also the existence of the risen one beyond all such projections—comes toward us, revaluing the names. The names can carry our own religious hopes and thus even

9. See my *Holy People: A Liturgical Ecclesiology* (Minneapolis: Fortress Press, 1999), 26–31, for a discussion of our current ideas of assembly and their possible juxtaposition to biblical critique.

10. See Edward Schillebeeckx, *Tussentijds verhaal over twee Jezus boeken* (Bloemendaal: Nelissen, 1978), 31–34.

ourselves, but the reversals and inversions of the names can carry us thereby into new and deeper meaning, saving us and saving even our religion. The resonances of the names—their great hopes—are still there, but broken and saved.[11]

Something like this very process seems to have gone on with the word *gospel*, whereby the announcement of the beneficence of emperors was broken to a new purpose, an astonishing proclamation of God acting in the cross for the sake of the life of the world. Hopes for a very wide world to participate in prosperity and peace were still there, but in an utterly new way.

The same method of gospel critique may be applied to our various assemblies for worship. So our gatherings for worship may be considered sacred communities or even holy clubs of a sort, with their own identifying communal practices, including religious prayer, with their own leadership, and with their own promise that engagement with them will lead to divine blessings for us. But when the Gospels are set next to these practices, inversions and revaluations occur. Think, for a moment, only of Mark. Mark 9:36 calls our group to attend to the marginal child, and Mark 10:30 promises us a hundredfold mothers and brothers and sisters and children and houses. Reading this book, our group is thus continually invited to be both permeable and linked to others beyond our boundaries, to revalue "community" and "family." In both Markan texts, the "more" that is in Jesus, the reality of Jesus beyond our projections, is coming toward our group and gifting it with change. The crucified risen one is received in the child, and so God is received. The new reign of God, as it is in Jesus and the gospel, breaks in to our world with a new sort of family and a new sort of house. Then, Mark 8:15 counsels our practices to avoid the yeast of the Pharisees and the yeast of Herod. If our practices include a shared meal of one sort or another, as is likely, then the "more" that is in Jesus, the reality of Jesus beyond our projections, is coming toward our meals and gifting them with a new meaning, calling them beyond purity and privilege. So also Mark 9:35 (and 10:41) addresses our leadership, continually inviting it to serve. Mark 11:25 addresses our prayer, inviting it to be for more than ourselves and to be linked with our forgiveness of others. And Mark 14:3-9 invites us to find our hope for blessing expanded to include our needy neighbor, the poor who are always with us. In all of these things, the reality of Jesus beyond our projections—the crucified one alive in the text, the

---

11. This "breaking" or this revaluation of names is what I have written of elsewhere as "the breaking of symbols." See, for example, my *Holy Ground: A Liturgical Cosmology* (Minneapolis: Fortress Press, 2003), 34–35.

Jesus present in the Gospel and inverting our ordinary projections—is coming toward our practices and transforming them.

One could engage in something very like this exercise with each of the other Gospels as well. Matthew's discourses, Luke's travel narrative, and John's final assemblies address our meetings and invite their revaluation. It is not that the Gospels give us much information about the actual activities of the assemblies to which they were originally addressed, as if we then might mimic those practices. It is, rather, that they give us remarkable voices for reform, addressed to diverse activities, calling them all to be broken for the purposes of the gospel.

These reflections must not be turned into idealism nor made the grounds for idealism's companion, compulsion. The words of the Gospels, by their juxtapositions to our practices, invite us to reconsideration, surprise us with gracious new meanings. They do not compel us. Our meetings for worship will continue to be groups or clubs with identifying communal rituals, a religious leadership and a hope for blessings from God. If we are not careful, however, even though they are called "churches," they can become highly boundaried groups with domineering leaders, practices centered in our own identity, reinforcing what we already thought, and prayers primarily for ourselves. But, to say the matter in faith, they may also find themselves, in the Spirit poured out from the crucified risen one, being reformed according to the gospel: their communal center may be determined by words, a meal, and a bath, continually reformed to speak of the crucified Christ; their prayers may be for others; their leadership may serve; their collections may send assistance to the hungry; and they may find themselves continually becoming God's own assemblies again: *ecclesia semper reformanda*.

Such reforms according to the gospel belong in all our assemblies, regardless of their otherwise great diversity. By this view, what our Sunday assemblies are for is telling the truth about the world and God, enabling a group of needy people to come to trust in God again through Jesus Christ, and so, by the power of the Spirit, beginning to make signs of witnessing love in the world.

Houses, Feedings, Appearances

This may be a new way for us to think about the Gospels. We are familiar with the idea that the New Testament contains some material that speaks directly about the church and its assemblies. The book of the Acts of the Apostles describes what the assembly does as its gathers around "the apostles' teaching and fellowship, the breaking of bread and the prayers" (2:42) and as it cares for those in need. Then the book tells stories of the founding of several such assemblies in the ancient world, implying these things as always providing the necessary center. Paul urges the assembly at Corinth, gathered for worship, to act "decently and in order" (1 Cor. 14:40) and proposes ways that this may be done. He criticizes and redirects the celebration of the Lord's Supper (1 Cor. 11), especially arguing against the exclusion of the poor. He also calls for collections of money in the assemblies, perhaps as a sign of solidarity and communion with the poor of the church in Jerusalem, perhaps as a more general enacting of his undertaking to "remember the poor" (Gal. 2:10). Matthew gives us developed rules for mutual correction and forgiveness in the life of the church as well as a surprising assertion about how small a group—two or three—may constitute the *minyan* of a Christian assembly (Matt. 18:15-22), because of the presence of the risen Lord among them. And the pastoral epistles provide our earliest models of the genre that becomes the "church order," documents seeking to organize the doctrine, worship, leadership, and life of the Christian assemblies. 1 Timothy, for example—in the passage that has become the source for the idea that the "rule of praying establishes the rule of believing," *lex orandi, lex credendi*—urges that the church in assembly make intercessions for everybody (2:1-4). All of these resources can and have served through the ages as continuing calls to ecclesial reform.

But we are not so familiar with the Gospels' coherence with assembly also making such proposals. Still, as we have seen, there are many images in the Gospel books that do urge communal reform, albeit more indirectly. The house at the center of Mark (9:30-50), the house built on the rock in Matthew (7:24-25), the disciples going to and eating at Emmaus in Luke (24:13-35), and both the farewell gathering and the final Sunday assemblies in John (13–17 and 20:19-29) all call to our assemblies. So do the images of the faithful and wise slave in charge of the household in Matthew (24:45-47) and the returning and serving master in Luke (12:35-38). So do many other stories. In thinking about how our assemblies might be reformed according to the gospel, we might for a moment consider the narratives in the house, the narratives of the feeding of the multitude, and the narratives of the appearance of the risen one with which the Gospels conclude. These narratives can make us think of our own assemblies. They can also challenge those assemblies.

These narratives, first of all, give us images for current assemblies. We have observed how the narratives of the house in the Gospels were probably, at the outset, intended to invite the readers to think about the very house-churches in which they were gathered. They still do so. The house, in the Gospels frequently a place of assembly, of healings, of teaching, and of communal meals, calls the reader or hearer of the Gospel book to imagine the house of assembly in which she or he participates as also a place of these very events, a place of the continuing presence and work of Jesus. But then the unique narratives that occur in the house are all the more important. For example, in Mark 2:1-12 the crowd at the house of Jesus is so great and so impenetrable that those who are bringing the paralyzed man must remove part of the roof in order to let him down on his mat before the healing and forgiving Lord. In connection with this story, it is fascinating to note that most of the actual remains we have discovered of the houses where house churches met demonstrate that the house had to be remodeled for the use of the church:[12] a *triclinium* was finally not big enough for the purposes of the Eucharist; a family space was not adequate for this new, more open family. This text from Mark might still be seen as the *locus classicus* for the remodeling of a church building. In any case, the readers and hearers of this narrative—including the readers and hearers of the narrative read in our assemblies today—may know that their assembly is indeed the place of healing and forgiveness, that here many people who are paralyzed in guilt and fear are enabled to rise and walk. That is what the Gospels mean: Jesus Christ in the power of the Spirit comes here, attending to the fearful and the sinful, bringing life, even against all religious strictures. Our assembly is this house.

Similarly, the narratives of the feeding of the multitude were seen, in ancient Christian teaching as in much modern exegesis, as reflections on eucharistic practice. Also in the assembly, Jesus takes, blesses, and breaks the loaves (Mark 6:41). Here the wilderness is green (6:39), the people are constituted as a new people of the exodus (6:40) or as coming from all the four corners of the world (8:3, 9), and they eat also the fish of the resurrection and of the end of chaos, perhaps Leviathan itself. Twelve and then seven baskets-full of fragments are left over, as if corresponding to the bread-serving leadership of the Jewish-Christian assembly and the Hellenistic-Christian assembly of Jerusalem—the "Twelve" and the "Seven"—reflected in Acts (6:1-6). And the Fourth Gospel uses the "sign" of this event to ground the great discourse on Jesus as the Bread of Life. No wonder painted images in the catacombs and mosaic images at Ravenna and on ancient Orthodox patens show the fish of these narratives—and of the resurrection appearance by the sea (John 21)—on the table of the Last Supper

---

12. See above, chap. 3, n.23.

or the table at Emmaus. Ancient patristic preaching saw this set of narratives as one important image for the church, gathered around the risen one, himself the bread of life in the wilderness, himself the *ichthus*-fish. Current lectionary preaching may use the same texts as images for our assemblies.

The narratives of the resurrection appearances at the end of the Gospel books also and especially give us a primary image of the assembly. The story of the appearance on the road to and at the table in Emmaus (Luke 24) seems to have been intended to give to the Lukan churches an assurance of the presence of the risen one, known in the reading and interpretation of the scriptures and in the shared meal in all of their Sunday assemblies. Indeed, our current liturgical pattern of Gathering, Word, Meal, and Sending seems to be anchored here, parallel to the narrative's welcome of the stranger, interpretation of all the scriptures, blessing and breaking of the bread, and running back with the news to the city of death. The original ending of the Fourth Gospel (John 20:19-31) is less liturgically clear, but the assembly imaged there does meet on the first day of the week and then again "a week later,"[13] a succession of meetings, Sunday after Sunday, that has come down to our own day. And our assemblies, as well, are intended for the speaking of Christ's peace, the breathing out of the Spirit, and the sending into the world with the word of forgiveness, all focused around the reaching out in faith to touch the wounds of this man who is our God. Our assemblies, too, read the books that are written so that we might come to believe, even though we do not see. Furthermore, Matthew's Gospel (28:16-20) gives us the assembly around the risen one in teaching and baptizing throughout the world—word and sacrament in its other primary form. And the risen one does not go away, but is with this assembly always, just as the text says earlier: "Where two or three are gathered in my name, I am there among them" (18:20). Finally, we have seen that the circular shape of Mark replicates the very shape of an assembly gathering and proposes the presence of Christ in that assembly.

These narrative images of the assembly are a great gift to us. They help us to see that, gathered in the assembly, we may be in that house, gathered with that multitude, assembled around the resurrection, sent with the word of forgiveness.

But these narratives are also a continuing challenge to reform. I think that they were intended to be so from the very beginning. The conclusions of Luke and John and Matthew and the whole shape of Mark meant to call the congregations for which they were written to an ongoing practice that understood the

---

13. Or "eight days later," as the Greek of John 20:26 reads.

presence of the risen one and the outpoured Spirit in the assembly itself, that set out word and meal in clarity every Sunday, that read centrally from the book that enabled faith, and that spread teaching and baptism throughout the world. The Gospels, especially in their conclusions, still call us to the practice of these central things.

More: the narratives of the feeding of the multitude have that astonishing challenge to the disciples: "You give them something to eat" (Mark 6:37). Then those baskets-full are left over, still to be passed out and given away, famine relief in the world. For Mark, that is what leadership of the churches *is*: people who serve the assembly with bread, servants of the assembly's meal—bread of the word, bread of the sacrament, bread for the poor. The disciples do not always clearly understand this. Nonetheless, they are called to this service. The Eucharist of the church always points toward a hungry world, begins to make a sign about God's intention for the sharing of food with the most needy. The Gospels call our presiders and other ministers to a continual reform of their understanding of office. They are to gather the assembly around the meal here and they are to call the assembly to turn with help to a hungry world. "You give them something to eat." Of course, the local assembly will not solve the world hunger problem, but it can begin to be a sign of God's intention, God's mission.

Then we may also see how the house narratives carry critical, reforming intent and did so from their first use in the Gospel books. The narrative of the paralytic and the removed roof, for example, seems to be an image for something very much like the critical concern of Paul about the assembly at Corinth, the concern that the poor and enslaved were being excluded, being left only to look in upon the excessive feast of the rich (1 Cor. 11:21-22). The immediately following story of the meal with tax collectors and sinners in Levi's house (Mark 2:13-17) provides another such image. When this story is then put beside the central Markan house narrative, the welcoming of the child into the midst as the very welcoming of Jesus (9:35-36; cf. 10:13-16), then the implications become stronger yet. We have seen that the child, in New Testament imagery, is not a sign to evoke our modern sentimentality. Rather, the child—the little one, the powerless one—is the consummate outsider, the marginalized, in Greco-Roman culture the unwanted one, the one frequently exposed to death or given into slavery to be rid of it. These stories urge the inclusion of the outsider and the marginalized at the heart of the assembly. They criticize the inevitable boundaries that a religious or ritual group sets up as it tends to become a "club." They enact in narrative image something like the very word of the Matthean Jesus who has the Son of Man, at the last judgment, praise the ones who feed and clothe Christ in the suffering outsiders (25:31-46). They give us an image for the passionate concern of the letter of James (2:1-7) for the permeability of the assembly, or, echoing James, the passionate concern of the third century Syrian book, the *Didascalia*. The *Didascalia* says: "If a poor man or woman should arrive, whether from your own congregation or from another—and especially if they are elderly—and there is no place for them, then you, the bishop, with all your heart provide a place for them, even if you have to sit on the ground" (2:58:6).[14] The very inclusion of the bishop's chair in this directive recalls the Markan narrative. The child is welcomed to the midst as a sign of Christ after the Markan Jesus counters the hierarchical pretensions of the Twelve with his saying, "Whoever wants to be first must be last of all and servant of all" (Mark 9:35).

These house narratives stand, then, as images for continual reform in the assembly. The house must be remodeled to welcome the excluded, as the roof was removed. The pretensions of powerful leadership must yield to service, as the marginalized are welcomed again and again into the center of the house. These reflections may lead in our time—as they may have in the ancient house churches—to actual building remodeling: accessible doorways and wheelchair-friendly floors; short pews or benches for children and their parents along with beautiful and movable chairs for a diverse assembly; a central table, perhaps at the lowest place in the room, with the assembly banked around it. In any case, the assembly must cease being a passive crowd, mere consumers of the holy things who are, at the same time, keeping others out at the door. The assembly must turn, rather, in service to the latest comer, to the least member, to the usually excluded, and together with them to shared participation in the work of the meeting. Indeed, if the death and resurrection of Jesus Christ are the very heart of the assembly, then that assembly must see that the sufferings of the marginalized are themselves embodiments and signs of that central mystery. As Mark 9:30-50 counsels, let our houses be places where the word of the crucified risen one is central, changing our ideas of God and of the world, and continually restructuring our meetings to be nonhierarchical, noncompetitive, welcoming the powerless and the outsiders, and at peace. Such are among the continuing challenges of the Gospels to our current assemblies.

---

14. Sebastian Brock and Michael Vasey, *The Liturgical Portions of the Didascalia* (Bramcote: Grove, 1982), 17.

Of course, we will fail. We have failed throughout history. Sometimes we have failed abysmally. Against the witness of these narrative images, the protection of the assembly by the so-called *disciplina arcani*, the extensive development of the ecclesiastical hierarchy, and the more recent centering of the celebration on our own identities are all such failures. Even more modestly, our simply trying to have a good assembly for liturgy will inevitably carry with it the formation of a group with boundaries. But the call to reform remains. So does the assurance that the Gospel narratives and the Gospel signs can set out God's mercy in the midst of all of our assemblies, no matter how often we fail.

Preaching, Eucharist, and Baptism according to the Gospel

But, besides these more general reflections about assembly, reading the Gospels as coherent with assembly also offers some concrete help to our actual liturgical practices.

Take preaching, for example. The question may rightly be raised whether what we have been seeing in the Gospels can be useful to us at all, given our attention here to the full structure of each of these books and the idea that originally each them might have been read as a whole in assembly.[15] Most of us, after all, read from the Gospels in short, scheduled lectionary sections, in pericopes, with little attention to the structure of the whole. But I have argued that the liturgical development that surrounded this reading of a Gospel pericope with acclamations to the risen Christ, as if the words of the book itself were the risen one in our midst, is a legitimate interpretation of at least the Markan and the Johannine understanding of the function of the book. Furthermore, the very situation of this reading within the structure of the Eucharist, with the eucharistic meal always representing the many meals of the Gospels and, especially, the meals that proclaim the passion, recapitulates something of the structure of a whole Gospel book. To be a participant in such a liturgy is to find oneself in the Gospel structure, held within the Gospel as a living event. Then the business of the preacher must include a willingness to make clear those connections across the circle of the Gospel book and the circle of the liturgy. The preacher must be willing to teach in the house,[16] knowing how to use the Gospel pericope to stand for the intention of the whole Gospel book. I think that such a full word-

---

15. Though one needs to remember Justin's "for as long as there is time."
16. Cf. Mark 4:34; 5:19; 7:17; 9:28; 10:10; as well as 9:33.

meal event, with a diverse reading of juxtaposed scriptures, is a better idea in our time than a new attempt to read interpretively the whole of one Gospel book, an attempt where the accent will likely fall on the interpretive skill of the reader rather than on the intention of the Gospel text.

The Gospel text is not a news report. It is a symbol of our actual need and, at the same time, a symbol of the crucified risen one alive in this assembly. Its function comes to clarity as it is set side by side with the other symbols in the assembly's liturgy—with the gathering itself, with all the readings, with the work of the preacher, with the assembly song, with the prayers, and with the meal. Preachers can help us see each Gospel pericope as such a symbol. They will do so the more as they renounce the literalism that so easily makes the story into an event unrelated to us or makes it vulnerable to the preacher's own psychologizing or idealizing. They will also do so as they avoid turning texts into "wide truths of life," even general religious and salvational truths, self-help advice for individuals. Instead, the preacher may help us see how the stories in the four Gospels always present an image of human need and, then, always carry us to the cross and so to the crucified one now, acting here. Preachers will be helped by deeply knowing the meaning-giving structure of each Gospel. By showing us how, in the structure of its Gospel, the individual pericopes open toward—indeed, lean toward—the gift of the cross, the meals of the cross, and the present assembly around the crucified, preachers can then interpret the entire word-meal liturgy as a Gospel event and sign, turning its "sending" toward the sharing of food and care with the hungry poor and so toward a new vision of the actual circumstances of the world.

In our assemblies—at least in those making use of a classic Christian lectionary —the Gospel pericope will also be read side by side with a text from the Hebrew scriptures and usually also with a text from Paul or one of the other early letter writers. Often a psalm will be sung as a way to receive and bridge these readings. There is an elegant beauty in this abundance of scripture and, with that beauty, a resistance to easy theme making. The several scriptures resound against each other, speaking differing images and ideas, refusing ideology and making space for the encounter with God. For the Christian preacher, the Matthean and the Johannine sense that Gospel events were in fulfillment of the scriptures (e.g., Matt. 2:17; John 19:36-37), the Johannine idea that the resurrection could be known from the scriptures (John 20:9), and the Lukan "Today!" of Jesus in relationship to the scriptures (Luke 4:21) all point toward the idea that the Gospel text will function as interpretive center for such reading in the assembly. So does the Lukan image of Jesus "beginning with Moses and all the prophets," interpreting to the disciples on the way to Emmaus "the things concerning himself in all the scriptures" (Luke 24:27). Such a hermeneutical center does not mean that the Gospel pericope is the "best" text. Nor ought it lead to ideas of religious progress or Christian supersessionism. Rather, the God who, in all the scriptures, justifies the ungodly, gives life to the dead, and brings into existence the things that do not exist—as Paul sums up the faith of Abraham and of Israel (Rom. 4:5, 17)—is the very God we meet now in Jesus, through the power of the Spirit, here. It is to this trinitarian encounter that the Gospel now gives witness in our meetings. And, according to the Gospels themselves, the scriptures provide imagery for who this Jesus is and what he does. The preacher can rightly draw on that imagery, in all of the Sunday texts—not simply in one, as preachers are so often taught today—to speak our need truthfully, to reorient our knowledge of the world and of God, and to call the assembly into that renewed trust in God that comes to be through Jesus.

Counsel for preaching according to the gospel, then, might be given to a preacher in this way: first read the Gospel text, considering how it stands in the whole structure of that Gospel book, how it moves toward and illumines the meaning of the cross, how it evokes the assembly, and how it may stand as a symbol for the risen one in the current meeting. Think, for example, of how the signs work in John, how the circle works in Mark, how the discourses and the meals work in Matthew and Luke, all moving us toward Christ in the present assembly. Then read all of the texts of the Sunday, including the Gospel again, in the original languages if possible, considering how each of the texts brings the current need of the world to expression and how each of the texts also expresses the abundant mercy of God, how each text can provide both words for the "law" and words for the gospel of Jesus Christ. Then read the prayer of the day from the liturgy to be celebrated, hymns and other texts from the same liturgy, and a variety of commentaries or lectionary helps, considering the whole shape of the liturgy, especially as that shape will recapitulate the shape of the Gospel book. Consider especially the meal, asking how your sermon may finally say in words drawn from the texts of the day the same thing that the meal will say in sign. Consider also baptism, thinking about how this bath which has constituted your assembly continually washes over us the meaning of these texts. Then think about the time of the church year, as it also carries the intention of the Gospels, and think about our own times. Know what time it is. Read the newspaper. Read current novels or poetry or watch current films. And read the social, biological, and physical environment around your assembly. In all of these latter readings, watch for the cry of need so that you can tell something of the truth about our world as well as the truth about God. Then imagine your assembly, and begin to consider how you will speak both these cries and the gospel of Jesus Christ, articulating again the meaning of your Sunday meeting, so that these very people may again come to trust in God with their lives. Such a preparation follows from the idea that the Gospels are coherent with the assembly and have words for it, indeed, that the Gospels propose the presence of the crucified risen one in the assemblies.[17]

In all of our assemblies, as diverse as they are and can be, preaching according to the gospel will speak the truth of our need and of God's mercy, as that truth is present in the Gospels, will bear witness to the crucified and risen Christ symbolized by the Gospel text and imaged by all the readings, and will aim at once again enabling us to believe.

Or take the Eucharist. We have seen that, while the meal practice of the ancient churches may have been diverse, the meal critique of the Gospels had a certain shared convergence. If, by thinking of the Gospels in relationship to paleo-Christian meetings, some light was cast on the origins of the Eucharist, it seems that several ongoing proposals for reform in our own churches inevitably follow. Of course, we are still in need of recovering the very idea that the Eucharist in our churches is a meal, in continuity with the meals of the Hebrew scriptures, the meals of Jesus, and the supper clubs of the paleo-Christians. We need to celebrate it every Sunday, with recognizable food at a recognizable if strong table, with staple food and festive drink, with generous and beautiful vessels,[18] and with beautiful table prayers. Diversity in practice will inevitably occur and is welcome here: in the words and patterns of the prayers, in the cultural resonances of the staple food and festive drink, and in the way the food is shared. That meal recovery is the first movement of reform. Each of these matters that belong to meal practice is worth attention. We simply cannot continue, for example, to use the wafer bread—the "hosts"—that were invented in the Western church, precisely with the prerogatives of the clergy and of "sacrificial" practice in mind, and have continued in use simply because of convenience.

---

17. For further reflections on preparation for preaching, see my *The Pastor: A Spirituality* (Minneapolis: Fortress Press, 2006), 41–58.

18. See Thomas O'Loughlin, "The Liturgical Vessels of the Latin Eucharistic Liturgy," *Worship* 82 (2008): 482–504.

But then, the words of the Gospels still speak critically to our meals. Having a beautiful dinner with beautiful food is not enough, certainly not when its abundance and beauty are only for us. What will unite us across our local diversities are the very themes of reform working in the midst of our various meals: that this is a "hungry feast," proclaiming the death of Jesus and the present gift of the risen one, open for all to come and eat and drink, but then sending both its participants and its necessary excess into a hungry world as signs of the life-giving and merciful intention of God. The Eucharist will not solve world hunger, but it will make a meaningful sign toward the poor and the hopeless. Such is a reform we still—and continually—need. The Eucharist ought not be centered on us and our consumption. It also ought not be centered on our offering anything to God, except the response of turning in love to our neighbor. It is to be centered on Jesus Christ, giving himself away for the sake of the life of the world, which center is a continually revealed gift. Still, that critical word ought not mean a crimped style of meal. The taste of the gospel rightly comes in a loaf of good bread and a shared cup of good wine—or in such basic eating and festal drinking made available in other, locally recognizable cultural forms—and in a gracious ritual practice, even as this food is shared here only in fragments, that a wider world may also live.

How shall the meal proclaim the death of Jesus? The so-called institution narrative (or "words of institution," as this narrative is called in many traditions) is perhaps best understood as liturgical catechesis about the meaning of the central Christian meal, not as originally a ritual text or a set of ritual instructions.[19] It has that role in Paul's letter to the Corinthians and in the Synoptic Gospels. Nonetheless, its content is an urgent catechesis, in need of being brought constantly before the faithful assembly. That it has found its way into most Christian thanksgivings at the Lord's table is an appropriate development, a strong proclamation of the central gift of Christian faith, an outstanding example of Christian tradition at work, even if that location has been misunderstood to be "consecratory." In correcting that misunderstanding, however, it is not wise simply to dismiss these words but, rather, to reinterpret them as proclamation. The words ought not now be so accompanied with manual acts nor so isolated uniquely, as if they were a magical incantation by the priesthood, forcing Jesus' presence. Still, the more urgent question is whether the words themselves have simply

---

19. Paul F. Bradshaw, *Eucharistic Origins* (London: SPCK, 2004), 14. See also John F. Baldovin, S.J., "The Usefulness of Liturgical History, *Worship* 82 (2008): 14–17.

become so formulaic as to lose their reforming power. How shall our meals indeed "proclaim the Lord's death until he comes"? Perhaps by includin words of this gift in a new and better "dispersed euchological way," to echo the recent Roman Catholic estimation of the practice of the Prayer of Addai and Mari among Syrian Christians.[20] Perhaps by better preaching conjoined with strong intercessory praying for a suffering world. Perhaps by remembering the poor. We should attend to what seems to be the counsel of both Mark and Luke, echoing Paul: hold no Eucharist without a collection for the poor and hungry beyond our assembly.

Make the meal clearly a meal, though only the fragment of a meal: a beautiful and evocative shared loaf and cup. But continually reform that meal on the trinitarian trajectory of the crucified and risen Christ, in the power of the Spirit, going out toward the life of the world before God. In such a way, eucharistic practice, in all of its diversities, will remain continually in touch with its origins. There is a start in listening seriously to the reforming Gospels, those first-and second-century books marked by a mutual coherence with the Christian assembly.[21] In all of our assemblies, as diverse as they are and can be, Eucharist according to the gospel will be a weekly meal that proclaims the death of the Lord and, as in the Gospels, enables the encounter with the crucified risen one, turning us in love and service toward the world.

Or take baptism. We have not extensively discussed baptism here, in the preceding chapters of this book. But we ought not be surprised if something like the same reforming intentions we have explored, addressed now to the initiatory practices of ancient assemblies, are also found in the Gospels. The Gospels are, after all, full of images for baptism. Here are a few from the many: Jesus is baptized at the outset of the Synoptics, in a revelation of the voice and the Spirit of God that can be taken as the primary New Testament image for the Trinity, but also in an act through which God's Son stands with a needy world, longing for God and God's reign to replace horror, oppression, and death. Then, it is no wonder that the death of Jesus is also called his "baptism" (Mark 10:38-39; Luke 12:50), where the same identification with need occurs, but where that reign also paradoxically begins to arrive. A young man runs away naked in the garden, as if he is being immersed in the narrative of the death of Christ that immediately

---

20. "Guidelines for Admission to the Eucharist between the Chaldean Church and the Assyrian Church of the East," quoted in Baldovin, "The Usefulness of Liturgical History," 14–15.

21. For further reflections on the reform of the Eucharist, see my *Holy Ground*, 143–46.

follows (Mark 14:51-52). Perhaps it is this same young man, now clothed in a white robe, who sits in the empty tomb and announces the resurrection (Mark 16:5-7). He invites the women—invites the church—to see anew, with fresh eyes, how the risen one goes before them into the world itself, will be seen in their meetings and in their welcome to the least. More: the demoniac is now clothed and in his right mind, as the Legion is drowned in the sea—and this man made whole is now sent as a witness in the mixed-culture towns of the Decapolis (Mark 5:15, 19-20). In John, a Samaritan woman is thirsty for more than the village well can give, more even than the traditional well of Jacob can provide. She encounters the source of the water of life, and turns to bear witness in her village (John 4). A man who is born blind and scorned by traditional religion is sent by the Sent One to the pool called Sent and comes back seeing (John 9). A man who was dead is unbound and given to the community again (John 11). And Matthew, at the end of the book (Matt. 28:19-20), presents the continuing task of the church, given it by the risen one, as baptizing the diverse peoples of the world into the very triune reality with which the Gospel book began and teaching the very teaching of Jesus with which that book is filled. The Gospel according to Matthew then looks like a kind of catechism, full of texts that are gifts for those coming to the water.

It may very well be that the communities of the Jesus movement continued to practice an eschatological washing, not unlike the baptism of John, as a way to sign their own eschatology, their own sense of entry into the last times and so the constitution of their own assemblies.[22] But then the Gospels were, in diverse ways, calling that eschatology to new anchoring in the death and resurrection of Jesus and in God as God is known in the death and resurrection of Jesus. This washing was not to be simply a purity bath for the practitioners' own salvation nor simply an exclusive entrance rite. It was to be reformed according to the gospel. That same call comes to us and to our initiatory practices.

Here is a way that one might speak today, in our terms, of the purpose of baptism as it is imaged in these Gospel sources: that the bath might constitute a people gathered by the Holy Spirit, identified with Jesus Christ, and standing before the face of God for the sake of all the needy world, and, at the same time, that this bath might be the continual resource for persons who, because of their encounter with what God has done in Jesus, are learning to trust God, to be unafraid of death, and are being moved by the Spirit to turn in witness and in

---

22. For another account of the origin of Christian baptism, see my *Holy People*, chap. 7.

service toward God's beloved world. Baptism is thus the doctrine of the trinity experienced, lived. So reformed, it is also the continual foundation of the church and of its unity.

But then our religious bathing practices also require ongoing reform. The images of the Gospels will refresh baptism among us, calling for more profound teaching associated with the water, for more water and a richer rite, for a sense that baptism identifies us through Christ with a needy world and does not distinguish us from it, and for its lifelong significance among us. Baptism will thereby be continually reformed to be an initiatory bathing that breaks with all the dangers of initiation: with the insider group; with the idea that we ourselves achieve the goal of the initiation; and with the gender divisions so characteristic of ritual initiations. The Gospels then do not so much report the "institution" of baptism. They call, rather, for its ongoing reform.[23]

In all of our assemblies, as diverse as they are and can be, baptism according to the gospel will thus echo the baptism of Jesus in the Gospels, gather us into his death, form us as a new community of the Spirit, and send us—like the Samaritan woman or the healed demoniac—to bear witness to our own cities.[24]

Four Voices for Reform

If the Gospel books do indeed invite us to the reform of our assemblies, then we will also want to note again that there are four of them. While these four do have much in common—including their great outline, their assembly coherence, their counterculturality, and especially, to use the Revelation image, the presence of the Lamb and the fire at their center—these four are not the same. Their very fourness has a mutually correcting, uniformity-resisting, ideology-destroying character. They call for reform in differing ways. Mark prepares the assemblies for persecution and even for death, celebrating the presence of grace and life under the form of their contrary in a profound *theologia crucis*. Matthew urges

---

23. For further reflections on the reform of baptismal practice, see my *Holy Ground*, 112–14.

24. We might go on. Healing is imaged in the Gospels and is practiced again in our assemblies. Prayer is found in both Gospels and our assemblies. In both cases, the Gospels invite us to hold our practice next to the crucified and risen Christ and so find its meaning widened and, often, turned inside out. Prayer is primarily for the other. The healed person, like the crucified one himself, may still die and, in any case, is still wounded. Healing is then God's gift of wholeness, not "cure."

serious ethical responsibility in the assemblies, while it also seriously counsels a discipline of forgiveness. Luke seeks to help the churches act as benefactors in a society where benefaction is valued. And John urges that the assemblies resist spiritualizing tendencies, setting out in the heart of their meetings the flesh of Jesus and both God's judgment and God's love for the world. These are not the same. Their images for assembly are different, and we need them all. We would be impoverished if we had only Matthew's reworking of Mark or only John's refiguring of Luke, just as we would be impoverished if we had only Mark or only Luke. We would also be impoverished if we had only Mark's house, only Matthew's two or three, only Luke's meals or only John's Sundays. These diversities may be both a symbol of and a source for the diversities in the practices of our assemblies.

Furthermore, the Christologies that the Gospels propose to the assemblies differ. Mark invites the assembly to meet the crucified one, knowing that meeting him is also, in a saving but hidden way, meeting God. John, following Mark's lead, makes this meeting yet more explicit: with Thomas, in assembly, we reach out toward the crucified risen one, saying, "My Lord and my God." Matthew and Luke would not quite say it that way. For Matthew, the crowd does not use the revealing words of Mark—"Who can forgive sins but God alone?" (Mark 2:7)—to wonder about the forgiving and healing of the paralytic, but rather glorifies God "who had given such authority to human beings" (Matt. 9:8). To Matthew, it really was "the prophet Jesus from Nazareth" who entered into Jerusalem before the passion (21:21). Luke's whole story is the account of a Spirit-filled man, a great prophet like the prophet promised by Moses (Luke 4:24; 7:16, 39; 13:33; 24:19). The assemblies of Christians have needed both ways, as Christianity has finally stated in the classic summary confession: Jesus Christ is indeed both "true God and true man." The richness of the diverse Gospel images, however, gives existential content to that confession.

Irenaeus was right to celebrate the four books and to caution against the easy slide into heresy that was possible by a devotion to only one as the sole truth. Indeed, the use of always at least two—John and one of the Synoptics—in any one year of both the Revised Common Lectionary and the Roman Catholic *Ordo Lectionum Missae* is a brilliant idea for our current assembly reading. John frequently is heard in the great festal cycles (or in Lent of year A and the summertime of year B), and the Synoptic Gospels are read on the Sundays through the year, so that the whole year has at least two significant Gospel voices. Indeed, in Holy Week we hear the passion account from one of the Synoptics on Passion Sunday, and six days later, on Good Friday, we hear from John. These accounts are not the same.[25] The ancient decision to keep the four books, to receive the four as a gift, to bind the four in a single codex and carry that fourfold book into the assembly, may be taken by us now as another word for our reform: let there be diversity in our unity, just as there is diversity in the Gospels themselves.

But let there also be unity in our diversity. These diverse books have a large degree of similarity between themselves. They not only share assembly coherence as well as a deeply similar outline. They are also, all four, interested in assembly reform. They all speak of the death of Jesus as their central story. Indeed, the correspondence of that passion account with the ongoing passion proclamation of the reformed central meal of the Christian churches may account for the preeminent valuing and ultimate canonization of just these four.[26] But they all, in diverse ways, especially also call the assemblies to know of the encounter with the crucified risen one in their midst. Around that encounter, because of that encounter, the books make their proposals for assembly reform.

Between all of our assemblies, as diverse as they are and can be, it may be that the shared call for reform of the assembly according to the gospel—in the light of the Gospels—will be the principal tool of unity.[27]

---

25. Similarly, on Maundy Thursday we hear two differing accounts of the "last supper" of Jesus: the Pauline account from 1 Corinthians and the Johannine account from John 13. These accounts are not the same.

26. Helmut Koester, *From Jesus to the Gospels: Interpreting the New Testament in Its Context* (Minneapolis: Fortress Press, 2007), 38, 227.

27. The seventh article of the Augsburg Confession points to both the presence of word and sacrament and that critique of their practice as the grounds for unity: "For this is enough for the true unity of the Christian church that there the gospel is preached harmoniously according to a pure understanding and the sacraments are administered in conformity with the divine Word. It is not necessary for the true unity of the Christian church that uniform ceremonies, instituted by human beings, be observed everywhere." Kolb and Wengert, eds., *The Book of Concord*, 42.

7

Leadership according to the Gospel

Leaders Criticized

This study has reminded us that the ancient Christian books that make up the New Testament canon were not, at origin, *organizational* books. They were not written as a sort of initial constitution for a society only beginning to meet. Rather, they are important, diverse sources for and records of an ongoing critique at various places in the early progress of a Christian movement already underway. They were intended as course corrections. Even as they presented foundational principles, they were *documents of reform*. The Pauline letters, for example, were written to existing Christian communities—some of which Paul himself founded, some of which he did not—and they were written with a still discernible reforming intent. The Lord's Supper had been going on at Corinth, but Paul was vigorously seeking to convince its celebrants about important changes they needed to make in their practice. Preaching had been taking place in Galatia, but Paul was seeking to refocus that preaching on what he calls "the gospel of Christ" (1:7). A similar purpose can be discerned in other texts, beyond the letters of Paul. Appointment to office had been taking place in the deutero-Pauline communities, but the author of the letters to Timothy was seeking, among other things, to reform and discipline the practice of office giving and office keeping. The examples could be multiplied. These written proposals, of course, became foundational documents as they took on canonical status amid the controversies of the second, third, and fourth centuries. But it is helpful for us to see again their early critical and reforming intent as we seek to hear them in our own day.

It is especially helpful to do so as we turn now to think about the office of leadership in our assemblies, the office of our pastors or priests. We can inquire how the reforming intent of the New Testament also reached to the critique of leadership in the ancient Christian communities and how that critique may still have something to say to us today.

So, what do the four canonical Gospels say? What do the Beasts roar about ministry? It is fascinating to see that all four Gospels openly criticize the earliest leaders. In the narratives of both the Synoptics and John, these leaders repeatedly do not understand, repeatedly get everything wrong, in spite of Jesus intentionally teaching them. Compare, for example, the question of Jesus in Mark 8:21—"Do you not yet understand?"—with the question in John 14:9—"Have I been with you all this time, Philip, and you still do not know me?" In the passion accounts of both the Synoptics and John, these leaders betray, deny, and forsake Jesus. Note the assertion of Mark 14:50—"All of them deserted him and fled"—alongside the saying of the farewell discourse in John 16:32—"The hour is coming, indeed it has come, when you will be scattered, each one to his own home, and you will leave me alone." While most of these very leaders were probably dead when the Gospel books were written, some of them were known to have once exercised leadership in some of the churches. These figures—Peter and James and John among them—still had revered names and remembered authority. If we then understand that the presence of these names in the narratives should probably be taken as symbolic for any leaders in the communities the Gospel writers knew, we will see the force of their critique.

And yet, here is the remarkable thing: none of the four Gospels seem to propose any alternative, better leaders. They are not books of schism, demanding a pure leadership. The Fourth Gospel may come closest to suggesting an alternative, with its ideas of the unnamed witness to the piercing of Jesus' side (19:35) and of the "beloved disciple" who reaches the tomb before Peter and who first comes to believe in the resurrection (20:2-9). But even these figures—or single figure?—are not exempted from the saying "You will leave me alone." Even if the book was written for the "community of the beloved disciple,"[1] in the Gospel also this disciple does not always get it right. Nor does the book more significantly denigrate the other primitive leaders. The Fourth Gospel still has Peter making a basic confession of faith (6:68-69), still has Philip and Andrew evangelizing (1:41, 45; 12:20-22), still has these original disciples as the company to which Mary Magdalene is sent and among whom the risen one appears. And the later "appendix" to the Fourth Gospel, chapter 21, probably legitimately develops the interest of the Gospel itself by presenting a story about the reconciliation and continued leadership of Peter who denied Christ, and by doing so side by

---

1. See Raymond E. Brown, *The Community of the Beloved Disciple: The Life, Loves, and Hates of an Individual Church in New Testament Times* (New York: Paulist, 1979).

side with an acknowledgment of the ministry of the "beloved disciple," indicating a sense of difference between the two leaders but not a sense of competition.

The Synoptic Gospels are clearer yet. The relentless criticism in these books—especially in Mark—of the misunderstanding of the leaders in the earliest community never goes paired with even the suggestion of some other, better leaders.[2] The most remarkable single Synoptic example of this may well be the heightened Matthean account of the confession of Peter. Mark's "Get behind me, Satan!" is still there, addressed to Peter (Matt. 16:23; Mark 8:33), but so also is now "On this rock I will build my church" (Matt. 16:18). Matthew holds both assertions together. This basic leader of the primitive church, this holder of the keys, this rock of church-building faith and confession, also becomes a rock of stumbling, an offense, speaking wrongly, getting in the way, even opposing God's own intention. Indeed, all three of the Synoptic "passion predictions" are marked by the misunderstanding disciples and, specifically, the badly misunderstanding Peter, James, and John. Yet, in one way or another in all three of these texts, the following narrative goes on to have Jesus teaching a reform in the way that leadership should be exercised in the community (cf. Mark 8:32ff.; 9:33ff.; 10:35ff.), not a replacement of these leaders.

The Gospel books are not primarily histories. We have been seeing that they are books about and themselves symbols of the meaning of Jesus in the current life of the churches. They were and are words into the present of the church, including important words of criticism for those who lead. If we understand that the Gospels were written in the late first and early second centuries and if we remember that these books were written primarily as theological proposals to the then current churches, we should see their critical, reforming intent in the actual life of the churches of the time, also in respect to leadership.

That this reforming intent about leadership is important and unique can be seen by comparison with two other ways that late-first-century or early-second-century Christian books chose to go. The Johannine letters demonstrate one alternate approach. For this writer, called the "elder," there are leaders who are wrong—"Diotrephes, who likes to put himself first," for example (3 John 9)—and leaders who are right—himself and the missionary "friends" or "brothers," for example (3 John 5, 7, 10). Here, the book envisions an alternative set of true leaders, not an ongoing reform of whatever leaders there are. The probably

---

2. *Pace* Theodore J. Weedon, *Mark: Traditions in Conflict* (Philadelphia: Fortress Press, 1971), 73ff.

second-century *Gospel of Judas* demonstrates yet another way. Here the disciples are indeed massively criticized, in language reminiscent of the Fourth Gospel ("How do you know me? Truly I say to you, no generation of the people that are among you will know me.").[3] But then here the rejection of the Twelve—who are presented as "priests" and teachers in the current church[4]—is paired not with an alternative leadership but with the announcement of a way supposedly without leaders, the Gnostic way of the star-guided, escaping, individual soul, the way of the "Jesus" and "Judas" of the book. Here not only leadership, but also assembly, shared meals, and creation itself are denounced.

I think that these two alternatives make the way of the four Gospels all the more precious to us. It is a realistic and flesh-affirming—*sarcophilic*—way, quite aware that communities will inevitably have leaders and religious communities will have sacred leaders. It is also a way of reform, setting out a continuing critique of leadership in Christian communities and a continuing set of criteria for that critique. It is a way we still need.

It is, of course, a paradoxical way. Peter is both Satan and the Rock. Indeed, sometimes I have wished that that in the dome of St. Peter's in Rome, above Peter's traditional gravesite and also above the ministry of the bishop of Rome, there might be inscribed not only TU ES PETRUS, ET SUPER, HANC PETRAM AEDI-FICABO ECCLESIAM MEAM, but also, in facing and equal-sized letters, VADE POST ME SATANA, SCANDALUM ES MIHI. Using only the first words does not accurately present the fascinating and essential dialectic of the narrative. But, in a certain sense, the four Gospels already inscribe this paradox above any leadership that proposes to be seriously and faithfully Christian: such leadership is potentially both Rock of building and Satanic stone of offense and stumbling. In a time like ours, a time of serious suspicion about any authority at all, this deep Christian acceptance and critique of leadership is an important gift. We may be often asking the late-modern questions: "Who says so? On what authority? And who is profiting from this authority? What is the hidden power?" But the way of the four Gospels, requiring as it does that the exercise of leadership in the Christian communities always be self-critical and continually transparent to its purpose, can be in responsible dialogue with precisely those questions.

---

3. Rodolphe Kasser, Marvin Meyer, and Gregor Wurst, *The Gospel of Judas* (Washington, D.C.: National Geographic, 2006), 21.

4. Ibid., 25–29.

Mark on Scribes and Rulers

Consider especially Mark, the book that we think invented the genre "Gospel." In that book, the community that is imaged seems to be an assembly that meets in houses and shares meals together, profoundly interested in the story of Jesus. The book urges that community to continue the meal practice of Jesus, to tell the story of his death, to welcome outsiders and sinners, and to understand itself as seeing the crucified and risen one in those very welcomed outsiders, in the "Galilee" of its life together and in the "Galilee" of this book being read to them. Such is this Gospel book's agenda for ongoing reform.

A further trait so urged is this: in the assembly the "messianic secret" is now to be spoken aloud, just as the Gospel book itself is doing. This mystery is the hidden lamp that is now to be put on the lampstand, the secret that is now to come to light (Mark 4:22), the meaning of the transfiguration that is now to be proclaimed (9:9), the word from the tomb that was supposed to be sent to Peter and the other leaders (16:7) for them to enact. Here, in the open meeting of the community, the leaders are now to proclaim what Jesus heard and saw at the Jordan and on the mountain, what the demons knew as they were being cast out, what the passion predictions promised, what the parables meant, what Peter confessed, what the dead and the deaf and the blind experienced, what the crowds ate, what even those who were killing Jesus attested to without knowing what they were saying, what left the women at the tomb terrified and amazed— all of this is to be spoken openly, clearly, boldly, without fear, in the power of the Holy Spirit (13:11). A crucified man is Messiah and Son of God, the Holy One and the Source of Life—just as an annual mustard bush is the tree of life with room for all the birds, just as Elijah has come first even though they killed him, just as an unnamed woman anointing Jesus for his death is at the same time anointing the Messiah, just as a sponge filled with sour wine and put to the lips of a tortured and forsaken man is the very fruit of the vine now drunk new in the arriving kingdom of God, just as the stone that builders rejected has become the cornerstone. In Jesus, God's forgiveness, life-giving mercy, and reign of justice are placed there where we thought they could never be, under the form of their opposites, in places of death, alienation, sin, and loss. God has acted and is acting for the life of the world.

According to this Gospel book, the community now is gathered around this very mustard-bush-tree-of-life, this very crucified risen one, and the book itself is the news the women were too afraid to announce (16:8). The book itself is the missing voice of those women now come into this assembly. The book itself is the very memorial of the unnamed woman, as if the words were a continued pouring out of her ointment on Jesus' head. The book is the secret—the "theology of the cross"—set free. As testimony to the resurrection, the book is the beginning and basic principle—the ἀρχή (1:1)—of the gospel of Jesus Christ now to be announced and enacted in the assembly and so openly in the world. The book is testimony to that single gospel, utterly different from and subversive to those imperial "gospels" of the divine emperor. The book is Galilee in which the assembly sees the risen one, now, doing in its midst what he does in the story. As the Anglican theologian Austin Farrer says,[5] the Gospel of Mark is itself that resurrection appearance of Jesus which its conclusion seems to lack but toward which the whole book points.

But if this reading of the Gospel according to Mark is correct—if, as we have argued, the assembly of the church is woven into the intention of the book—then the book also has significant things to say about the leadership of that church. We have already implied several of these things. Leadership can get and has gotten matters quite wrong. The message of the gospel, the gospel that fills the book, the gospel that openly reveals the identity and presence of the crucified one, is entrusted nonetheless to these leaders. The humility of that entrusting makes up part of the theology of the cross: these frail leaders are all we have. But there is more. The leaders themselves, in the manner of their leadership, need to be called and to call themselves continually to correspond to that paradoxical gospel. For one thing, to take language from Mark, they are not to be like the scribes. For another, they are not to be like the emperors or other rulers of the nations. The most available, symbolically powerful leadership models—the learned religious leaders of the Jews and the great men of the Greeks and Romans, the model of professionally interpreting authoritative texts and the model of powerfully organizing human affairs—are simply inadequate.

According to the narrative, Jesus himself speaks with an authority unlike the scribes (1:22; cf. 1:27). Whatever that authority means,[6] in Mark it must not include the things presented as characteristic of the scribes: thinking or saying that the forgiveness of sins is blasphemy (2:6); wishing to exclude sinners from

---

5. Austin Farrer, *The Glass of Vision* (Westminster: Dacre, 1948), 145.

6. The Gospel of Matthew uses the idea of astounding teaching, with authority unlike the scribes, as a summary of what has been encountered in the Sermon on the Mount (Matt. 7:28-29).

the community's meal (2:16); insisting on purity regulations (7:1ff.); or turning religion into a public show and an uncriticized despoiling of the poor (12:38-40). This may be excessively hard on people who were actually Jewish textual scholars during Jesus' lifetime and may demonstrate the prejudices of one ancient Christian writer. It is more likely, however—and more interesting!—that the author of this Gospel is not so much telling a history of the conflicts of Jesus as using "scribe" as a current narrative symbol for a religious leadership that is skilled in writing, copying, and debating the significance of texts. Indeed, it is likely that there were Christian communal leaders, knowledgeable about texts, who were engaged in the very things that the Gospel book is criticizing. In any case, when the narrative has Jesus himself exercising authority exactly by forgiving sins, casting out demons, restoring life, welcoming the outsiders and sinners, and speaking for the poor, and when this very authority is then given to the disciples (3:14-15; 6:7), it becomes clear that a contrary role for leadership is being imaged.

The Christian community does indeed have something like "scribes." Is not the writer of the Gospel one? Do not arguments from the scriptures play a role in the text? Are not our preachers also scribes? And does not the Gospel of Matthew speak of scribes in the church and scribes sent by Jesus (Matt. 13:52; 23:34)? If that is so, then they are to be scribes who are not scribes, scribes in another way. Christian leaders are not simply to know the texts and then give lectures on various possibilities for religious meaning. Nor are they to find their primary work in drawing or debating the lines between the insiders and the out, the righteous and the sinners, the pure and the impure, the rich and the poor. The leaders in the community are to speak the gospel of Jesus Christ, as if Jesus himself and the Spirit that is upon him and from him (Mark 1:8; 13:11) were present and acting in the words. They are to enact this gospel—known in the text of the Gospel book itself and testified in the ancient scriptures—in announcing forgiveness, in welcoming the excluded, in healing and acting for the sake of life, in resisting and testifying against evil, and in attending to the lot of the poor. The living voice of this "new teaching" (Mark 1:27) actually casts out the unclean spirits that possess people. This authority actually gathers human beings, like fishers gather fish (1:17), rather than dispersing, cataloging, and alienating them. The leaders are to act and speak with authority. But it is not just any authority, not simply the authority of their office or their learning, not traditional religious authority. It is, rather, the quite specific authority for proclaiming the gospel of Jesus Christ for forgiveness, gathering, and life.

But besides being scribes who are not scribes, in Mark the leaders of the assembly are also to be rulers who are not rulers. We should attend to the trilogy of passion predictions that delineate the center of the book, the heart of its ring construction. The first Markan passion prediction leads to the criticism of Peter and then an appeal to the disciples and the crowd—to anyone who wants to follow Jesus—to take the way of the cross (8:32-38). The second passion prediction leads to a criticism of the quest for greatness by any of the community's leaders, to an invitation for these leaders and the entire assembly to welcome the marginalized and powerless of the world, and to a criticism of John for trying to forbid others who are doing the work of Christ but not following his own group (9:33-42). But the third passion prediction leads to an even more explicit criticism of the leaders—first of James and John and then of all the leaders (10:35-45). Instead of the desired places of power, James and John are offered the paradoxical cup and baptism of Jesus. These are, of course, symbols of the central rites of the community, rites in which the leaders of the assembly preside. But, in Mark's Gospel, they also strong symbols of Jesus' death. Indeed, the seat "at the right hand and at the left," the supposedly powerful places that James and John are coveting but that they do not understand and that Jesus cannot give, are the very places reserved for executed bandits (15:27). Power here is never what it appears to be. Then the rest of the Twelve, imaged as angry because they also want a share of the power, are also invited to the way of service. Among the nations, leaders act as lords and tyrants. It is not to be so in the Christian community. Rather, leaders are to be table servers, *diakonoi*, and slaves to the well-being of the community, just as Jesus also serves at table and gives his life for the great crowd, *the many*, the *hoi polloi*.

The story then turns toward the account of the passion itself and does so utilizing a fascinating turning point, the story of the healing of Bar-Timaeus, the son of Timaeus (10:46-52).[7] Just as we have had scribes in the story up to now, symbolic of values contrary to those of the needed leadership in the Christian community, so now we come across a leader from the nations. Or, rather, we come across such a leader's son, functioning here—like the scribes—as a symbol. Literate, Greek-speaking people of Mark's time knew that Timaeus himself, the primary speaker in the *Timaeus*, the most widely read of Plato's dialogues and one of the most widely read books of the ancient world, was supposed to be both

---

7. For the following interpretation of the Bar-Timaeus narrative, see also my *Holy Ground: A Liturgical Cosmology* (Minneapolis: Fortress Press, 2003), 30–38.

a Pythagorean philosopher and a statesman from the Greek city of Locri in Italy. He was thus one of those "among the Gentiles whom they recognize as their rulers . . . and their great ones." Here, however, far from perceiving the mysteries of the cosmos and ruling over the peoples, his son has been reduced to blindness and begging. In Jesus Christ he comes again to sight and follows him into the story of the cross. He stands as a model for James and John and for us all. Tyrannical leadership and such theory as serves only the interests of the great ones together make up a kind of blindness. When the gospel gives sight, leaders will follow Jesus, together with the rest of the community, into life-giving service.

The leaders of the community, then, are to lead like Jesus leads from the cross. To use the imagery of the much later Revelation to John, they are to rule like a slain lamb rules (Rev. 5:12). Of course, this is impossible. Taken literally, this counsel seems to propose a kind of suicide. It is a counsel that very likely arises, like the counsel of the first passion prediction to "take up the cross," from the Markan expectation that persecution and death were just around the corner. Still, what the great ones and first ones of the community are actually given to do is the sharing of that cup and that baptism in the assembly. They are given those tables to serve. That task is still true for us. They are indeed going to be seen as important among us. They do indeed preside—but as servers at the communal table and as baptizers in the water. And then they need to follow where that cup and baptism both lead—into the serving and life-giving death of Christ. Like the cup and the baptism, they need to love and build up his community, not their own power. They are not to be simply servile. False modesty, feigned weakness, and fawning ways can often be, after all, yet another means, a passive-aggressive means, to build up one's own power. Rather, they will still openly be those who would be "great" and "first." They will be leaders. But the cross of Christ will always continue to be the impossible standard of criticism for their leadership. Even more, in the midst of the life of the community, in the words of the gospel and in the cup and the baptism that enact it, the very crucified risen one himself will be serving table and giving himself for the life of the many. In such a community, the leaders are rulers who are not rulers.

Here, as W. H. Auden says of following Christ, are unique adventures. Scribes who are not like the scribes, rulers who are not like rulers—such is the leadership of the Christian community in the reforming image of Mark. These leaders will exercise an astonishing authority that is not finally their own authority. With the open secret of the gospel on their tongues—with the risen Jesus

Christ in the power of the Spirit on their tongues—they will speak to resist evil, gather outsiders, forgive sins, enable a community of multiple houses and multiple siblings (Mark 10:30), and give life. And these leaders will serve with a service that is not servile, bathing those who come, serving the bread and the cup, and pointing to the one whose gift of life is at the heart of this service.

The paradoxical proposal of Mark about leadership remains immensely important for us. Then, in addition, there are the three other Gospels and there are yet other, concurrent images for and ideas about leadership in those books. Matthew, for example, repeats the Markan passion predictions but also adds the words about the "faithful and wise slave" (Matt. 24:45-51) who, put in charge of the household of the Lord, distributes food fairly and refuses to act in self-serving and abusive ways. Luke gathers all of these ideas together into that Gospel's account of the Last Supper, where Jesus is "among you as one who serves" (Luke 22:27), himself a model for leadership in the community to which he gives that "kingdom" which is most properly imaged by a shared table (22:29-30). John gives us the foot washing, as if summarizing all of these ideas (John 13:1-17): "You call me Teacher and Lord—and you are right, for that is what I am. So if I, your Lord and Teacher, have washed your feet, you also ought to wash one another's feet." But the Markan paradoxical proposal about scribes and rulers remains especially helpful to us. That proposal accords with the Markan understanding of both the gospel itself and the church around that gospel, with both the Markan "secret" and the Markan ecclesiology—and so it invites us to see ideas about office and ministry as woven into whatever we will try to say meaningfully about the gospel and the church.

Ministry: Leadership according to the Gospel

This Markan proposal also accords with the classic Reformation proposal about ministry. The Augsburg Confession, the core Lutheran document, for example, welcomes the traditional Catholic Christian way of appointing ministers. Its fourteenth article says, "No one should teach publicly in the church or administer the sacrament unless properly called."[8] At this point, as at many others,

---

8. In German, *ohn ordentlichen Beruf*; in Latin, *nisi rite vocatus*. See Robert Kolb and Timothy J. Wengert, eds., *The Book of Concord* (Minneapolis: Fortress, Press 2000), 46–47. Cf. *Die Bekenntnisschriften der evangelisch-lutherischen Kirche* (Göttingen: Vandenhoeck & Ruprecht, 1963), 69.

Lutheran churches are quite conservative. They do have regularly called and appointed bishops and priests. On the grounds of this confessional point, there is no reason at all why Lutherans cannot gladly rejoice in the use of the historic succession or the practice of quite traditional ordination rites or the ministry of bishops. Ordinarily, barring all emergency, they will do so. But such call and appointment do not guarantee that the authority of these leaders will be exercised as the rock of building rather than the satanic stone of stumbling. The Augsburg Confession also requires continuing reform, also requires of this ministerial power that it be broken to the service of the gospel and the sacraments. Article five of the Augsburg Confession, about the means of grace that enable faith, is called *Vom Predigtamt* or *De ministerio ecclesiastico*—"Concerning the Office of Preaching" or "Concerning Ministry in the Church."[9] Article seven, about the church around these means of grace as we have seen, makes clear that those ministers serve the church by the right preaching of the gospel and the administration of the sacraments in ways that accord with the gospel—the church is a participating assembly in which "the gospel is purely preached and the holy sacraments are administered according to the gospel."[10] This sentence sounds like Mark's sense of the authority of the gospel in the mouths of the leaders and the service of baptism and cup and table in their hands. At their best, the Lutheran Confessions speak a yes and no about ministry, without any intention to build an alternative ministry, but with a call to the continuing reform of the ministry, not unlike our metaphorical dome or not unlike Mark's rulers who are not rulers. Such a Catholic affirmation of ministry combined with a Reformation critique, such "Catholic substance and Protestant principle" ought to be available to all of our churches.

But the Markan proposal also accords with the traditional rite of ordination. The rite in most churches includes actions that seem like the outright bestowal of authority and office. Indeed, the laying on of hands itself seems like an action of imparting the office by contagion. But the rite also includes actions that seem to be about waiting for God, openness to a transcendence larger than our decision, invocation of the Spirit, singing the *Veni Creator Spiritus*. And, as the laying on of hands is accompanied by prayer, the touch can also seem simply like an indication of the one for whom we are begging: "O God, make use of this one."

---

9. Kolb and Wengert, eds., *The Book of Concord*, 40–41; *Die Bekenntnisschriften*, 58.

10. *Bei welchen das Evangelium rein gepredigt und die heiligen Sakrament lauts des Evangelii gereicht werden.* Kolb and Wengert, eds., *The Book of Concord*, 42; *Die Bekenntnisschriften*, 61.

Both things are true: giving the office; praying for its right use.[11] Also in this rite, there is a dialectic about ministry that can be illumined by setting it next to the Markan texts.

But the Markan proposal seems especially to correspond also to the need of our late-modern times. It is right, this Gospel book seems to say to us now, to be suspicious of leadership and authority. It has often been used for tyranny, for personal power, for division, and for despoiling the poor. But we will fool ourselves to think we can do without leaders. They will rise up all the more, in disguises we will not recognize and in situations where open criticism is not possible. Rather, in all human life our leaders need to be obvious, open to critique, and able to present themselves in ways that do not contradict the communal purposes of their leadership. But, in the church, we may take joy in the public but paradoxical office of self-critical authority, of serving leadership. Who says so? A crucified and powerless man, according to Mark. On what authority? On the authority that welcomes the unincluded, forgives the sinner, washes and gives life to the dying, and serves the table of the poor, the very authority of the triune God as known in Jesus Christ. This is the only true authority pastors or priests have, and they must always be seeking to break the power they are given by their public and religious role to the purposes of this authority. The comfort is that even if they do not succeed in doing so, even as they misspeak and mislead, God can nonetheless use also their stumbling leadership—if their words are somewhere near the words of the Gospel books and their actions somewhere near the cup and the baptism given to James and John. God can also use these frail leaders to build up the assembly as a real witness to mercy for the life of the world.

The announcement of forgiveness of sins and new life in Jesus Christ: this is the priest's only true authority. The gospel and the sacraments according to the gospel: these communal actions are what the pastor's ministry is for. These communal liturgical tasks, this bit of bread and cup of wine, this pool of water, these words, this responsibility and presidency in their use, this enabling of an assembly to practice them together—and this extension of their practice into places of individual need that can be connected to the community's purpose—these are the matters that are given to James and John and Peter and the rest of the ancient leaders and to our current priests and pastors and bishops. There, in those tasks, they will find the possibility of a lively exercise of the paradox that describes

---

11. Further on this dialectic in Christian leadership, expressed in the rite of ordination, see my *Holy Things: A Liturgical Theology* (Minneapolis: Fortress Press, 1993), chap. 8.

them: scribes who are not scribes, rulers who are not rulers. Seminary curriculum needs to explore this paradox, allowing more time to the central practices of ordained ministry, more space to both the yes and the no in Christian leadership, and more honesty and depth to a study of the purpose of the Gospels.

Such a fascinating profession or vocation is one that can be gladly and honestly taken up by some people of late-modern times. It will be in need of a "spirituality" to sustain it, a spirituality of paradox, like that sketched by Archbishop Rowan Williams, in his *Christian Spirituality* (or *The Wound of Knowledge*),[12] as the continual questioning and reorienting of religious meaning in human life that occurs in the encounter with Jesus Christ and the words and symbols that carry his presence. But such a spirituality was already quite present in the reflections of the nineteenth-century Danish pastor and theologian Nicolai F. S. Grundtvig, when in 1863 he tried to answer his own question, "Will the Lutheran Reformation really be continued and completed?"[13] Note how he writes of the tasks of the leaders of the church as largely liturgical tasks. But note how he also writes, embracing the paradoxical reorientation in ways of seeing leadership and, for that matter, seeing the world:

> When it happens that the priests stand at the baptismal bath as Zion's watchers in the power of the Spirit, and the bishop stands at the altar-table truly representing the Good Shepherd who lays down his life for the sheep, while the congregation gladly lets the light shine in good works, and the learned keep watch over the book with their lamps lit from the flame on the altar and keep watch that the church has open doors for going out as well as for coming in, then is everything in Christian order and then is the . . . Reformation complete.[14]

Perhaps, in our times, we would be a little less sure about "Christian order" or about anything being "complete." But there are those priests and that bishop, with the cup and the baptism of James and John; rulers that are not rulers. And

12. Rowan Williams, *Christian Spirituality: A Theological History from the New Testament to Luther and St. John of the Cross* (Atlanta: John Knox, 1980); the British edition is titled *The Wound of Knowledge: Christians Spirituality from the New Testament to St. John of the Cross* (London: Darton, Longman and Todd, 1979).

13. Nicolai F. S. Grundtvig, *Skal den Lutherske Reformation virkelig fortsættes?* (Copenhagen: Schauberg, 1863).

14. Ibid., 115–16. Trans. from Gordon W. Lathrop and Timothy J. Wengert, *Christian Assembly: Marks of the Church in a Pluralistic Age* (Minneapolis: Fortress Press, 2004), 50.

there are those learned ones—who, in the present time, include our educated and skilled pastors and priests—caring for the book, the book of the Gospels not least, the book full of the very content of the altar, and thus also caring for the door opened for gathering and sending, not for excluding; scribes who are not scribes. And there with them is that congregation. Here is a reform of leadership from the Gospels, a continuing and unique adventure.

8

The Reforming Gospels

Renewing the Biblical-Liturgical Movement

The Bible and the Liturgical Movement

In the middle of the twentieth century, Louis Bouyer, a French Roman Catholic scholar who had once been a Lutheran pastor, argued that the Roman Catholic liturgical movement of that same century had been much strengthened when it was joined with the similarly vigorous and similarly unfolding biblical movement.[1] Bouyer was thinking especially of the work of the Austrian priest Pius Parsch, a popular interpreter of the Bible as it was used in the Roman Catholic liturgy and of the Roman Catholic liturgy as it made use of the Bible. Bouyer was also thinking of the depth in liturgical renewal that came from a union between history and Bible, a union between, say, the profound liturgical scholarship of places like the German monastery at Maria Laach, where Ildefons Herwegen and Odo Casel worked, and a new popular awareness of biblical meaning and biblical texts as this awareness was encouraged by Parsch's community of Klosterneuburg.[2] Parsch had envisioned better biblical understanding among all the participants in a liturgical assembly as one strong means for an increase in active liturgical participation, a major goal of the liturgical movement. One of Parsch's tools for this knowledge, a tool he borrowed from patristic

---

1. Louis Bouyer, *Liturgical Piety* (Notre Dame: University of Notre Dame Press, 1955), 65–67. See also my article, "A Rebirth of Images: On the Use of the Bible in the Liturgy," *Worship* 58/4 (July 1984): 291–304.

2. Another example of such a union between liturgical historical studies and reflections on the biblical typology so important to patristic-era and medieval liturgy, the very typology being popularized by Parsch, can be found in another French work: Jean Daniélou, *Bible et Liturgie* (Paris: Cerf, 1951); English trans., *The Bible and the Liturgy* (Notre Dame: University of Notre Dame Press, 1956).

preaching, was "typology," the idea that events in the life of Christ and sacraments in the life of the church had been prefigured in earlier biblical history.[3] For Bouyer, this broadening and deepening change in the liturgical movement was to be applauded for at least three reasons: because thereby people could come to grasp "the full significance of the liturgy itself by uniting it once more with its chief source," the Bible; because the practice of a biblically grounded and biblically rich liturgy could promote "the direct and abundant use of God's Word" in Christian life; and because the Bible, heard in the context of the liturgy, would be provided with "that living commentary without which it cannot be properly understood."[4] For Bouyer, this emergence of thought about the Bible uniting with thought about and experience of the liturgy promised to yield a new phase in the liturgical movement, a "third phase,"[5] one that brought about actual reform by linking research in the history of the liturgy with the Bible alive in its celebration.

Something similar happened also in Protestant circles. In the 1940s in Sweden, for example, several New Testament scholars—notably Anton Fridrichsen and Olof Linton—contributed significantly to the creation of a "new view of the church," a view grounded in their exegesis. This "new view" then itself became the source for new thought about liturgical practice.[6] At about the same time and influenced by this thought, Gunnar Rosendal published in Sweden a set of reflections very much like and influenced by Pius Parsch's important, multivolumed consideration of the use of the Bible in the liturgical year, now turned to a consideration of Lutheran liturgical practice.[7] Furthermore, the inquiry into the

---

3. The New Testament *locus classicus* for this idea is 1 Peter 3:21, though scholars debate what "prefigured" means here.

4. Bouyer, *Liturgical Piety*, 66.

5. A phase, thus, after and yet uniting the historical and theological inquiry of Maria Laach and the biblical popularization of Klosterneuburg; see ibid., 67.

6. See Anders Nygren, ed., *En bok om kyrkan* (Stockholm: 1942); English trans., *This Is the Church* (Philadelphia: Muhlenberg, 1952). See also Sven-Erik Brodd, "Liturgy Crossing Frontiers: Interplay and Confrontation of Ecclesiological Patterns in Liturgical Change during the Twentieth Century," in Oloph Bexell, ed., *The Meaning of the Liturgy: Studies on the Liturgy of Church of Sweden* (Grand Rapids: Eerdmans, forthcoming).

7. Gunnar Rosendal, *Nådens År: En Kyrkokalender*, 3 vols. (Osby, Sweden: 1940–41). The commentary on the liturgical year by Pius Parsch was first published in 1923 as *Klosterneuburger Liturgiekalendar*. This work was later much expanded, called *Das Jahr des Heiles*, and published in several editions (the latest, Würzburg: Echter, 2008). In English, it appeared as *The Church's Year of Grace*, 5 vols. (Collegeville: Liturgical, 1964–65).

possible cultic origins of many biblical texts, found, for example, in the research of scholars like the Norwegian Sigmund Mowinckel and the Swede Harald Riesenfeld, may well have also encouraged a recovery of the linkages between Bible and liturgy, becoming one of the sources for ritual renewal. Similar linkages might be traced between, say, the biblical scholarship of Austin Farrer in Oxford and Anglican midcentury liturgical interests, or between the salvation history accents of American biblical theology and Presbyterian worship renewal. The scholars who were later accused of being "panliturgists" and whom we have discussed[8] also made their contribution to the linkages between Bible and liturgy.

Still, one might argue that Bouyer's third phase has, for all of us, come and gone. It came with the liturgical reforms of the second part of the twentieth century. Only slightly later than the expression of Bouyer's hope or the Scandinavian "new view," the Second Vatican Council did indeed engage in articulating linkages between Bible and liturgy and in creating the circumstances in which a new three-year lectionary was brought to birth. The lectionary was to function in the liturgy as "richer fare . . . at the table of God's word," as the Council itself called this project.[9] This Roman Catholic lectionary was profoundly influenced by Protestant biblical studies from the early part of the twentieth century, perhaps as much as it was also influenced by the patristic use of biblical imagery to express liturgical meaning. Then, in its subsequent ecumenical rebirth as the Revised Common Lectionary,[10] the three-year lectionary has come to matter immensely in many churches and to form one of the pillars of liturgical reform in many places. Furthermore, various churches not only adopted versions of this richer reading from the scriptures in their assemblies. They also used that adoption as a stimulus to work on the quality of preaching and on the recovery of biblical imagery in their prayers.

Among the fruits of the biblical-liturgical movement of the twentieth century one might thus list the lectionary, lectionary-based preaching, widespread lectionary-based studies and discussion groups, collects with richer biblical imagery,[11] an explosion of new hymnody making use of the same imagery, and

---

8. See above, chap. 1.

9. Second Vatican Council, *Constitution on the Sacred Liturgy* 52, http://www.vatican.va/archive/hist_councils/ii_vatican_council/documents/vat-ii_const_19631204_sacrosanctum-concilium_en.html.

10. Consultation on Common Texts, *The Revised Common Lectionary* (Nashville: Abingdon, 1992).

11. Cf. the "prayers of the day" in *Evangelical Lutheran Worship* (Minneapolis: Augsburg

many new prayers of thanksgiving at both table and font similarly marked by a shift to a fuller biblical rhetoric. That "richer fare" envisioned by the Second Vatican Council and by Bouyer's third phase has indeed been set out. The Old Testament has returned to Christian Sunday worship. Preaching has at least been challenged to be more biblically responsible. And juxtaposed biblical imagery has become a frequently used model for our praying and singing.

One could even argue that other matters among us have stemmed from this biblical-liturgical movement. The important use of the word *assembly* in talking about congregational worship has arisen from reading Paul again and from thinking about the *qahal*—the assembly of Israel—in the Hebrew scriptures. The recovery of the liturgies of the Three Days with their extensive biblical readings has been much influenced by a new seriousness regarding the uniqueness and diversity of the four passion accounts, by an interest in letting John stand next to one of the Synoptics in Holy Week each year, and by a recovery of the many ways that ancient Christians read the Hebrew scriptures to interpret the resurrection. The widespread use of the baptismal garment, the alb, to clothe leaders in many different assemblies, replacing the black academic gown, has had at least some support from the New Testament texts that speak of baptismal clothing metaphorically and perhaps even actually.[12] The recovery of leavened loaf bread in eucharistic practice echoes an awareness that many biblical bread stories—not least the stories of feeding the multitude—have mattered to eucharistic meaning, and that Christians only began to use unleavened bread in the ninth century, and then only in the West. Seriousness about women's participation in the assembly has been supported by reading of those early house churches in Paul—in Romans 16, for example—and by his baptismal refusal of gender distinctions in Galatians 3:28. And an accent on liturgical leadership as service, as we have seen, has deep roots in the Gospels. All of these changes have arisen at least partly due to a new reading of the Bible in our communities. These effects of the biblical-liturgical movement remain with us.

But Bouyer's third phase can also be said to have gone—or, least, to have been seriously challenged. The mid-twentieth-century movement was remarkable,

---

Fortress, 2006), 18–63; and *Revised Common Lectionary Prayers* (Minneapolis: Augsburg Fortress, 2002).

12. E.g., Gal. 3:27; Rom. 13:12; Mark 14:5-52 and 16:5. See Martin F. Connell, "Clothing the Body of Christ: An Inquiry about the Letters of Paul," *Worship* 85/2 (March 2011): 128–46.

moving, deeply important, but it could not finally continue as it was. The biblical reflections of Parsch and Rosendal, read today, seem naïve, missing any sense of critical reading or knowledge of the origins of the books being read. The use of biblical typology, so important to these works, now seems to us to run the danger of being an illegitimate attempt to know the mind of God—as if God planned the flood in order to provide images for baptism—or an irresponsible exercise in "supersessionism," implying that Christianity has replaced Judaism in a kind of divinely blessed religious progress. The more critically careful work of the Scandinavian exegetes who advocated a new view of the church has never had much hearing in North America or elsewhere outside of Sweden and is now overwhelmed by a widespread secularism in Scandinavia itself. The extent to which this exegesis supported a remythologizing of the biblical stories and a concomitant recovery of ritual practice has also come under suspicion, not least because so much of biblical studies has taken its lead from Germany, and Germany's experience with the myths and rituals of national socialism left a strong antimythological bias among its scholars. As we have seen, the "panliturgists" had their hypotheses largely rejected. Furthermore, the attention in New Testament studies in more recent times, especially in North America, has very largely turned to inquiries behind the texts, to attempts to establish what can be known of the historical Jesus. The stereotypical observation that liturgists do not know much about biblical studies and biblical scholars do not care much about worship is unfortunately often true. The lectionary and its fruits remain in place, but Bible and liturgy seem to have gone their separate ways.

Indeed, the liturgical movement itself is currently challenged. Given the huge shifts in worldview since the time of the movement's origins, this should be no surprise. Among Roman Catholics, the reforms of the Second Vatican Council are being rethought and even reversed as a massive and officially sanctioned conservative retrenchment has taken power. Among Protestants, romanticism, the source of so much desire for liturgical recovery in the nineteenth and twentieth centuries, is long since dead. The modernist scholarly contributions to a unified biblical theology and a unified view of liturgical history, also much used in articulating the goals of liturgical reform, have yielded to a postmodern accent on diversity. Interestingly, one of the few matters biblical study and liturgical study hold in common in our time is this very interest in diversity. Faced with such an interest, it may be that "movement" of any sort is problematic now, as if it presents too much a kind of totalizing dream.

In an article written near the end of the twentieth century, the Lutheran pastor and scholar Frank Senn argues that the liturgical movement of that century had accomplished much, as is evident officially in the many reformed worship books of diverse denominations, but that "there is a widespread feeling that it has spent its course, done its job, or simply run out of gas."[13] For Senn, that widespread feeling has arisen because liturgical reform has come up against the American spirit of individualism and pragmatism and has even come to be actively opposed by proponents of "church growth." Still, for him the movement has not at all "gone as far as it can go." Most significantly, he notes that the movement's vision of the liturgical assembly has still not been fully realized, that "the roots of the liturgical renewal have not been deeply planted and that its fruit is in danger of withering for lack of nurture."[14]

I do not think that the liturgical movement is over, nor that the importance of the Bible to that movement has passed. On the contrary. Used carefully, Bouyer's call to understand the Bible as the Christian liturgy's chief source and Senn's urging that the roots of liturgical reform need to be more deeply planted can be held together as important proposals to our own time. We can know a recovered and deepened liturgical movement, its fruits nurtured by biblical texts and biblical knowledge. Of course, ours can no longer be the project of an easily united biblical theology, nor of a supersessionism that triumphantly proposes Christian superiority, nor of a typology that literally believes that such types disclose the mind of God or the truth of history. But I think that critical biblical study and the recovered experience of mystery in Christian assembly can go together. Reading the Bible and singing and enacting its images have long made up central practices of Christian worship. The juxtaposition of biblical images in a rhetorical typology, one text borrowing the images and language of other texts in order to heap up meanings,[15] has belonged to the best of liturgical poetics. But now, honesty about the Bible and about the possible communal meanings of its many books and seriousness about the ways in which the faithful Christian assembly can use, critique, and be critiqued by those meanings can help demonstrate anew

---

13. Frank C. Senn, "What Has Become of the Liturgical Movement? Its Origin, Current Situation, and Future Prospects," *Pro Ecclesia* 6/3 (1997): 319.

14. Ibid., 319–20.

15. Sometimes, such use of one text making allusion to other texts can be called "intertextuality." See, for example, Sipke Draisma, ed., *Intertextuality in Biblical Writings: Essays in honor of Bas van Iersel* (Kampen: Kok, 1989).

how biblical texts are still the Christian liturgy's chief source. This honesty and seriousness can also help to plant the roots of reform more deeply among us now, responding to the movement's critics while also seeking to make ongoing liturgical renewal a more central matter in Christianity—indeed, a *biblical* matter.

The kind of biblically grounded reform we want to consider in our assemblies is no longer the recovery of a golden age of liturgy nor the assertion of a single model of practice. It will not be built on either romanticism or modernism. It also ought not be built on biblical literalism or biblical naïveté. Rather, all of our diverse assemblies need to be invited to use the Bible faithfully, which is to say not as a law code nor as a history book but as scripture, as grounds for the encounter with the triune God in assembly. Such faithful use means employing the biblical symbols in support of Christian faith and engaging the biblical texts in a dialogue of critique with our assemblies. The biblical books can be used to say a lot of different things, not all of them good. The devil can quote scripture, as many have observed. In critically sorting those diverse uses of the Bible, the Gospels themselves can help us see again what scripture in the assembly may mean. Mark's use of juxtaposed symbolism can show us with clarity how biblical texts often work. Matthew's acceptance and yet critique of the old scriptures can provide one model for our own critical hearing.[16] So can John's assertion of the purpose of the Gospel book and Luke's image of the disciples seeing the risen one with burning hearts in the midst of the interpreted scriptures. And the mutual coherence between the four Gospels and assemblies can refresh our understanding of what Christians see as the liturgical purpose of all of the biblical books.

Indeed, the biblical canon is the list of books that Christians have agreed may be read with authority in the assembly, and the Bible itself is a one-volume collection of those very books. The Christian Bible was originally a book for worship. At its best, it still is. That being so, then biblical texts, for us, come into their own as they are read in the assembly. While the Gospels are by no means the only books on this canonical list, the assembly's use of the Gospels and the Gospels' own understanding of their purpose in assembly can assist us to think about the purpose of all the Bible when it is brought into Christian liturgy. Such thought can lead us to a deeper understanding of what Christian worship actually is.

---

16. For example, Matthew frequently quotes the scriptures, but also has the devil quote the Psalms (4:6) and, in the Sermon on the Mount, has Jesus counter the scriptures with "But I say to you" (5:21-48).

This volume about the diverse ways in which the four Gospels are coherent with Christian assemblies, addressing those assemblies with reform in view, inviting them to see the risen one in their midst, intends to be one small contribution to thought about the relationship of critical biblical studies and liturgical renewal. Bouyer's "third phase" may yet be ahead of us and may go paired with a new honesty about the Bible.

The Gospels and the Biblical-Liturgical Movement in Our Time

The four Gospels of the New Testament address assemblies, have an interior coherence with assemblies. In diverse ways, they call for the reform of those assemblies. Believing our current assemblies to have some continuity—and even communion—with the assemblies at the origin of the Gospels, we can also hear those counsels of reform in our present time. Such has been the argument of this book. Of course, this approach to the Gospels does not exhaust their meanings. They remain sources for reflection and thought beyond our concern here for assembly renewal, beyond our single question about their relationship to assembly. The present interest in weighing and sorting the texts of the Gospels in the quest to learn what can be accurately said about Jesus in his own context has been very important to us all, even though it runs the danger of considerable projection on the part of the researchers. People engaged in this quest have often been accused of finding mostly themselves and their own preconceptions at the end of their study.[17] But Christians do not think that Jesus is only a projection of our religious belief. He did really live and die, and repeated attempts to say what can be said historically about that life and death, for all of their fragmentary character and risk, do intensely matter to us. Still, the Gospels were written for assemblies and had to do with the meaning of Jesus for those assemblies. Then our inquiry about those communal meanings and their implications for ongoing reform corresponds, at least in part, to the intentions of the books themselves.

But if the Gospels are to be newly read as part of a biblical-liturgical movement, as one way to approach such a movement anew, can we summarize what

---

17. So already, Martin Kähler, *Der sogenannte historische Jesus und der geschichtliche, biblische Christus* (Leipzig: Deichert, 1896). More recently, see John Dominic Crossan's reflections on the charge that Jesus researchers may be engaged in a kind of looking at their own faces reflected in a deep well: in *The Birth of Christianity: Discovering What Happened in the Years Immediately after the Execution of Jesus* (San Francisco: HarperSanFrancisco, 1998), 40–46.

they might be saying? I think we can. Of course, they are saying different things and saying these things best in an actual encounter with the narratives of each book. Mark wants the communities of Christians to be ready for persecution, to know how to negotiate between horror and hope. Matthew wishes them to have their lamps ready for the return of the Lord. Luke argues for the constant repetition of the meal at Emmaus. And John gives the assemblies resources to resist incipient Gnosticism. This diversity can itself be a resource for us today, urging us to know that also our assemblies and their circumstances may indeed be different from each other, but also urging us to put those differences into a dialogue with each other. This is the kind of dialogue that the maintenance of the four books—the refusal to keep only one—also required of the books themselves, even though the individual books seem to have originally presumed that such a dialogue was not needed.

Still, for all of their differences, the books also tend toward unity. They share an interest in the assembly. That is already a great deal. But they also share more. We might summarize what we have been discovering about the Gospels on assembly in this way: they call diverse assemblies to reform. They propose that the heart of this reform must be the encounter with the crucified risen one. They make this risen presence to be the central mystery in the assemblies, the genesis of what later generations of Christians will call "sacramentality" as well as what will be called "the doctrine of the Trinity." They make symbol, metaphor, and verbal juxtaposition the most basic ways they articulate the meaning of Jesus and of the Spirit poured out in the assembly from Jesus. And they mirror the openness they call for in the assembly by the open-ended character of each book.

Let us say a little more, as one sketch of some of the characteristics of a biblically based liturgical movement in our time.

The Gospels call diverse assemblies to reform. And so they call us. We have encountered some of the concerns of this call: that the assemblies be focused on scripture reading, shared meals, prayer, healing, teaching, and baptism in such a way that all of these practices faithfully bear witness to Jesus Christ and to the mercy of God as it is known in Jesus; that the poor be remembered and actively assisted; that leaders in the assembly serve; that the assembly avoid competition; and that the doors be open. These are to be the central matters of a Christian assembly. But these calls to reform are addressed to a variety of different groups, at different times in the development of early Christianity. Inevitably, these were groups with different ways of eating together, different practices in baptism, different accents in teaching, probably different ways of gathering together at all. Nonetheless, the common interest of the Gospels in reform remains. There is for us here an important model. We, too, have diverse assemblies, existing often side by side in the same town or city, in any case in the same time. Our time has rightly been marked by a new welcome to this diversity.

But the call to reform can unite us as well. It is not that, by reading the four different Gospels, we are urged toward a single model. It is, rather, that those very diverse books, held as scripture by all of us and held together, do urge a few shared things upon us and do urge us to see, encourage, and rejoice in our unity-in-diversity. Martin Luther's reforming "marks of the church"—his counsel about how anyone might be able to tell whether a given gathering is actually a Christian assembly[18]—are already foreshadowed in what the Gospels urge. Luther's list of these marks includes the preaching of the gospel, the practice of baptism and of the supper, the announcement of forgiveness, the use of prayer, and the appointing of ministers. These all find parallels in the counsel of the Gospels to the assemblies. Remembering Mark, so does Luther's surprising seventh mark: that a genuine Christian community suffers, or, at least, that it does not hide from suffering, its own and that of others. Urging that these things stand forth in clarity in all of our diverse worshiping communities belongs to an ecumenically recovered biblical-liturgical movement.

Ask: Are these "marks"—especially as they are elaborated in the Gospels— centrally present in our assemblies? Might we join together in a movement both to recover their centrality and to see how the Gospels teach us that word, table, and bath can associate us with a needy world?

The Gospels propose that the heart of this reform must be the encounter with the crucified risen one. And that proposal comes to us. All of the other reforms are centered here. The central passage of the Markan ring composition, the Matthean "where two or three are gathered together," the meals of Luke, and the repeating Sundays of John all urge the assemblies to see the crucified risen Christ at the heart of preaching, scripture interpreting, praying, meal making, healing, forgiving,

---

18. Martin Luther, "On the Council and the Church," in *Church and Ministry III: Liturgy and Hymns*, ed. Eric W. Gritsch, Luther's Works, vol. 41 (Philadelphia: Fortress Press, 1966), 148–78; see also Gordon W. Lathrop and Timothy J. Wengert, *Christian Assembly: Marks of the Church in a Pluralistic Age* (Minneapolis: Fortress Press, 2004), 39–43.

baptizing, and turning toward the marginalized and the poor. The Gospels have a diversity in this theme: the crucified and risen Christ is encountered in the Gospel book, in the welcomed child and in the wretched poor, in the meal, in mutual forgiveness, in the assembly itself, and in the apostolic ministers. But the encounter with that presence is both what all four of the Gospels mean by the resurrection and the very heart of what they urge as reforms for the Christian groups of the late first and early second centuries.

The resurrection, then, is not the resuscitation of a corpse somewhere, somehow, a resuscitation not particularly connected with us. Nor is the resurrection some assertion that we will ultimately get out of this earth or even that we will survive death. Rather, it is the living one himself, meeting us in spite of death, inviting us in the power of the Spirit not to be afraid and to live gladly and lovingly here, now, before God. It is the promised reign of God already dawning, at least in down payment, in the one who has made death and horror and godforsakenness to be the place of life. Then the reforming way in which the Second Vatican Council summarized a major concern of the twentieth-century liturgical movement by accentuating the "presences" of Christ, not only in the bread and wine of the Eucharist but also in scripture reading, in baptizing, in the praying and singing assembly, and in its ministers,[19] may be taken also as responding to an idea already found in the Gospels. Such an accent on the presence of Christ in assembly belongs centrally to a biblical-liturgical movement in our time.

Ask: Is the interest of the Gospels in the risen "presences" of Christ the primary interest of our ongoing liturgical reforms? Might we join together in a movement to encourage each other in seeing those presences?

The Gospels make this risen presence to be the central mystery in the assemblies, the genesis of what later generations of Christians will call "sacramentality" as well as what will be called "the doctrine of the Trinity." In the Gospels, "church" is coming to be as various gatherings or clubs are transformed by the presence of the crucified risen one, in the power of the Spirit, changing the practices of these meetings and drawing these assemblies to be people before God on behalf of the world and witnesses in the world to what God is doing. Thus, it is the resurrection that continually is founding and creating the church. Thus also, the question of the "institution" of the Eucharist or of baptism, as if one could find the

---

19. *Constitution on the Sacred Liturgy* 7 (see n. 9, above). See Judith M. Kubicki, *The Presence of Christ in the Gathered Assembly* (New York: Continuum, 2006).

historical moment of the creation of these sacraments, is no longer a very helpful question. The Lord's Supper is being created wherever the word and presence of the crucified Jesus Christ and the Spirit poured out from him are encountering and changing our meal practice. Baptism is being created wherever the word and presence of the triune God—God as God is known in the Gospel story of the baptism of Jesus and the Gospel account of the cross of Jesus as a baptism—are encountering and breaking open our initiatory practices, our ways of joining people to our assemblies. "The word comes to the element and so there is a sacrament," as Augustine said.[20]

Thus diverse meal practices and diverse initiatory practices inevitably describe the churches. Meals are always local. So are ways in which communities are constituted. But what unites us is the shared critique of the Gospels and the gospel, the shared challenge to our practices and their shared transformation when the God we know in the Spirit of Jesus Christ comes near. This enveloping nearness of the holy Trinity is the central mystery of Christian worship, making our ritual practices to bear the very presence of the one who is transforming death and sin into life and reconciliation, the one who is turning us toward the needs of our neighbor. Thus these practices come to be called "sacraments." And "Trinity" may be considered as the way Christians, because of the resurrection, come to know God encountered in assembly as God for us and for all the world. Such trinitarian challenge and transformation of our practices belong to a biblical-liturgical movement in our time.

Ask: Are we always learning again the richness of faith in God as God is known in the Gospels? Are our liturgical reforms trinitarian? Are our sermons trinitarian? Might we join together in a movement "to make the liturgical experience of the churches again one of the life-giving sources of the knowledge of God,"[21] that is, the knowledge of God as God is known in Jesus and encountered both in the sacraments and in places where we thought God could not be?

The Gospels make symbol, metaphor, and verbal juxtaposition the most basic ways they articulate the meaning of Jesus and of the Spirit poured out in the assembly

---

20. *Accedit verbum ad elementum, et fit sacramentum.* Augustine, *In Johannis Evangelium* 80:4; cf. http://www.newadvent.org/fathers/1701080.htm. See my *Holy Things: A Liturgical Theology* (Minneapolis: Fortress Press, 1993), 164ff.

21. Alexander Schmemann, *Introduction to Liturgical Theology* (New York: St. Vladimir's Seminary Press, 1973), 19.

from Jesus. Thus such symbol and juxtaposition have become primary means of liturgical meaning also for us. Biblical speech patterns well before the Gospels were marked by what Austin Farrer has called "a rebirth of images," metaphors and stories intertextually linked in reinterpretive chains.[22] Biblical speech is also noted for what Harold Bloom has called "parataxis," putting one phrase next to another, one image next to another, in a way that both builds meaning and creates space, like the space between the cherubim on the ark, the "mercy seat" where God meets Israel (Exod. 25:17-22). The Psalms, for example, have "a way of juxtaposing phrases that is central to Biblical Hebrew," establishing speech about God as "a living labyrinth of parallelisms and parataxis," and setting out "a way of thinking that is not ours."[23]

This is the way of thinking alive in the Gospels. Mark's ring composition demonstrates the large pattern of juxtaposition set out to carry the meaning of the book. Beyond that structure, yet further parallel images occur. The whole action of Mark, for example, occurs between the torn heavens of the baptism (1:10) and the torn curtain of the Temple (15:38), as if these were the new cherubim to a new mercy seat. The recurring image of water in John, the recurring "welcome" of Luke—from Simeon welcoming the child to Jesus welcoming the crowd and then the thief and then the Emmaus pilgrims who also welcome him—and the reuse of the biblical idea of five books in Matthew all set out examples of meaning by rebirth of images and by parataxis. That water of John, for example, flowing at Cana, at the well in Samaria, on the temple mount, in the pool at Siloam, at the foot washing, and from the side of the crucified, and thereby echoing and rearranging many other biblical uses of the water image, speaks to us of Jesus himself, of the Spirit that is from him and of the baptism that is into him. Such poetics of juxtaposition belongs to the history of Christian liturgy.[24] Its continued recovery in prayer texts, in hymnody and music, in preaching, in the visual arts on the walls of the meeting room and in the gracious kinetic arts of assembly presiding belongs to the biblical-liturgical movement in our time.

Ask: Are we teaching the use of biblical imagery as we teach the practice of the liturgy? Are we helping people see that such a poetics holds life into hope in ways that

---

22. Austin Farrer, *A Rebirth of Images* (Philadelphia: Westminster, 1949). See also my *Holy Things*, 24.

23. Harold Bloom, "Who Will Praise the Lord?" *New York Review of Books* 54/18 (November 22, 2007): 20–21.

24. Lathrop, *Holy Things*, 82.

are far more profound and far more lively than biblical literalism? Might we join together in a movement that welcomes the poetics of the Gospels as a model for the arts of our celebrations?

And the Gospels mirror the openness they call for in the assembly by the open-ended character of each book. Each of the Gospels tells an open-ended tale. At the same time, paradoxically, at the heart of this openness and enabling it we find a decisive encounter with the risen one.[25] Mark's women-witnesses run away afraid, leaving the story to us while also urging us back to Galilee to see Jesus risen. At the heart of Galilee is an encounter with Jesus in the house meeting of 9:30-50, where the cross is to be preached, the leaders are to serve, competition is to be renounced, and Christ is received in the child. Around this decisive meeting circles the open story, and the meeting itself is to be open. Mark, in the very structure of the book, images an assembly of strong center and open door. Something like the same structure is found in each of the other Gospels. Matthew ends with "I am with you always" (28:20). There is no going away. The book simply ends there, openly, yet thereby the meeting where "two or three are gathered in my name" (18:20), the meeting of a disciplined reconciliation, is recalled. Luke's ending presses us on to Acts, and yet Acts itself does not really end, opening up to the continuing works of the risen Christ, the Christ who breaks the bread and interprets the scriptures, in all the churches. And John's Sunday meeting after Sunday meeting opens onto our continuing Sundays, while nonetheless exercising the judgment, the life-giving *krisis*, that comes with any encounter with the risen one in the heart of these meetings. Open meetings, centered on the crucified and risen Christ and thus on the triune God, imaged and convoked by the Gospels, welcoming the child or the Emmaus pilgrims or Thomas or us all, belong to the biblical-liturgical movement of our time. Open meetings, centered on Jesus Christ, inevitably find that they are centered on the one who identifies with all of the excluded, all of the marginalized.

Ask: Might we join together in a movement to make of all the diverse Christian assemblies places of strong center and open door?

The recovered central matters of the church; the accent on the presence of the risen one in those central matters; the mystery of the Trinity understood as

---

25. Harold W. Attridge, "Genre Bending in the Fourth Gospel," *Journal of Biblical Literature* 121/1 (2002): 19.

the mystery of the assembly's gathering and the assembly's sacraments; the continually recovered poetics of parataxis and juxtaposition; and renewed work on the strong center and open door of our meetings—such are some characteristics of a biblical-liturgical movement in our time that will have learned from the Gospels and their coherence with assemblies.

This movement will, first of all, be concerned with what happens on Sunday, when the Gospels are read in assembly. At the heart of the proposals from the Gospels to this assembly, we have seen, again and again, this urging: the risen one, the one around whom the meeting gathers, is the crucified one. Mark, by means of the secret and the ring construction, asserted this identity of the risen one already, echoing Paul (Mark 16:6; cf. 1 Cor. 1:23; 2:2) and establishing the Gospel purpose and the Gospel genre. But the same assertion, the same refusal to forget the cross, is there, also for example, in Matthew's image of the last judgment and Luke's image of the serving Lord. The same assertion recurs in the risen one showing his wounds in John. Why does this matter so much? Why is it the constant theme of all four Gospels? Not because it means to center our assemblies on a cult of violence. On the contrary. Rather, the repeated Gospel interest in proclaiming the crucified risen one means to anchor our assemblies in truth telling about our sin and death and, at the same time, truth telling about who God is. The resurrection is not a fairy tale nor a wish dream. It is an encounter with the God who takes on the awful need of the world and transforms our place of death into the place of life. Because of this repeated theology of the cross, the Sunday assemblies are called to let the words of the meeting tell the truth, the prayers of the meeting be for far more than ourselves, the meal of the meeting proclaim Jesus' death as life giving and so also remember the poor, the bath that constitutes the meeting be seen as a bath that makes us dirtier with the needs of all of our neighbors, the boundaries of the meeting be porous, the tone of the meeting be deeply joyful while avoiding triumphalism, and the leadership of the meeting serve.

While these proposals from the Gospels come to all of our Sunday meetings, give meaning to all of our Sundays, they may also be seen in a particularly clear form in the current movement for the recovery of the classic liturgies of the Three Days: Maundy Thursday, Good Friday, and the Great Vigil of Easter.[26]

---

26. For recent versions of these liturgies see *Evangelical Lutheran Worship*, 247–70; *Evangelical Lutheran Worship Leaders Edition* (Minneapolis: Augsburg Fortress, 2006), 611–53; and *Book of Common Worship* (Louisville: Westminster John Knox, 1993), 268–314.

Some medieval and early modern patterns for the observance of these Three Days included keeping the Thursday Eucharist as if it were a reenacting of the institution of the supper, reading and preaching on the "seven last words" in a three-hour service as if all of the Gospels were a single historical book, celebrating a liturgy of *tenebrae* as if it marked the moment of the death of Jesus, and either avoiding the Vigil in favor of a sunrise service or seeing a moment in the Vigil as if it were the moment of the resurrection of Jesus. That "as if," that attempt to journey to "Jesus-then," formed a major part of such liturgies.

But a recovery of the Three Days in the light of the biblical-liturgical movement avoids such pretending. We keep this annual feast now, in our own time. Jesus has already died and is risen. Into our present celebration comes the content of the Gospels, taken seriously as individual books speaking to present assemblies. All of the central practices of the assembly are here—open meeting, scripture reading, praying, baptizing and remembering baptism, the meal, collecting for mission and for the poor—but these are seen exactly as carrying the central encounter with the crucified and risen one, with God as God is known in Jesus. The experience of the assembly, thus, is exactly that the sacraments have their origin and continued font in the resurrection of the crucified one coming here, to this meeting. It is he who is at the heart of our washing each other's feet on Thursday, our praying for everything we can think of in the light of the victory of the cross on Friday, and our reading scripture, baptizing, and keeping the meal on the night from Saturday to Sunday. One Gospel is read here primarily, the Gospel according to John. The passion story from the Synoptic Gospel of the year has been heard on the preceding Sunday. Now we hear John, juxtaposed to that story, unfolding that story in another way. The foot washing on Thursday extends into our time; we are urged to turn toward each other in mutual service. The passion account on Friday makes the story to be about Christ's victory and thus grounds our intercessions for all the current world. And Mary Magdalene, who is remembered for encountering the risen one and being sent to tell the disciples, comes also here to this assembly in the text of the Gospel at the Vigil. But the patterns we know from the other Gospels are also here, in dialogue with John. With Luke (and with Paul) there is an open meal. With Matthew there is a stunning reinterpretation of the Hebrew scriptures, read in chains of images throughout the whole three days but especially at the Vigil. With Mark there is an awareness that Galilee is here, that the secret is proclaimed openly on this night, and that the risen one is the crucified one.

This meeting is where the risen Christ comes, already serving on Thursday, with the suffering world on Friday, in the book itself at the Vigil. And with all the Gospels, these liturgies evidence a life-giving labyrinth of reborn images and verbal parataxis, one thing next to another, and the holy Trinity meeting us in between. The recovered Three Days belong to the biblical-liturgical movement of our times.

The Four Beasts Again, Not Tame

When Irenaeus chose to use the image from the Revelation as a way to speak about the four Gospels and when the ongoing Christian tradition delighted in that choice, making it a recurring image, it was probably the fourness of the image that most recommended its use. Against the choice of only one Gospel and against the amalgamation of the four into one, perhaps even against the intentions of the original authors of the books, the four themselves, in all their diversity, were celebrated. But beyond fourness, we have also found an excess of meaning in the image. There are four and they are different. But they share a common vocation. They are themselves not the Lamb. They bear witness to God and to the Lamb, lead the assembly in praise of God and the Lamb, and the Lamb—"standing as if it had been slaughtered" (Rev. 5:6)—is the one who opens the book. Like the Beasts, the Gospels bear witness differently but together to the crucified and risen Christ. Part of that witness is the trust that the awful cross of Christ is the key to all the scriptures. Like the Beasts, the Gospels belong in assembly, lead the assembly in expressing its faith. Like the Beasts, the Gospels call out "riders" who speak the judgment of God against social ills throughout the world. Like the Beasts, the Gospels are not tame.

We have not tamed them here. The Gospels are far more than we have explored, far more dangerous to any social or political status quo and to any uncritical, self-focused religion than we have had space to explore. The Swedish poet and bishop Nils Bolander (1902–1959) said it like this:[27]

> Christianity used to be an eagle gospel
> springing out of the nest on the highest peaks
> with great, bright wings of flight.
> But we pruned its daring feathers,

---

27. Nils Bolander, "Kristendomen var ett örnevangelium," trans. Gordon W. Lathrop.

professionally straightened its raptor's beak,
and see—it became a black bird,
a talkative and tame crow.

Christianity used to be a lion message,
constantly hunting for warm and living prey
a young lion of Judah.
But we clipped its sharp curled claws,
quieted its thirst for heart's blood
and made it into a purring house cat.

Christianity used to be a wilderness sermon
sharp and cutting as the piercing wind,
burning as the desert sand.
But we made it a pleasure garden,
daisies, hyacinths, and pious roses,
a sentimental inclination among the flowers.

Lord, deal with our pious failure!
Give it agile eagle's wings and sharp lion's claws
Give it the smell of wild honey and the dusty wind
and say then with the Baptizer's voice:
This is the victory that overcomes the world.
This is Christianity!

But when they are allowed to be untamed and undimmed by pious cowardice, then among their other great dangers, the Gospels do speak in reforming voices to the assemblies for Christian worship. There, in assembly, they do bear comforting and challenging witness to the Lamb. They do give an ever-new poetics to our song, calling it to be a genuinely truth-telling, life-and-death song, not a sentimental mood. They do wash our eyes to see our world and our neighbors in new ways. In such an assembly, the lion's claws and the eagle's beak are still sharp.

I am quite aware that the Gospels have not always been used in this way. Stories are told in Christian history, for example, of the book of the Gospels being carried in victorious joint ecclesial and military processions that intended precisely to subjugate others.[28] Stories can still be told of words from the Gospels being used to exclude and condemn, to close rather than open the meeting. But then, I think, the texts of the books themselves have not been honestly read. Or they have not been read in their fourness, in their remarkable and mutually correcting tension with each other, in their wildness, and in their calls to reform. The books have not then been seen for what they are.

When a text from the Gospels is read at the heart of a Sunday liturgy, with the whole assembly gathered around the reading, it may stand for all four of the Gospels among us, roaring, the Beasts around the Lamb. Today it maybe Mark or Matthew or Luke, but soon it will be John again, as the unfolding year sets the evangelists here in a tension-laden, yet rich, dialogue. Today it may be the raising of the daughter of Jairus or a passage from the Sermon on the Mount, but set next to the supper and in the assembly, it is also the whole story, indeed the whole trinitarian presence of God. As we hear the reading, we hear its witness to the presence of the crucified risen one among us. The Gospel text is not Jesus Christ, just as the Beast is not the Lamb. Yet, in the words of the Gospel, we encounter the crucified and risen Jesus, just as we do in the bread and wine of the Eucharist. In another sense, the Gospel reading is Jesus Christ here. The Gospel calls our assembly to reform, with the particular accent of the evangelist we are reading, yet with the other voices also in our memory. That call to reform is not tame. We are reoriented toward the world. We are turned toward the wretched, as Matthew tells us the parable of the last judgment. We are turned toward the child, as Mark tells us of the assembly in the house. We are welcomed and invited to welcome others, as Luke tells of the feeding of the multitude. We are centered on the crucified, and so our center always lets in a larger world. But we are also given the unutterably astonishing gifts from Jesus appearing on those final Johannine Sundays: peace, forgiveness, the Spirit, a mission—water welling up to life. Then the Gospel text continues to give a center to the remainder of the meeting: an interpretive key for the other scriptures; a ground for our intercessions for the needy world; an impetus for our greeting of peace to each other; words for what we will eat and drink; and a pattern for our being sent. Our assemblies are made coherent with the Gospels.

---

28. See, for example, the story of Bishop Porphyry of Gaza destroying opposition, carrying the Gospels in a militarily protected procession in fourth century Palestine, discussed in Annabel Jane Wharton, *Refiguring the PostClassical City: Dura Europas, Jerash, Jerusalem and Ravenna* (Cambridge: Cambridge University Press, 1995), 102.

Remembering the epigraph with which we began,[29] we have indeed seen rare beasts in this study. Mark especially has been a land of unlikeness, but so have the others. Presiding at a service will continue to be a unique adventure. So will Luke's welcoming meals and Matthew's "just as you did it to one of the least of these . . ." and John's signs on Sunday. More: we have also seen why it is that many Christians have found the Gospels to be like the Beasts of Revelation's heavenly city. Reading the Gospels in assembly, we begin to come to that astonishing, welcoming city of God, surrounded by all the others through time who have also found these to be the most important books we have. And we find that city already now, here, in this earth, coming among us with the one who meets us in these texts, welcoming us home.

---

29. See above, page xvii.

Index of Biblical Texts

Index of Names and Subjects

Douglas, Mary, 26, 62, 76, 81–82, 85, 87

eschatology, 25–26, 42, 53, 56
Eucharist, 169–71, 202
    origins of, 54–57, 201–2
Evangelical Lutheran Worship, 193–94, 205
Farrer, Austin, 29, 51, 97, 111, 182, 193, 203
Fitzmyer, Joseph A., 109
footwashing, 136–37
Fridrichsen, Anton, 192

Gospel, the, 15–17, 19, 22–23, 30, 32, 86, 157
Gospel procession, 3, 154–55
Gospels, the four, 37, 153–54, and *passim*
    summary characterizations of, 130, 146, 160, 173–74, 186, 197, 199, 200, 203, 204, 205
Goulder, Michael D., 29
Grossouw, Willem, xiii
Grundtvig, Nicolai F. S., 189–90

Harland, Philip, 12, 19, 20, 42, 119, 121
Horsley, G. H. R., 17
Horsley, Richard A., 7, 86
house, 4, 6–7, 10, 25, 32, 61, 82, 83, 136, 137, 143–44, 161–62, 164–65
    See also Mark, houses in

Ignatius of Antioch, 35
imperial cult, 6, 14, 17–19, 20, 27, 31, 121
imperial gospels, 17–18, 53, 61, 182
institution narrative. *See* Words of the Institution
Irenaeus of Lyon, 33, 36–37, 145, 147, 174, 207

Jeremias, Joachim, 45
Jesus-then as Jesus-now, 8, 27, 37, 48, 61, 89, 142–43, and *passim*
John, assembly in, 130–33, 134–45, 146, 160, 174
    meal reform in, 53–54, 136–37
    origin of, 30, 125
    outline of, 134

signs in, 128, 133–45, 168
    use of Synoptics in, 125–30, 137, 142–43
Johnson, Luke Timothy, 13, 42, 119, 131
Josephus, 17
Judas, Gospel of, 43, 180
Just, Arthur A., 47
Justin Martyr, xi, 4, 14, 36, 40, 50, 90, 166
juxtaposition, xiv, 33, 75, 76, 77, 79, 173, 196, 197, 202–3

Kaddish, the, 45–46
Kähler, Martin, 106, 198
Koester, Helmut, 17, 30, 34–35, 56, 154, 175
Kümmel, W. G., 11, 108

Lange, Dirk, 56
leadership, 177–90, 194
lectionary, 3, 139, 167–68, 174–75, 193, 195
Leitourgia, 14, 39
lesser entrance. *See* Gospel precession
Linton, Olof, 192
liturgical history, 43–44
liturgical movement, 191–98, 199–207
liturgical pattern, 90, 163
liturgical theology, 43
living creatures. *See* Beasts, the Four
Lord's Prayer, the, 45–46, 54, 99, 105, 106, 113
Luke, assembly and, 146, 160, 174
    cultural accommodation in, 119–21
    Jesus as benefactor in, 117, 120, 121
    long text of Last Supper in, 47, 116
    meal reform in, 47–48, 109, 114, 118–19
    origin of, 29–30, 94
    outline of, 109
    travel narrative in, 110–16, 118–19
    use of Mark in, 93–96, 110, 111, 112, 114, 116
    use of Matthew in, 94, 96, 110, 114
    worship in, 118–19, 121–23, 168
Luther, Martin, 154–55, 200